The German Failure in
Belgium, August 1914

The German Failure in Belgium, August 1914

*How Faulty Reconnaissance
Exposed the Weakness
of the Schlieffen Plan*

DENNIS SHOWALTER,
JOSEPH P. ROBINSON AND
JANET A. ROBINSON

McFarland & Company, Inc., Publishers
Jefferson, North Carolina

All images from the collection of Joseph A. Robinson.

LIBRARY OF CONGRESS CATALOGUING-IN-PUBLICATION DATA

Names: Showalter, Dennis E., author. | Robinson, Joseph P., 1955– author. | Robinson, Janet A., 1946– author.
Title: The German failure in Belgium, August 1914 : how faulty reconnaissance exposed the weakness of the Schlieffen Plan / Dennis Showalter, Joseph P. Robinson and Janet A. Robinson.
Description: Jefferson, North Carolina : McFarland & Company, Inc., Publishers, 2019 | Includes bibliographical references and index.
Identifiers: LCCN 2018058322 | ISBN 9781476674629 (softcover : acid free paper) ∞
Subjects: LCSH: World War, 1914–1918—Campaigns—Belgium. | Schlieffen Plan. | World War, 1914–1918—Germany. | Military reconnaissance—Germany—History—20th century. | Military planning—Germany—History—20th century. | Moltke, Helmuth von, 1848–1916. | Germany. Heer—History—20th century. | Operational art (Military science)—Case studies.
Classification: LCC D541 .S56 2019 | DDC 940.4/21—dc23
LC record available at https://lccn.loc.gov/2018058322

BRITISH LIBRARY CATALOGUING DATA ARE AVAILABLE

ISBN (print) 978-1-4766-7462-9
ISBN (ebook) 978-1-4766-3437-1

© 2019 Joseph P. Robinson and Janet A. Robinson. All rights reserved

No part of this book may be reproduced or transmitted in any form or by any means, electronic or mechanical, including photocopying or recording, or by any information storage and retrieval system, without permission in writing from the publisher.

Front cover: A proud German cavalry tradition, represented by a hussar squadron on the move superimposed on a map showing German cavalry movements in Belgium, August 1914, did not hold up to planning and execution expectations (map by Florin Safner, photograph from author's collection).

Printed in the United States of America

McFarland & Company, Inc., Publishers
  Box 611, Jefferson, North Carolina 28640
    www.mcfarlandpub.com

Dedicated to the Lord our God who gives us strength.

Blessed be the Lord my strength, who teacheth my hands to war and my fingers to fight.—Psalm 144:1

Acknowledgments

Many of these wonderful people have spent a lifetime in the military, be it American or that of another nation. Dr. William Nance was very obliging in pointing the way to several great resources and references. Internationally, Dr. Jack Sheldon guided us and opened himself to a series of probably inane questions. Col. (Ret) Merle Tiedeman, a professional logistician, has always made us think of the "wait a minute" problems associated with logistics as opposed to our overzealous saber waving operations. Col. (Ret) Barbara Eager, the options lady, kept whipping us to consider other options and get back to work. This started out as a joint project with Francis Hendricks, the Belgian enthusiast. Unfortunately, for personal reasons he left the project. He certainly contributed early on. Edwin Van Bloois from Holland provided a great deal of information and photographs about the crossings at Lixhe and Dutch neutrality. Lars Alfers, a Dutchman from Norway, provided a unique set of pictures and some analysis of locations from Google Earth. Our proofreader, Donna Magnani, has been a real pleasure to work with now for our second book together. She really looks at everything with a gimlet eye. The wonderful maps we have are all the creations of Florin Safner. He lives in Venezuela and has suffered through some of the difficulties of that nation. We can heartily recommend his services.

Table of Contents

Acknowledgments   vi
Preface   1
Introduction   5

1. Concept   7
2. Structural Issues   16
   Cavalry Heritage   16
   Jaeger   17
   Reconnaissance   17
   Heereskavallerie vs. Divisionskavallerie   21
   Integration of Aviation   32
   Communications Failures   37
3. Operational Issues   41
   Enemy Situation   41
   Ultimate German Objective   46
   Single Point of Failure: Staff Plans   55
   "Technical Problems"   59
   Number of Cavalry Divisions   71
4. Preparation for War   74
   July 29   74
   July 30   75
   July 31   75
   August 1   76
   August 2   77
   August 3   83
5. Handstreich   88
   August 4   88
   August 5   98

August 6	112
August 7	120
6. Reducing Liège	126
August 8	126
August 9	132
August 10	134
August 11	136
7. Prior to the Final Advance	141
August 12	141
August 13	146
August 14	150
August 15	150
8. Advance	153
August 16	153
August 17	154
August 18	158
August 19	164
9. Bad Deployment Strikes Back	166
August 20	166
August 21	170
August 22	175
August 23	181
Conclusion	185
Appendix: Peacetime Organization of the GGS as of May 1, 1914	191
Glossary of Terms and Abbreviations	193
Chapter Notes	195
Bibliography	204
Index	209

Preface

Analyzing the military system that Imperial Germany took to war—or perhaps vice versa—in August 1914 remains an academic and military cottage industry. If wars were handicapped like baseball seasons or horse races, Germany would have been a clear favorite: a century-long record of impressive victories, a general staff that was the envy of its rivals, a sturdy base of public support that made the military the Second Reich's de facto national symbol, an obliging administration and executive—in the colloquial phrase, "What's not to like?"

Germany's relative failure in 1914 was a corresponding surprise even to the victors of the Marne and First Ypres. That failure by 1918 metastasized into a catastrophe whose explaining engaged military and intellectual energies for most of a century. The major military emphasis was on the Schlieffen Plan: in particular, the failure of Schlieffen's successor Helmuth von Moltke to apply it as intended. Those who found that explanation too narrow turned to the Second Reich's diplomatic, political, and socioeconomic shortcomings, and the extent to which they enabled the armed forces to assert a privileged position they were unable to justify in the ultimate challenge of a war they conceived and midwifed but could not win.

The passage of time, combined with a second world war and a threat of thermonuclear Armageddon, generated more nuanced perspectives. Recent historiography presents the Great War in the context of contingencies: mistakes, misjudgments, misperceptions—a kind of sleepwalking campaign structured at its focal points by interlocking military and political elites whose power exponentially exceeded their capacity to use it. The consequence was sets of decision chains, improvisations made less from consideration of Thucydides' triad of honor, fear, and interest than by what seemed like good reasons at the time. The result was global war.

In contrast to this emphasis on systematic, structural contingencies, the German Army has sustained its unique position—interpreted negatively. The army was under fire for projecting itself and being accepted as "competent by definition": possessing unique skills as a military instrument. In fact, critics now argue, the vaunted "Schlieffen Plan," if it existed at all, was anything but a recipe and a template for victory. At most, the "plan" was based on a position paper intended as a response to Germany's precarious strategic position. That position was understood and defined as being "a mollusk without a shell," exposed to the possibility of a two-front war on exposed frontiers. Perhaps the diplomats might mitigate that geographic situation politically. They could not eliminate it.

Germany's geostrategic circumstances were thus the inverse of the contemporary United States and the "free security" it enjoyed thanks to the Atlantic and Pacific oceans and the weakness of its immediate neighbors. Germany, its soldiers reasoned and argued, could assure its security not only by radically increased military spending, but also by applying that spending to secure a swift, decisive victory—a victory, if you will, of annihilation.

Momentum was more important than procedure. Speed must supersede method—or better understood, must *become* method. Instead of playing to its continental enemies' strengths by a series of frontal encounter battles in the pattern of the Wars of Unification, Schlieffen argued, the German Army must force the next war's pace to a point where its opponents would be only able to react. Even sieges were increasingly conceptualized in a context of tempo: "rapid siege operations." In the context of field warfare, German planning in the 1890s for both western and eastern theaters increasingly tested the potential of concentrating against an enemy's flank, then driving against and across his lines of retreat. Tactically, operationally, and strategically, France, whose geographic and political structures alike impelled concentration forward along the frontier, was clearly most vulnerable to the systematic application of shock and speed. And the best way of securing and institutionalizing these capacities involved management.

Deliberately limiting their participation in the greater worlds of policy and diplomacy, the soldiers concentrated their energies downward. Operational and tactical effectiveness became foci of the multipliers expected to overcome the geographic and strategic challenges of preparing for a two-front war against superior forces. And on that level, the German Army has generally been accounted comprehensively successful in the Great War's decisive theater during its opening rounds. From the checking and countering of the French offensive in Alsace-Lorraine through the bitter battle of the Frontiers from the Ardennes to Charleroi, the Germans remain credited with superior competence that reflected prewar preparation. Even their encounters with the British Expeditionary Force (BEF) at Mons and Le Cateau, however enshrined they have become in British military mythology, in sober fact "reflected what happens when an army that has neglected doctrine and ... training meets up with an army that has made a religion of both."[1]

And yet, and yet—the military historian's favorite questions remain "yes, but ..." and "are you *sure*?" The *Schwerpunkt* of the German offensive was its right-wing sweep through Belgium. In turn, the focal point of that operation was Liège. The German Army had to break *through* the Liège defenses and break *out* into the Belgian plain, then *find* and *fix* its enemies—all against an ever-ticking stopwatch. There was no room for error, no time for "fog and friction" to do their silent work. It all depended on that sector, the way a massive door might hinge on a single bearing.

And that was only the operation's initial stage. No less vital was the envelopment—indeed the destruction by envelopment—of the Allied left wing. And by mid-August that meant dealing with a BEF that had set itself up as an "obliging enemy": one whose enemy's decisions so positioned it that they might as well have emanated from its opponent's headquarters (HQ). Having no strategic concept beyond a scheme for landing in France, inadequately commanded even by the marginal standards of 1914, at sixes and sevens with its still nominal allies, the BEF lurched forward almost at random. It deployed in an overextended and underdeveloped position around Mons and Jemappes—with its left flank exposed to a tactical counterpart of the strategic and operational "envelopment of annihilation" that was at the core of the German grand design and that might almost, in spite of its defects, transform the echeloned French offensive into Belgium to a successive collapse of dominoes standing on their edges.

But again, that prospect hinged on *finding* and *fixing* the French left flank—not approximately, not more or less, but *precisely*. Here too there was no room for approximations. And that placed responsibility squarely on the German Army's two weakest links: the horsemen and the airmen. Never let it be said that Bellona does not have a sense of humor!

Hindsight, supported by the Battle of the Marne, says the German Army of 1914 did not fulfill its assigned and assumed mission. To date, however, the "why" of that failure at the sharp end remains largely neglected, rushed, or misinterpreted. This book proposes to examine in detail the German Army's performance at the decisive time and the decisive place of its history. Given the specialized, not to say arcane, nature of much of the data, the authors offer benchmarks around which readers may structure evidence and draw conclusions:

1. Information

Successful execution of the operation and the overthrow of the BEF depended above all on securing and transmitting information across a full spectrum from tactical positions to railheads and march routes. Securing that information depended on reconnaissance by an incongruous mixture of retrograde old and cutting-edge new: cavalry and aircraft. Would there be *enough* cavalry for simultaneous complex missions? Could horsemen operate effectively in an age of firepower? Could airplanes and airships, fragile and untested, sustain operations in an environment of daily missions as opposed to planned performances?

2. Transmission

Could the information collected be communicated to the relevant HQ and operational units within relevant time limits? And might randomness and immediacy combine to confuse HQ and officers used to thinking and acting in slower, more measured contexts?

3. "Planholes"

Recent analysis of the "Schlieffen Plan" indicates it was more a structure of suggestions than a detailed program of operations. Did change on one level call for changes further down the planning chain? The most obvious subject in the context of this study is the General Staff's decision not to risk sacrificing the Netherlands' neutrality by crossing Holland's vestigial "Maastricht Appendix." That in turn transformed Liège from an obstacle to a bottleneck—a bottleneck that *must* be cleared, comprehensively but above all quickly. There was no time for maneuver, little opportunity for "mission tactics" or subaltern initiatives. Could a managerially oriented system reprogram its *mentalité* accordingly? Could an already limited number of already overworked general staff officers think appropriately "out of the box?" Or would there be a tendency, an unconscious tendency, to rely on the system? To believe "It'll be all right on the night"—even for an army of virgin soldiers?

The Great War's most crucial operation would turn out to be more of a coin-flip than even a Clausewitz might have predicted. That development in turn highlights the irregular internal dynamic of the German Army of 1914—an instrument of war, to be sure, but an instrument imperfectly and unpredictably tuned.

References for this work frequently ran afoul of what is called the three language balancing act. They employed French spelling, Dutch spelling and German spelling. The first thing to understand when referencing German texts is that the German language was not standardized until 1939. Just as the individual states retained much of their unique cultural foundations, so did the language. The myth that one could just look things up in a standardized dictionary was far from the truth. There were a slew of dictionaries and official languages that followed state of dialectic (*Mundart*) lines such as the *Wörterbuch der Elsässischen Mundarten*. As a result of two conferences in 1901 and 1902 some changes were generally accepted. However, many publishers did not change their typeface. That is why there are different spellings in texts written between 1871 and 1918. We have tried to smooth all this out. No doubt we failed and the fault is ours.

Introduction

"Inconceivable!" was the exclamation repeatedly used by Vizzini in the iconic movie *The Princess Bride*, and it could have been uttered loudly when describing the initial failure of the German right wing during the attack on Belgium in August 1914. The Germans represented the most powerful and most respected military system in the world. Their army was sent into motion at the presumed will of their political masters, and victory was assumed as automatic. On paper and on maps, an overwhelmingly strong right wing was certainly poised to crush the French in a battle of annihilation when it came down on France's open left flank. The small, relatively insignificant British Expeditionary Force (BEF) expected to intervene and could extend the French left wing but in turn would expose itself to outflanking. All the Germans had to do was find the allies' left wing, envelop it operationally, and crush it tactically. None of these seemed beyond their army's power.

This plan for a strong German right wing has since been commonly called the Schlieffen Plan. Modern scholars increasingly debate its existence or its prewar acceptance by its creators. What is not debated is what Bucholz, Robinson, and Robinson call the von Schlieffen Doctrine in their 2013 book, *The Great War Dawning*.[1] The Germans had to perform the largest outflanking movement in the history of war. Failure to find and get around the French left wing invited inconceivable catastrophe.

The true hero of *The Princess Bride*, Inigo Montoya, repeatedly told Vizzini, "You keep using that word [inconceivable]. I don't think that word means what you think it means." Yet in August 1914, the inconceivable happened. The Germans not only failed to execute the leverage point to turn the allied left flank easily, they failed entirely to find the BEF. But how was this possible? The Germans had systematic redundancy, superior numbers, apparently ample cavalry, and an efficient air arm. No force as large as two corps could cross the English Channel and go unnoticed. The exact position and strength of the BEF could easily be found. Failure in this mission was inconceivable! Yet it happened, and the Great War veered off on an uncharted course.

The difference in this book from others is that it is viewed through the lens of an army planner. Joe Robinson never maneuvered World War I armies but, unlike many academics, he has planned many operations in the modern day. Most of this was done as the G3 of the U.S. First Infantry Division as well as of Multinational Division North in Bosnia. So rather than recount historical facts, this book examines historical events through the eye of someone who has planned operations. It examines the most dangerous and the most probable choices facing the German Army at the sharp end of its defining operation in August 1914. It will become apparent that this operation was somewhat less than perfectly planned and was in fact quite risky at best. We are talking about only twenty days in August 1914. World War I started in Belgium on August 4, 1914. Readers of *The Last Great Cavalry Charge*[2] will have a sense that things were not going well for Germany, or at least not as well as they needed to go through August 12, 1914. Could things continue to decay in eleven more days until the main German army literally stumbled into the BEF? Were the reconnaissance problems structuring that decay the consequences of oversight inconceivable or were they inherent in the German system?

It is not our intent to discuss the strategic issues facing Imperial Germany in 1914. Gallons of ink have been spent explaining the whys and wherefores of Germany's strategic plans. We simply accept the fact that the Germans decided to use an attack in the west that would feature a strong right wing. We focus instead on the planning and execution of the attack—a bit complex because the chief of the Great General Staff—often translated as German General Staff (GGS) operated in a political environment deeply intertwined between politics and operational art.[3]

1

Concept

> *It is a very easy matter for a school man to make a plan for flanking a wing or threatening a line of communications upon a map, where he can regulate the positions of both parties to suit himself.*—Antoine-Henri Jomini[1]

The Great War in Belgium started on August 4, 1914. The BEF was fully involved by the battle of Mons on August 23. The army of Imperial Germany had only to find and destroy a small force: four divisions altogether in a war where divisions were counted by dozens. The allies, moreover, were an "obliging enemy." The French high command, its attention focused on Alsace-Lorraine and the Ardennes, virtually ignored its left flank in the war's first weeks. The British deployed almost haphazardly, with little idea of where the French were and no notion at all of the German positions. Relations between the high commands ranged from chilly to prickly to overtly antagonistic. Overall, it posed not quite what German slang would call a "set table" (*gefundenes fressen*), but certainly offered a promising opportunity.

Envelopment, whatever its specifics, was a necessary condition of the "fresh and glorious war" postulated by the Second Reich. It did not happen. Something went terribly wrong between August 4 and August 23. To explain why a highly possible sequence of events was not realized, this study focuses on a crucial but neglected subject: reconnaissance. Whether the German war plan was a comprehensive recipe for decisive victory or a farrago of unacknowledged improvisations, it depended on one vital aspect: envelopment of the French left wing. Whether this involved a massive strategic sweep beyond Paris itself or a more modest series of direct tactical-operational maneuvers against the flank itself, reconnaissance was a vital prerequisite: finding and enveloping the enemy—in this case, the BEF—was the goal of the mass flanking maneuver by Schlieffen's "strong right wing," This was a requirement of the still amorphous area between strategy and tactics: operational art.

Carl von Clausewitz said: "The primary purpose of every theory is to clarify concepts and ideas that have become, as it were, confused and entangled. Not until terms and concepts have been defined can one hope to make any progress in examining the question with clarity and simplicity and expect the reader to share one's view." As we use words like "levels of war," "strategic," "tactical," and "operational," we should realize that what we understand as those terms did not always exist.

Clausewitz divided war into two realms. He defined tactics as the "principles of how to use forces in battle," and strategy as "the principles of how to use engagements for the purpose of war."[2] All the noted military writers of the Second Reich—Moltke the Elder, Sigismund von Schlichting, Colmar von der Goltz, Friedrich von Bernhardi, and Alfred von Schlieffen—used some form of the term "operational." German military doctrine and regulations, however, did not have a definition of "operational" for decades after World War I. Therefore, when using the word "operational," there is always a certain amount of variance between its meanings in modern analysis and in quotations from the World War I era. Over the years, terms like "operational level of command" were used differently by different theoreticians and writers. This remains true. Clearly standing between tactics and strategy, operations is an O-ring, an ambiguous concept. For example, Clausewitz's concept of applied strategy as stringing together engagements is today generally considered "operational." But when Clausewitz talks about strategy in terms of national objectives and policy, he is talking strategy in the contemporary sense. And he presents the two in the same continuum, not as separate entities.[3]

A long-term two-front war was Germany's strategic nightmare. Schlieffen noted as late as 1912, "All of Germany has to throw itself on one opponent, that one that is the strongest, most powerful, and most dangerous, and that can only be France–England. Austria can rest assured: Russia's army intended to go against Germany will not march to Galicia before the dice have been cast in the west. And Austria's fate will not be decided upon the Bug, but on the Seine!" Helmuth von Moltke (the Younger), Schlieffen's successor, took that principle further and eventually abandoned all planning for an eastern deployment, focusing only on the west. Moltke the Younger could not ignore the threat from Russia in concrete planning as Schlieffen had in a theoretical exercise. Nevertheless, a plan for war on two fronts required considering the amount of force going in each direction. Schlieffen in his famous 1905 memorandum had all of it going to the west. Moltke allocated forces to the east— albeit limited forces. From April 1913,[4] Germany had only a single strategic plan to be implemented in case of war; a plan that left seven of eight numbered armies in the west and only one in the east to support Austria.[5] It is correspondingly necessary to look at the differences between the operational points of Schlieffen and those of his successor Moltke the Younger who actually carried out the attack in August 1914.

At the beginning was operational planning. The GGS offered a war plan that did not work, was in fact too risky to be workable—and they had to know it. The strategic offense built around an overwhelmingly strong German right wing is presented in every military school and repeated in virtually every book on German plans in World War I. Holger Herwig, a leading historian of Imperial Germany, summarizes the most familiar contemporary evaluation: that the Germans had forty days to execute their grand design in "one throw of the gambler's dice."[6] Other scholars are more critical. Did, for example, the German General Staff realize there was no chance to win and thus commit "suicide from fear of death?"[7] The Schlieffen Plan was supposedly based on Schlieffen's written 1905 *Denkschrift*, which he in fact completed in early 1906. However, many key documents were supposedly destroyed during World War II. In his 2002 book, *Inventing the Schlieffen Plan*, Terrance Zuber goes so far as to assert that there never was a Schlieffen Plan.[8] What is clear is that the 1905 *Denkschrift* conceptualized a one-front war where almost all the German forces would launch a hammer blow to flank the French Army and eventually pin it against Switzerland.

The key document, however, is not the 1905 *Denkschrift* but the *Aufmarschplan* for the mobilization year 1906–1907, the last year when Schlieffen had personal responsibility. The *Aufmarschplan* was based on the operational planning of the 1905 document. The mobilization plan of a year earlier, however, featured a reinforced left wing and a weak right wing. In the 1906–1907 document, First Army covered the right flank against Antwerp and Second Army advanced toward Brussels. This deployment indicated a right-wing envelopment operation covering Belgium and Holland. In other words, the GGS was not yet planning a deep offensive into Belgium. The 1906–1907 document also shows two separate iterations of the required force structure: *Aufmarsch West I* dealt exclusively with western opponents and *Aufmarsch West II* watered down the western force structure to deal as well with an eastern opponent.[9] So, while Plan I followed the concept of the *Denkschrift*, Plan II already accepted the possibility of a two-front war. The *Denkschrift* was only for one front.[10]

The *Denkschrift* envisaged a force concentrated on the western front amounting to 48½ army corps and ten cavalry divisions, supported by 26½ brigades of Landwehr [second line reserves]. He expected the two numbered armies on the extreme right of the line to deliver the decisive blow upon which the hope of speedy victory depended. To these two numbered armies of the northern group, Schlieffen allocated sixteen army corps and five cavalry divisions.[11] This was a significant increase in previous projected deployments. In the 1906–1907 *Aufmarschplan*, a total of eleven cavalry divisions were available to Schlieffen. In the West II variation with its context of a two-front war, two of those cavalry divisions were assigned to the east and four more allotted to the right wing north of the Meuse River. Two other cavalry divisions could lend support from south of the Meuse. This was a powerful mounted force by turn-of-the-century standards. But what was it expected to do?[12]

Several distinctions emerged between the Schlieffen Plan as envisioned and what was eventually executed in the Moltke Plan. The first and most important of Moltke's modifications was his decision to respect Holland's neutrality. Instead of crossing the corner of Dutch Limbourg that projects into Belgium, the Maastricht Appendix, as Schlieffen had planned, Moltke decided to restrict the German right wing armies to an invasion of Belgium. This fundamental change of avoiding Holland is generally described as caused by Moltke's fear of the British naval blockade. If the war lasted for any length, Moltke reasoned, Holland would be the last opening that would allow American strategic resources to be imported into Germany. This is difficult to reconcile with the Schlieffen Plan's alleged postulate that the victory would take place before the blockade had any chance of seriously impacting Germany. Herwig says that this change brought to the fore several "technical problems." This study will show that is a major understatement.[13]

The 1908 Deployment Plan was the first one to avoid violating Dutch territory, though this option was retained as a fallback Plan B in case the attack on Liège failed. If the initial *coup de main* failed and the forts had not been captured by the eighth day, a second attempt with more strength was planned. If that also failed, First Army would enter Dutch territory to cross the Maastricht Appendix.

Moltke's revised plan, when excluding crossing the Maastricht Appendix, necessitated crowding two numbered armies into the area around Aachen, thereby increasing mobilization and supply problems. It also required immediate reduction of the Belgian fortress in Liège as a prerequisite for the main advance of the German armies and their columns. And Liège would prove an obstacle exponentially more formidable than Moltke anticipated.[14]

Squeezing two large armies through the gap blocked by Liège would require a lightning strike, a *coup de main,* to take the fortress. Schlieffen's plan had avoided this by marching through Dutch territory. Moltke thought that Germany had to take the risk of not invading that part of Holland—even though the speedy defeat of France was the only militarily operational solution to worst-case contingency of a two-front war in which Germany had to fight both France and Russia.[15]

Here we see a consequence of the "Clausewitzian continuum" referred to earlier between operations and strategy. In a 1930 letter, Gen. Gerhard Tappan asserts to the Reichsarchiv:

Colonel General von Moltke assessed the possibility of a victorious performance of a war against France without violating Belgium's neutrality multiple times. The large winter war game 1913–1914 [maybe already 1912–1913?] was based on such a situation. The negotiations and talks in 1912–1913 with the Ministry of War and the Artillery Inspection Commission took place precautionary and proactively in case the Belgian east front, with French funding, was as strongly developed and fortified as the French east front and that then a circumvention of this fortified belt could only take place by violating the Dutch neutrality. Colonel General von Moltke did always speak out implicitly against such a violation of neutrality.[16]

Schlieffen's concept of the operation was to outflank the French Army by marching around the west side of Paris while simultaneously pinning the enemy down along the rest of the front. According to his calculus, 33½ corps would be needed only to tie down the French between Paris and Verdun, apart from the fifteen more needed for the sweep west of Paris. The German Army was significantly short of anything like that establishment. Schlieffen maneuvered imaginary divisions. He established no strict timetable. However, marching to the west of Paris could easily take several months, not the forty days so often quoted in later sources. We must keep in mind that the railheads were limited in their advance and such a spacious envelopment movement would require substantial railroad construction.[17]

In 1914, Moltke attacked Belgium and France with thirty-four rather than the 48½ corps Schlieffen projected. Moltke had insufficient troops to advance around the west side of Paris. He was criticized heavily for putting too many troops on the left flank as well as too many on the eastern front. Moltke said in May 1914 that he wanted to defeat the French "in six weeks from the start of operations." The Schlieffen Memorandum did not include that deadline. Schlieffen's two-front thought was that troops had to be moved quickly from the west to the east. Six weeks was too long to wait before that transfer if Moltke's right wing was operating east of Paris. Even then, the German right wing armies were operating one hundred kilometers from their railheads. This required horse-drawn supply vehicles to make weeklong roundtrips.

Eventually, the Schlieffen Plan became defined in conventional German military lore as *sui generis* in the history of war making: a plan so brilliant it would guarantee success if only it had been followed. But in Schlieffen's fourteen years as the chief of the GGS, the massive right-wing attack through the Low Countries is featured in only three general staff exercises, two deployment plans, and the famous December 1905 memorandum.[18] Nevertheless, the plan became viewed as the golden elixir of victory.

Operationally, despite all the subsequent analysis of force structure and deployment, the number of divisions committed, or whether the attack went west or east of Paris is inconsequential. If the French Army was the objective, as Clausewitz teaches us, then scholars and soldiers have argued for a century about the placement of trees when we could not see the forest. What had to

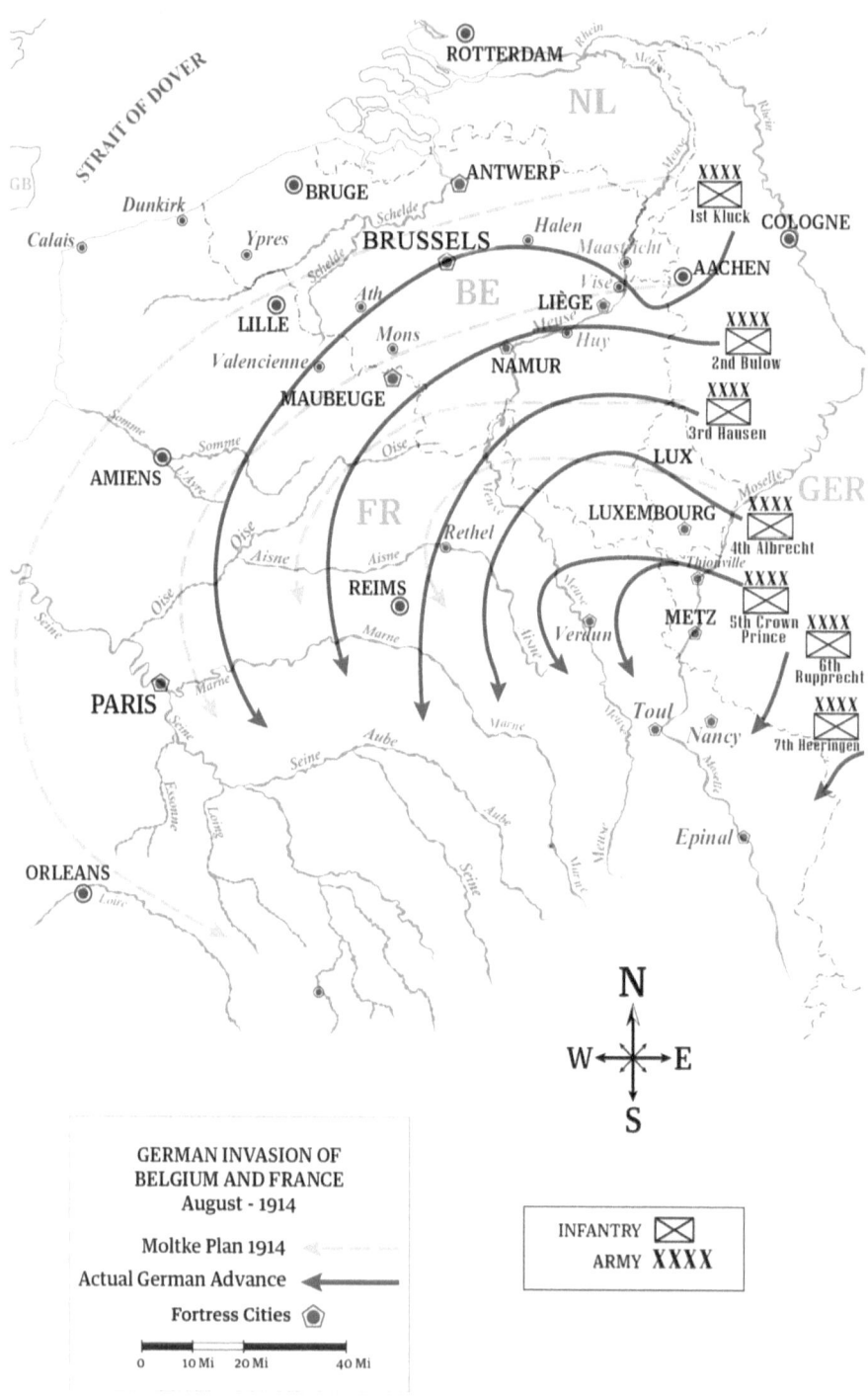

Two different plans: one going through Liège, one going around Liège.

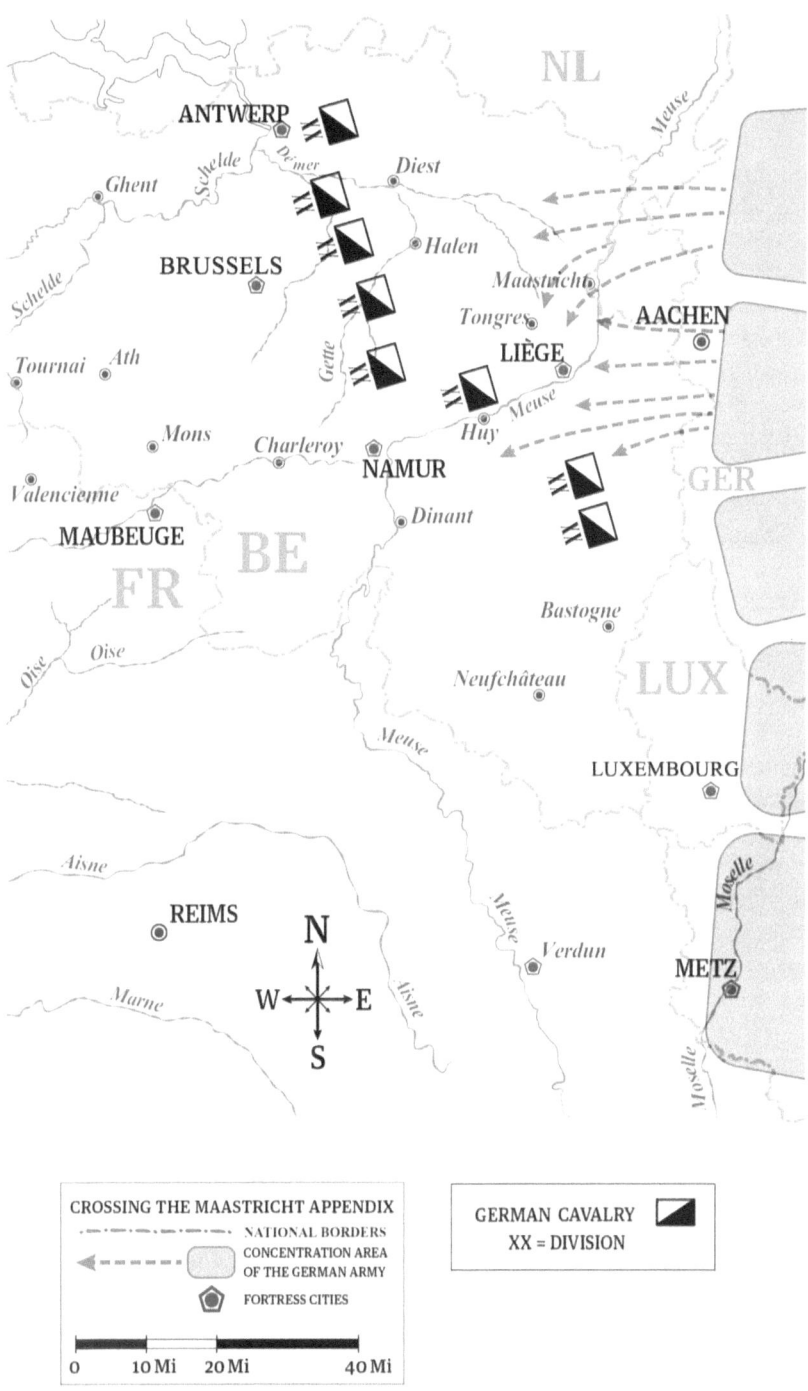

Schlieffen's eight cavalry divisions on the right flank.

happen is that the left flank of the French Army had to be identified. After it was identified, the maneuver forces had to be put outside on the French left flank in order to envelop the enemy army. An enveloping force supported by highly mobile cavalry forces would be in position to rout a larger opposing force when they entered its rear area. From a planning perspective, these essential tasks were also sequential. Commanders of German armies had to find the flank of the French Army before they could maneuver to envelop it. Therefore, the ultimate task was to find the end of the French Army's line. If that line was extended by the BEF or the Belgian Army, those factors had to be dealt with. So, it really did not matter how many days the envelopment took or the size of the maneuver forces allotted—as long as they were adequate to the mission. The location of the "enveloping hook" and where it made contact with the end of the line did not matter. What mattered is that the force would be able to envelop the enemy with sufficient resources to destroy the enemy army, achieve victory, and exploit decisively. This could not be done without operational and tactical intelligence—provided by reconnaissance. Reconnaissance must indicate where to make the attack. Reconnaissance had to do this in a timely enough fashion to allow the maneuver force to get into striking position. This process is spelled out in detail in Book 1, Chapter 2 of *On War*: "The fighting forces must be destroyed: that is, they must be put in such a condition that they can no longer carry on the fight. Whenever we use the phrase destruction of the enemy forces this alone is what we mean." A little bit further on, Clausewitz clarifies this point: "If we wish to be a total victory, then the destruction of his armed forces is the most appropriate action and the occupation of his territory only a consequence." The object of the German plan had to be the enemy armies, not where those armies were located. Therefore, all the discussion about west of Paris, east of Paris, and force structure pale in significance before the objective of destroying the enemy force.[19]

What needs to be understood above all in this context is that the German Army was not practiced in the execution of war at this scale. In peacetime, there were no organized armies. Therefore, there were no army commanders. Nobody had to administer, command, or integrate the resources of such an increasingly complex, increasingly large force, incorporating strong infantry, an unprecedentedly powerful artillery, and vital mobile elements—cavalry and aviation. The highest peacetime *command* position was the army corps commander. These commanders had both geographic and training responsibilities. Their organic cavalry, however, was not designed or trained for operational level reconnaissance. Rather, the corps cavalry was considered more as a screen, defensive in nature, to protect the corps. Its reconnaissance reports were "close in" by nature. Aviation was little more than a phantasm.

Schlieffen in *Aufmarsch West II* had nine German divisional-level cavalry units on the west front, with the clear majority on the right flank. There were three different *Höherer Kavallerie Kommandeur* (HKK): two HKK totaling six divisions north of the Meuse and a two-division HKK south of the river. As detailed in the deployment plan of 1906, HKK 1 consisted of four divisions—the First, Fourth, Guards, and Ninth—and HKK 2 included two divisions, the Second and Fifth. HKK 3 consisted of Third and Sixth Divisions. The Bavarian Cavalry Division seems unassigned to a HKK and is not counted but was located close to HKK 3. The Moltke Plan on the other hand had only three cavalry divisions on the far right. The lack of cavalry divisions would weigh heavily upon operational reconnaissance in 1914.[20]

Where are the cavalry units in operational planning maps? Clearly, they are the more maneuverable and speedier, yet they are not always there. There are no cavalry units on the great Schlieffen map shown by Gerhard Ritter in 1930. A detailed map of the *Denkschrift* shows the positions of each army-corps sized unit, but not the cavalry divisions or the HKKs. When Gerhard Gross lists operational maps, the cavalry shows up at culminating points but not during the reconnaissance. The German official history does a better job but compares it to the well-known English-language maps from the West Point Atlas. Why? If the tasks are sequential, if the end of the line needs to be identified and then decisive force moved into a position to envelop the enemy, why is the reconnaissance necessary to structure those movements not considered primary in the operational maps? Certainly, it could not be that the commanders of the numbered armies were entirely reliant upon the army corps reconnaissance assets. In looking at Schlieffen's often-cited model of the Battle of Cannae—or perhaps casting forward to France in 1940—we see indicators of the mobile forces enveloping flanks, striking the enemy, and rolling him up. The similar maps for the Schlieffen plan do not include that data.[21]

2

Structural Issues

In war only what is simple can succeed. I visited the staff of the Cavalry Corps. What I saw there was not simple.—Hindenburg[1]

Cavalry Heritage

Two other institutional factors influenced the cavalry's approach to operational doctrine. One was heritage. Prussian-German cavalry had established itself in the eighteenth century as a battlefield instrument, mounting decisive charges in the style of Seidlitz and Ziethen—a mindset culminating in the 1870 "Death Ride" of General von Bredow's brigade at Vionville-Mars la Tour. That role had been complemented in the Wars of German Unification by an intruded emphasis on reconnaissance and screening. This was an essential aspect of Moltke the Elder's principle of marching divided and fighting united, which required accurate knowledge of the enemy's positions and systematic concealment of one's own. And as modern firepower rendered large-scale, battle-deciding charges increasingly improbable, security missions sustained the dash, the panache, and the *coup d'oeil* basic to the cavalry spirit. On the other hand, the German experience did not include any significant heritage of using cavalry in large numbers for independent operations at medium or long range, in the pattern of the American Civil War or the style increasingly considered by Tsarist Russia in the latter nineteenth century.

Nor as noted can financial questions be overlooked. Imperial Germany's military budget was under an increasing number of mutually exclusive constraints—and cavalry was disproportionally expensive to raise and maintain. The army had to make the kind of case for every increase in the number of mounted regiments that rendered it easier to put the issue on the backburner until the appropriations.

Jäger

There is no question that, while the German cavalry training in dismounted combat and rifle marksmanship improved in the decade prior to World War I, they were at best second in the league tables. The British were far ahead, as they would demonstrate in the closing months of 1914. That imbalance is frequently mentioned as a significant reason why an increase in the mounted component of the German right wing was unlikely to have produced significant results. There is, however, an overlooked factor. The German Army included eighteen independent battalions of Jäger riflemen. A legacy of the era when most small arms were smoothbores, the Jäger of the Second Reich had an honorable history but an undefined role. That role, indeed, had a significant civil element: producing Germany's supply of foresters, game wardens, and similar woodland specialists. In a standard army corps, however, they were vestigial—no one was quite sure what to do with them in the next war, but their status was too high to permit condign disbandment.

Almost by default, in the first weeks of the war most Jäger battalions were more or less attached to the HKKs—which also had little idea of what to make of them. But a Jaeger battalion in 1914 was a formidable combined-arms unit: in addition to the standard four rifle companies, it included a cyclist company and a six-gun machine gun company. In the ad hoc situation of August 1914, the cavalry HKK would use its Jäger to fix an enemy while the mounted regiments sought to envelop the flanks. Or Jäger could be used as at Halen to make initial attacks, with the cavalry to support or exploit their success. The improvisations worked well enough to invite the question of why they were not institutionalized in peacetime doctrine and training. While again, the answer is opaque, branch-of-service rivalry combines with mutual low priority for a reasonable explanation. But the disconnect would exact a price on the German right wing.

Reconnaissance

Reconnaissance in 1914 was nothing like modern-day reconnaissance. Aviation and horse-mounted reconnaissance were entirely separate. All the cavalry organizations had a glaring absence of aviation. The same higher staff would have to analyze the results, but they came from completely different sources. Cavalry reconnaissance, moreover, depended on the unit training of man and horse. A trained rider could not compensate for an untrained horse. Using the word "improvised," Balck went as far as saying that generally cavalry could not be regenerated during wartime—not quickly, at least—

because the horse had to be trained. Cavalry, in short was not an expendable asset. Reconstitution was not easy even when possible.[2]

Riding hard with fresh horses, a cavalry regiment could cover 50 miles (eighty kilometers) a day. Distances of eighty to one hundred miles were not unheard of in a twenty-four-hour period—and all with the horse's average load of 250 pounds (113 kilograms).[3] A standard cavalry division was supposed to cover between 12 and 20 miles or up to 32 kilometers per day, with the most frequent marching gate the walk—about three and one-half miles per hour. While infantry moving very quickly could match that speed, the horse could keep up the pace for a very long time. The horse's speed could be increased when required to a trot, or about eight miles per hour. However, a very short burst of a gallop or extended gallop could be used for several hundred meters.[4]

A cavalry division would deploy for reconnaissance at three different levels: patrols, reconnaissance squadrons, and the main body of the regiments. The furthest and smallest point of the spear was that of the reconnaissance patrol. These patrols came from a specifically assigned "reconnaissance squadron" that operated as backup in case their patrols needed to replenish ammunition or exchange horses. A cavalry division could have two or three of these squadrons,[5] and each squadron could dispatch as many patrols as needed. The main body of a cavalry regiment followed a reconnaissance squadron. The reconnaissance squadron could come from a different regiment than the one following it, and regularly no more than one reconnaissance squadron would be appointed per regiment. After a couple of days, the reconnaissance squadrons had to be withdrawn and replaced by other squadrons to rest the men and horses.

In theory, the divisions had reconnaissance squadrons patrolling a strip 15 to 20 kilometers wide. In fact, these sectors could be much wider, increasing to 35, even up to 70, kilometers per squadron as the tactical situation required, as shown by the reconnaissance exercise in eastern Prussia in 1905.

The reconnaissance patrols also came in three types: close-distance, long-distance, and officer patrols. Close-distance patrols were the primary method used in cavalry reconnaissance. They scouted terrain and situations close to the front of the reconnaissance squadron, and the reconnaissance squadron could easily reinforce them.[6]

Long-distance patrols routinely operated 40 to 50 kilometers away from the reconnaissance squadron but could go farther. As these patrols were independent from reinforcement; they had to be of some strength. They usually comprised a platoon with an officer in charge. Long-distance patrols supported raids and infrastructure destruction. They were doctrinally limited to the most important missions because of an ongoing debate about how difficult it was to get the report all the way back to the cavalry division staff using relay riders. Clearly, this was a very dangerous and unreliable reporting method. A long-distance patrol could take the light radio set and thus, theoretically, report to the division staff's heavy radio set. However, patrol leaders and theoreticians resisted having a radio with the patrol because a wagon-mounted radio system would slow down a fast-moving patrol. The net result was doctrinal limiting of long-distance missions that were considered exceptions to the rule in the reconnaissance manual. Radios also made reporting reconnaissance results much faster but less secure. Although reports were supposed to be encrypted before sending, they were very often sent not coded to allegedly save time—and the enemy was eager and able to read them.

Officer patrols consisted of two to three lieutenants together with a few noncommissioned officers (NCOs) and troopers. These officer patrols were sent to accomplish special missions, mainly to clearly identify strength and probable intention of an enemy believed to be in a certain location.[7] After the battle of Halen (August 12), patrolling also changed dramatically. It was found that the dispatch of mixed-arms patrols supplied with guns, machine guns, and bicyclists did far better than did cavalry-pure reconnaissance squadrons. In addition, officer patrols were eliminated due to the high loss of leaders.[8]

Army-level reconnaissance orders were issued in writing and delivered to cavalry staff by horse-mounted dispatch riders. The cavalry patrol leaders noted reconnaissance results in pencil on response forms. The HKK or the cavalry division combined these forms into reconnaissance reports and delivered them—again by messenger—to Army HQ. The Army HQ condensed them into a picture about the enemy situation. Reconnaissance results delivered that way were usually between six and eight, sometimes even twelve, hours old.

Cavalry reconnaissance in 1914 was considered far superior to any kind of aviation reconnaissance. The mounted orderly or messenger, not the aircraft, was still the primary method of transmitting orders and reports. However, strategists considered aerial reconnaissance a useful complement to the cavalry reconnaissance, especially behind enemy lines in a war of position. "On the other hand, it is only the powerful cavalry units which are able to give the reconnaissance the necessary persistence and drive capable of sweeping back the enemy reconnaissance organs and thus achieving a superiority on the advanced battlefront."[9] This argument was included in an endeavor to keep aviation assets out of the cavalry formations and assigned directly to the army command.

Compared with the French Army, the Germans started late building up their air power and when the war came, they were relatively weak. By 1914, the active corps had an aviation section that for the first time allowed the commander of the corps to reconnoiter in depth. The resulting information was available but it had to be synthesized and passed up and down the chain of command. The army commander also had an aviation section that could reconnoiter independently. That information had to be digested along with the information presented by the army corps aviation elements. This army command position did not exist in peacetime. This staff that had to do the analysis did not exist in peacetime. As an added complication, the cavalry divisions and the HKK had no aircraft. These type units also did not exist in peacetime. Any ground generated reconnaissance reports coming from the HKK had also to be analyzed by the staff of the numbered army. There was no integrated analysis—a guaranteed source of delay in a situation where speed was of the essence. As you can see, there was no practice in peacetime before the war.[10]

Reconnaissance improved with experience but in general during the initial operations failed the German requirements. One usually ignored fact is that the larger cavalry formations tasked to provide reconnaissance were either assigned to report to the *Oberste Heeresleitung* (OHL) or to an army command. Nothing that the cavalry did went directly to the army corps commander. Each army corps had a small organic contingent of cavalry but these were not the formations tasked to form reconnaissance squadrons. On the other hand, the active army corps had a squadron of six mainly Gotha and Albatros biplanes for reconnaissance, as did each numbered army HQ. The aircraft had a flight endurance of two to three hours and mounted two 25-centimeter cameras for surveillance. Reports from the higher cavalry formations had to be sent down to the army corps. Reports from aviation assets had to be sent up to the army when gathered by the army corps. Who got the initial report and the actions that could be taken often revolved around what level the reconnaissance report came in at? No mechanism was in place to share information between the aviation assets of the different army corps. The army corps had no radio. So that the primary way an aviation report could be spread up to the army HQ or to the adjacent HQ was through messenger. There was supposed to be telephone communication with the higher army HQ, but as we shall see, that link was tenuous at best.

Cavalry reconnaissance in large scale and long range was further complicated by logistics. A German army corps required 280 railroad trains and more than twelve thousand railway cars to move to the deployment area. Of these, 2,960 railway cars were outfitted to transport only horses. The standard ration for a horse was twenty-two pounds (ten kilograms) of feed and fodder. In First Army alone, this required 840 tons of feed for its eighty-four thousand horses—compared to the 555 tons of daily rations required for the troops of the same army, 260,000 heads. To make that sink in, First Army needed 50 percent more food for the horses than for the men—even though there were three times as many men needed for the initial campaign on the western front.[11]

Heereskavallerie vs. Divisionskavallerie

After 1900 and the introduction of machine guns, the role of the cavalry shifted even more heavily from a "battle cavalry" (deciding battles by mass attacks as in the *Kaisermanöver)* to a reconnaissance cavalry. This development also blurred the distinctions between the different cavalry types in favor of *Einheitskavallerie* (unitary cavalry). Functionally, by 1901, cavalry was all equipped and employed in a similar fashion but each had different uniforms and histories. Taking the tradition of Hussars, Uhlans, Kürassier, and Dragoners into consideration, together with the egotistical noble tradition of many regiments, one might imagine how painful this melding process must have been.

This meant that all individual cavalrymen were equipped and trained in a similar fashion. The uniforms were completely different but there was no difference functionally between a Hussar and a Dragoon or any other kind of cavalry. Gone were the days of the Napoleonic cavalry where uniforms and equipment varied with the missions of the mounted units. In 1914, they all did the same thing. The Allies called all German cavalry Uhlans regardless of their uniform, perhaps because they all carried nine-foot-long lances. Within the cavalry, however, there was a great deal of difference between army cavalry (*Heereskavallerie*) assigned to cavalry divisions and the infantry divisional cavalry (*Divisionskavallerie)*. Though the regiments may have had the same equipment and function, the divisional cavalry was limited to very local reconnaissance and direct protection of the divisional force. Local reconnaissance had a significantly different focus than its long-range *Heereskavallerie* counterpart. "The primary objective in local reconnaissance is to protect a force from surprise."[12] The use of *Divisionskavallerie* reconnaissance focused less on determining as much as possible about the enemy than on protecting the main body. In effect, the *Divisionskavallerie* reconnaissance performed more of what is now considered a security task, such as screening or guarding larger forces of foot and guns.

However, the really big difference between the two was that any intelligence reports from *Divisionskavallerie* went to the army corps commander to which it belonged. They did not go to the HKK. There was no mechanism to send a cavalry intelligence report from the *Divisionskavallerie* to the HKK. Internal aviation reports as well as these cavalry reports went to the army corps staff. Only if the corps decided to do it was the army informed. Nor was there an army-level clearinghouse that combined the reports from the HKK cavalry, the *Divisionskavalleri*, and the still unprocessed aircraft. There seemed to be a belief that somehow information found by a patrol was automatically transmitted to every organization in the relevant army. Therefore, one of the most basic understandings must be where the cavalry regiment was assigned. Information from cavalry assigned to the infantry divisions would be geographically restricted. Army cavalry reports from cavalry divisions would be more concerned with deeper reconnaissance. The reports were not analyzed by the same people and, correspondingly, poorly integrated instead.

Heereskavallerie Was Ad Hoc

Although—or perhaps because—serving in a cavalry regiment denoted a higher status for officers than did other troop assignments, German cavalry found it more difficult to adapt to the needs of modern warfare than did the infantry and artillery. Cavalry commanders before 1914 were generally more conservative than their infantry or artillery counterparts. This old-school attitude resulted in manuals and operational concepts that were unsuitable to the demands of modern warfare in 1914. Ironically, the experiences of 1866 and 1870–1871, when cavalry bodies formed upon mobilization and did not fully meet General Staff and War Ministry expectations, were repeated in 1914.[13]

After the war of 1870–1871, three cavalry divisions with their divisional staffs were included in the peacetime structure of the army. In 1887 and 1890, all but the Guard Cavalry Division were dismantled; the highest peacetime formation was again the cavalry brigade.[14] Cavalry divisions were only formed temporarily during autumn exercises, and cavalry corps were only formed for one day during the exercises in 1905, 1909, and 1912. Due to high costs and collateral damage caused to countryside and farmland, the participation of larger cavalry formations was reduced every year. In 1909, seven cavalry divisions and a cavalry corps were assembled during the exercises. These numbers were reduced to only two divisions and one corps in 1912. In the same year, the War Ministry clearly refused to allow four or six cavalry divisions to exercise in the open countryside by pointing out the high costs of collateral damage (*Manöverschaden*) they caused.

Cavalry inspectors usually led the cavalry divisions during exercises.[15] Although the General Inspection of the Cavalry clearly saw the problems caused by the lack of leadership experience in the cavalry divisions' commanders, neither the War Minister nor the chief of General Staff opposed the permanent introduction of peacetime divisional commands for the cavalry. These two organizations differed in their desires for organizations higher than division and how they would operate. Filing an *aide memoire* to the War Minister on August 4, 1908, the General Inspector of the Cavalry, Gen. der Kavallerie Georg Fredrich von Kleist, asked for the formation of six permanent cavalry divisions in addition to the Guard Cavalry Division. The proposal was turned down, and Kleist waited until 1912 before he used his right to approach the kaiser directly (*Immediatvortragsrecht*) to raise his point again. Kleist wrote to the kaiser that he found the role of cavalry division commander to be one of the most difficult to fill—certainly more complex and more difficult than the role of an infantry division commander. *Kleist felt these division commanders would fail in war without proper peacetime training and without being personally familiar with the performance and the leadership style of his regimental and brigade commanders.*[16]

In early 1913, the General Staff finally started planning to mobilize a cavalry command structure above the divisional level. This command structure operationally should lead the assigned divisions and give orders to the cavalry divisions directly—as the cavalry corps had done during previous exercises—but without interfering with high command (OHL) authority. This concept of HKK, not a "real" corps, created an extremely difficult situation for their leaders who would be taking over an organization with no peacetime practice and leading cavalry divisions formed only upon mobilization. The German wording *Höherer Kavallerie-Kommandeur*—Higher Cavalry Commander—makes it clear these commanders were not on par with the commanding generals of the army corps. The units had no peacetime rehearsals. They deployed upon mobilization and then begin active operations on the third day of mobilization at peacetime strength. Not only were these unrehearsed and untested organizations, but also none of the organization leaders or their superiors had any experience utilizing them.

Ironically but logically, Moltke discussed the general idea of the HKKs with Gen.Lt. Georg von der Marwitz,[17] the General Inspector of the Cavalry, but refused to inform Marwitz about the intended operational details of the mobilization plan. After receiving a request for further information, Moltke answered Marwitz, "Regretfully, I will not be able to meet Your Excellency's [Marwitz's] wishes to be briefed about the tasks of the big cavalry formations upon mobilization. But during the winter war games led by me and during the general staff rides, similar tasks of the cavalry will be analyzed. In case Your Excellency wishes to join personally or to send a delegate on your behalf, it would be my pleasure to follow this wish."[18]

The minimal and random planning, structure, and training of the HKK was such an obvious flaw as to be almost unbelievable. No planning was conducted until 1913. Then, the chief of the GGS would not share the plans with a potential commander who was inspector general of the cavalry at that time! No wonder wartime reconnaissance was poorly conducted.

The introduction of the HKKs into the mobilization plan of 1914–1915 seemed to be the exclusive initiative of the GGS. The cavalry department of the War Ministry still opposed the idea of the HKKs in an *aide memoir* (*Zur Frage der Höheren Kavalleriekommandeure*) written in January 1913. The War Ministry did not want mobilization plans higher than cavalry divisions.

Although the GGS wanted larger cavalry formations, they also wanted to ensure those formations carried out the OHL missions—even if that meant bypassing the army commands. The War Ministry, on the other hand, wanted cavalry divisions operating under the direct command of their numbered armies and, therefore, only under the indirect control of the OHL. The General Staff succeeded in getting its cavalry corps type organization but at the expense of confusing command structures among numbered armies, HKKs, and the OHL. The consequences decisively shaped German cavalry operations in Belgium in 1914.

In contrast to the regular army corps, the ad hoc cavalry HKKs possessed neither corps troops nor trains or logistic columns. Instead, cavalry HKKs consisted of two or three cavalry divisions. Although the divisions possessed a small staff to cover all necessary functions and departments, the HKKs did not even have a staff. As a result, the commander was not designated a commanding general but rather a senior cavalry commander. This designation meant his authority extended only into the area of tactics and strategy, not logistics. A chief of staff was assigned to the HKK but had no logistical role— all logistics were at the division level. Thus, the HKK was a reporting HQ that established tactical and operational parameters, much like the U.S. Army's corps in World War II. Within that umbrella, the division commanders had to provide for their own supply and administration.[19]

Little official information on the HKK structure exists. It is not even explained in the General Staff Officers' Pocket Book,[20] which informed the reader of everything about everything—except the HKK. Writing after the war, even Gen. Maximilian von Poseck in his seminal work on the German cavalry did not discuss the structure.[21] The only source that mentioned mobilization of HKKs was the cavalry reconnaissance manual from 1914 (issued before mobilization) issued not by the War Ministry, but by the General Inspection of the Cavalry with permission of the War Ministry. This limited information again illustrates the institutional struggle over cavalry mobilization that was fought within the military. The manual described the role of the HKK as a weak intermediate command position, with the function to coordinate the operations of several cavalry divisions temporarily formed to accomplish a joint mission. The HKK commander (here again named *Commander* and not *Commanding General*) had a purely coordinating function that was aided along if he joined one of his cavalry division staffs and then made use of their staff command and communications infrastructure.

The task of the HKK commander was to keep the cavalry operations in line with the overall situation of the army they supported and to follow the army commander's intentions. The manual emphasized that this role was not to slow delivery of reconnaissance results to the army commanders. If necessary, important messages were to be delivered from the cavalry divisions directly to the army commands, bypassing the HKK. Thus, the HKK commanders found themselves in a weak and ambiguous position when operations started in 1914.[22]

The HKK was a corps-sized unit but not an army corps. Many works refer to these as cavalry corps based on an easy but inexact English translation. Some works used the word *Heereskavalleriekorps*.[23] That is incorrect and gives the wrong impression. *Heereskavalleriekorps* describes what the HKK became in 1915, after the organization received a staff and a logistical function. Later renamed, they became much more like normal corps—but that is not what they were in 1914. Interestingly, the editors of a 1940 book attributed the term *Kavallerie Korps* to HKK 2 Commander Marwitz in their commentary designed around his letters.[24]

The first impression might be, "Who cares? What's in a name?" But that dismisses the issue. At the very top of the organization was the kaiser. The individual in charge of executing his war plan was Chief of the General Staff von Moltke, who was trying to control eight separately numbered armies. In peacetime, the individuals who were destined to become army commanders were the commanders of the eight army inspections. Each inspection oversaw about three army corps. Each army corps (with the exception of the Garde Corps) had geographical responsibility over a specific corps area. These commanders were extremely powerful men. The army corps commanders, the so-called commanding generals, and the inspectors each had the right of immediate access (*Immediatvortragsrecht*) to the kaiser—and they could exercise this right without anyone else being present.

When mobilization occurred, these inspectors were mobilized as numbered army commanders.[25] In peacetime, the cavalry had four cavalry inspections and each cavalry inspector took over a cavalry division after mobilization. The inspector general alone, however, had the same immediate access to the kaiser as the commanding general of an active army corps. By this right alone, the commander of the HKK was not on the same level as the commanding general of an active army corps or of a numbered army. Commanders of HKKs were either division commanders or inspectors of the cavalry. Cavalry division commanders were either cavalry inspectors or commanders of cavalry brigades before mobilization.

Cavalry Divisions

Like the HKKs, cavalry divisions were also assembled upon mobilization. The disbanded cavalry brigade staffs (made redundant by assigning their regiments as divisional cavalry) were used as cadres around which to form cavalry division staffs upon mobilization. An exception was the Garde Corps, in which a Guard Cavalry Division existed in the peacetime structure.

7. Eine Kavallerie-Division setzt sich in der Regel wie nachstehend ersichtlich zusammen:

	1.	0—24—3.
3.	2.	1.
U. 1.	H. 1.	D. 1.
U. 2.	H. 2.	D. 2.
Nachr. A. m. f. Funk. St. 1, 2 " f. " " 1, 2	Pf. A.	1.　　M. 1.
	f. M. K.	
Kav. Kw. Kol. 1.		

Durch Mobilmachung höherer Kav. Kdre. ist die einheitliche Führung mehrerer Kav. Div. vorbereitet.

This chart comes from the "red donkey," or General Staff Officers' Handbook. These handbooks were issued to general staff officers personally and individually and were not for general distribution. Remember, with one exception, these units did not exist in peacetime.

Unlike infantry divisions, cavalry divisions had two general staff officers. One (Ia) was responsible for operations and all tactical issues. The other (Ib) was responsible to liaise with the HKK and the numbered army responsible for information, intelligence, and all supply issues.

Confusion also arises because of nomenclatures used in 1914. Not only is the meaning of HKK often misunderstood, a further language anomaly causes even more problems: the translation of the word *Abteilung*. Many dictionaries translate *Abteilung* as "detachment" or even as "section." In both cases, these translations give the impression that the *Abteilung* was a subset of a unit and relatively small. This inference is incorrect. The word *Abteilung* has several meanings; it is a multipurpose word in the German military language. Within a staff, it translates to "department." In a field artillery regiment, it is "battalion." For example, *Reitende Abteilung* means the horse artillery battalion or *mounted battalion* of a field artillery regiment that went to a German cavalry division upon mobilization. Such a "riding battalion" was comprised of three batteries of four field guns. The reduced strength of four guns per battery together with the higher number of horses that enabled mounting the entire crew was the major difference compared to a regular six-gun field artillery battery.

Another example, a MG-Abt equated almost exactly to a machine-gun company. A mobilized MG-Abt was comprised of a gun detachment (*Gefechtsabteilung*) with six mounted guns and three ammunition wagons; a fighting baggage of one large four-horse ammunition wagon, one material wagon, and eleven surplus horses; and heavy baggage of a two-horse baggage wagon, one food wagon, and one wagon with horse rations.[26] The oft-misused word "section" is significantly misleading in this context.[27]

For a while during the great advance, the Second Army commander was given operational control of the right wing, to include First Army and HKK 2 as integral elements. The HKK 2 operated on the right flank and in front of First Army. At the time of the advance, HKK 2 was to revert to OHL operational control and send intelligence reports to First Army. Therefore, First Army was geographically between HKK 2 and Second Army. As a result, a numbered army HQ that was not contiguous with the area of operations had a command relationship with the cavalry forces. Alexander von Kluck called that an "unfortunate decision."[28] To clarify, the HKKs had no radio. There was no way to communicate electronically between Second Army and HKK 2. The cavalry divisions had radio equipment, but the HQ that controlled them did not. Messages between Second Army and HKK 2 had to traverse the geographic area of First Army. The only electronic communication would be if, by chance, the HKK commander was collocated with the radio equipment of one of the divisions.

Logistics Failures

The cavalry divisions had only very small supply units trailing behind them. The attached horse artillery battalions had their unit loads of ammunition—the combat load carried in the gun limbers and the basic load carried by the light ammunition columns. The artillery and combat formations had their heavy baggage and fighting baggage—and that was all. It was assumed that the cavalry divisions would be able to live on the resources of the theatre of operations. Each division carried, in a cavalry motor transport company, sufficient oats to last its horses one day. Replenishment was to be obtained from an army corps specially designated by the army. With the exception of the attached Jäger battalions, none of the artillery or cavalry units had mobile field kitchens as the infantry had; nor was any supply infrastructure mobilized. Cavalry troops and artillery batteries had a forage wagon each, which belonged to the field train. Ration wagons would carry at least one day's rations, while the forage wagons were loaded with approximately one day's supply of oats.[29]

Consider the effect of a simple change in command relations. Operationally, it would not be important if one day a soldier were assigned to one unit and, the following day, to a different unit. But when considering logistics, a huge problem arose. The soldier was supposed to draw his supplies through the communication zone of the numbered army to which he was attached. As long as the cavalry divisions operated with one particular army, it was possible to establish a working relationship with the supply line. However, in the event of a change of army, the logistical relationship had to change as well. Because the HKK had no logistical function, the entire logistics burden fell upon the divisions—which were in turn attached to an infantry corps for supply purposes. That would generally be an ad hoc function because the cavalry divisions were not organic. The HKK were considered "a constant burden on the army corps so unfortunate as to be responsible for them." Add in the time involved for horse-drawn convoys to reach the rear echelon supply source and consider the lack of efficient communication, and it is clear that resupply would have been a highly precarious matter worsened by constantly changing army affiliations.[30]

The entire trains-and-columns organization integral to the army corps was missing in these improvised cavalry corps. The only supply formation cavalry divisions had was the light motor transportation columns—one per division, created upon mobilization. A participant from Second Kürassier Regiment remembered the ration situation:

> The quartermaster's provisions could not reach us on the road leading to Lüttich [Liège]. A foot column marched by and their field kitchen cooked peas and bacon. We were still standing hungry in clayey mud, thinking they are better off than we are as they can cook while on the move. Tonight, they well might find dry shelter but they have to walk while we can ride! Cavalry did not know the field kitchen then; they cooked on the campfire in the bivouac. Who knows where these will burn tonight and when we can be able to renew our supplies?[31]

When it came to food, the HKK was at a distinct disadvantage. The HKK had no mobile kitchens, which in infantry units were part of the combat trains. The cavalry units had to wait for the arrival of their field trains to receive food, normally late in the day or at night. This timing led to a method of feeding that had an operational effect. In order to "meet the field trains," cavalry units generally had to withdraw and bivouac at a location behind the front. This meant breaking contact with the enemy. Food would be issued and prepared at the squad level; feed for the horses would also be issued, if available. The alternative was to fall back to living off the land, which would mean time lost from reconnaissance in order to search for food, and more time lost preparing it in something resembling edible fashion.

There were also requisitioning issues, all the dangers surrounding a breakdown in discipline, and potential looting.[32] Another point about living off the land was the belief that, except on rare occasions, only meat "on the hoof" could be procured in sufficient quantities. Bread, the major staple of

Standard German transport truck loaded with horse fodder.

the soldiers' diet, probably would never have been obtainable. Rations that could not be found locally, such as bread, were supposed to be drawn from the subsistence companies of the army corps. The HKK did not have such a company—it was assumed that cavalry divisions would be able to live entirely off the land. That meant a breadless existence for the troopers in an army where bread was a diet staple.

Each cavalry soldier was issued three reserve rations (so-called *iron rations*) and two or three grain rations for their animals. This was soon exhausted despite orders to use it only in emergencies.[33] Each division carried in its motor transport company sufficient grain and oats to last the horses one day. After that day's supplies were used, the divisions were supposed to draw replenishment from a designated army corps or directly from the communications zone. This arrangement was inherently weak. Because the army corps' supply situations were already heavily strained by the pace of the advance, this additional and unpredictable demand had serious implications for the supply situation and resulted in severe shortages. The cavalry was consistently reduced to begging the nearest army corps for what support it could spare.

Furthermore, the communication zone was so distant from their mounted operations that the divisional truck organization was not likely to be able to reach it and return in one day. On one hand, their logistics structure kept the cavalry divisions very small and mobile; on the other hand, it deprived them of the logistical assets necessary to ensure a systematic supply of food, fodder, and ammunition. Because the motor-transport columns were much too small to secure the supplies of the highly mobile cavalry divisions, soldiers had to either live off the countryside or make use of the iron rations designated for emergency use.[34]

Living off the countryside without having a reliable supply chain behind led to further mobility problems:

> The transportation of the cavalry divisions caused a good deal of trouble on more than one occasion. The mobility of the cavalry trains, in particular, is greatly impaired by requisitioning from the inhabitants' vehicles of every description. The commanders of the train seem to think that this practice was necessary in order to meet the difficulties of supplying ammunition and subsistence and of transporting men without mounts. As a rule, the cavalry ammunition companies and trains were required to make long marches in order to keep up with the advance by bounds of the cavalry divisions. The final outcome was that the cavalry divisions were to a greater or lesser extent always short of ammunition, probably because the hauling of supplies could not keep pace with the march performances of the cavalry. For this reason, the cavalry divisions eventually were an actual burden on Second Army Corps.[35]

The haphazard movements of the cavalry trains contributed to the congestion of roads that were planned for other columns of the army corps cooperating with the respective cavalry divisions:

> On a few occasions, we [Third Corps] were embarrassed in our supply by the cavalry.... Up to September 1, the HKK, because deliveries in its own supply, occasionally came into our assigned area and requisitioned supplies from the inhabitants, to the detriment of our own requisitions. Furthermore, on August 26 near Cambrai, the HKK made an urgent request for ammunition, thereby upsetting all our own dispositions and reducing seriously our stocks that, because the numerous daytime encounters, had been greatly depleted. But those requests had to be put up with. The independent cavalry had to rely for its supplies on the nearest army corps since it could not be encumbered with the trains.[36]

Although men were well kitted out and horses had state-of-the-art leather gear, a cavalry bivouac gave the impression of a gypsy camp.[37] The Eighteenth Dragoner Regimental History recounted, "The lack of field kitchens was experienced in an unpleasant way ... as the bivouac was occupied and the horses tied—unsaddling was prohibited and, when ordered, only per squadron. Then strong parties were dispatched. One party went looking for potatoes, another one cauldrons for cooking. Others drove cattle to be butchered on the spot. Water for the horses often had to be supplied from far away."[38]

The most compelling logistical problem was most acute for the cavalry, but it extended to all units equipped with horses. The issue was fodder. The ratio of men to horses, approximately four-to-one during the Franco-Prussian War, had decreased to three-to-one by the 1914 campaign. The warning signs raised by fodder issues in 1870–1871 went unheeded.[39] No special arrangements were made or even contemplated. The problem was too complex, too difficult, and overshadowed by operational matters. The simplest solution was to hand it down to the lower-level commanders to solve—which in the early days of campaigning proved no solution at all. The sheer quantity of the total fodder requirement for the German Army in 1914 was so huge that trying to bring it up through the communication zone would have rendered the campaign impossible. As a result, the German Army entered the campaign with little or no arrangements to feed any horses.

Given that the right wing was the main German effort, no quartermaster would be well advised to consider juggling at near random the logistical responsibility for cavalry divisions from one numbered army to the next. Yet, unbelievably, that is exactly what was done with this uniquely high-maintenance elite force. The staffs had planned mobilization details down to the number of cups of coffee at train stops, but apparently not for the care of their horses. Horses were far from well cared for and fed. Frequently, horses were fed local green grain that sickened them. Reportedly, some artillery team horses died even before crossing the border into Belgium. Logically, a corps-level unit would be logistically tied into its respective numbered army HQ. By these means, reordering supplies, ammunition, and feed for the horses could be made relatively routine. Instead, in the case of the cavalry, the plan was for each division individually to create ad hoc links directly with its army. A participant brought other problems to light, writing, "Such a nightly ride in double column hour by hour on cobbled roads tormented the horses. Horseshoes were often cast off caused by the frequent change of walk and trot. The call for the farrier then often rang out loud."[40]

Ammunition and weaponry replacement created a unique problem for the cavalry at regimental level. Captured Belgian stores could not replace the precision-made ammunition and spare parts that the cavalry units required. The horse-drawn ammunition columns could not keep up with the pace of movement. Therefore, motor transport was required once again. Further, the prioritization of ammunition created by Great War battle conditions caused a strange anomaly. Because the movement of ammunition took precedence over all other classes of supply including gasoline, the drivers frequently could not find fuel for the vehicles intended to haul the ammunition.[41] Hew Strachan shows that the General Staff did not develop a logistical concept to support operational mobile warfare. Instead, they simply ignored the inevitable consequences. They ignored the problem! As a result, logistical problems were marginalized in operational planning.[42]

32   The German Failure in Belgium, August 1914

Integration of Aviation

Few histories of early airpower cover reconnaissance in detail. Generally, they tend to be popular, anecdotal, and concentrate on "knights of the air" or early fighter pilots. Some research was conducted on bombing but in 1914, forward firing machine guns were a thing of the future. This book focuses on the time before air-to-air combat, when aviation was used solely for reconnaissance.

The Wright brothers made their first flight in December 1903, and aviation's embryonic technology was one that every military wanted to embrace—but in different ways. Between 1909 and 1911, the Germans made distinct choices between dirigibles and airplanes. The press represented the Zeppelin dirigible simultaneously as a symbol of German inventiveness and as a wonder weapon. Dirigibles subsidized by the German Army developed alongside military aviation. A series of tragic accidents in 1910 and 1911, however, gave the dirigible a black eye. Three commercial ships, as well as the army airship Z2, were lost and in September 1911, the army airship M3 burned during the Kaiser maneuvers. Simultaneously, airplanes challenged the reliability of dirigibles, especially as smaller airplanes displaced smaller nonrigid airships for tactical reconnaissance. The nonrigid dirigible model's inade-

1914 Italian aircraft recognition guide.

quacies in strategic reconnaissance and bombing overshadowed its advantages of field use and transportability.[43]

Heavier-than-air development was quite different from that of dirigibles because airplane manufacturers had no civilian market. Instead, they had to look toward military contracts for funding—and the German military was very slow to award such contracts. Generally, the contracts favored firms that had won various aircraft competitions. That meant military contracts favored large firms that could afford aerial teams to support unreliable aircraft over small firms.

The biggest transition for this very adolescent group was that aircraft were incorporated into the transport troops. The higher HQ or Inspection of transport was not considered on the same tier as a General Inspectorate—a legacy of its noncombatant role and low social status. At the suggestion of the chief of the GGS, this changed starting in 1910. The Transport Inspectorate became a General Inspectorate with a subordinate Inspection for Aviation and Motor Vehicles. This sub-inspectorate had a small allocation of 130,000 marks for airplane procurement, which amounted to thirty aircraft by the end of 1911. This number was not adequate for the survival of small manufacturers. Thus, larger companies such as Rumpler, Aviatik, and Albatros emerged on top. The 12,500 members of the Air Fleet League, along with the sixty thousand members of the Aviation Association, pushed for national funding starting in 1912.[44]

The German Army preferred airplanes because they were easier to handle, service, and prepare than were the dirigibles. The War Ministry, which controlled the budget, favored airships, considering them safer and longer range and therefore more suitable for reconnaissance. However, in a 1911 quarterly aviation magazine, Maj. Herrmann Lieth-Thompsen cautioned against relying on airships. He argued that airplanes would prove better in aerial reconnaissance and foresaw reconnaissance skirmishes similar to the cavalry in screening operations.

This debate led to a proposal by the chief of the GGS in fall 1911. Moltke the Younger suggested diverting funds away from airships to purchase airplanes. War Minister Josias von Heeringen and Transport General Inspector von Lyncker disagreed. The War Minister advised Kaiser Wilhelm II that it was most important to maintain Germany's edge over France in airships. He argued that France already had an advantage in airplanes. The kaiser agreed, and the War Ministry continued to fund airships. Airships were by then a major cultural symbol of German aerial creativity and superiority. The manufacturers Zeppelin and Parseval, as well as their subcontractors, had superior connections with the War Ministry. They also threatened to sell their ships to potential enemies.[45]

The difference between the two positions was large. Moltke wanted 112 airplanes in 1911. The War Minister wanted thirty-four. Whereas France spent most of its aviation budget on airplanes, Germany spent only about half. In a November 1912 letter to the War Ministry, Moltke compared airships to fixed-wing aircraft for reconnaissance purposes: "The maneuvers in Thorn clearly demonstrated the importance of aerial reconnaissance in cooperation with photography. The defense will make the airship mission difficult; they or their hangars will soon fall prey to enemy artillery or enemy bombing. The stationary balloons are also severely threatened by artillery fire. The airplane remains the only means of aerial reconnaissance."[46]

The German Office of Aviation Troops published the first aviation manual in March 1913. The number one mission of all aircraft—dirigible or fixed wing—was strategic and tactical reconnaissance. Most larger ships were expected to carry radio apparatus for communication within a range of three hundred to five hundred kilometers. For fixed-wing aircraft, the expected airspeed ranged between seventy and 120 kilometers per hour with an altitude between three hundred and eight hundred meters. This manual also provided a concrete expectation of what could be observed from the air. Although today this may seem obvious, the following quote provides good insight into what was possible in those embryonic aircraft:

> In good visibility, observation from airships is easy. One can observe to distances of twenty kilometers and farther. Aerial photos can be made at distances of twelve kilometers and farther. The higher the aircraft flies, the easier it is to see through low-lying ground haze. Fog, cloudbanks, and rain are detrimental to aerial observation effectiveness and require lower altitude flying. Moving troops, columns on the march, or troops building fortifications are easily recognized.
>
> Weather provides good cover against observation. Troops in column marching cross-country, in open fields, and away from the roads, are easy to find. Dust clouds assist the observation; rain makes it more difficult. Bivouac troops are often not observed, especially one-day camp in villages, edges of forests, rows of trees, or in shadows. Light brush provides minimal, and a forest almost total, concealment from observation. Packs and stacked rifles in an open field are easily recognized, as well as concentrations of vehicles and horses. It is difficult to differentiate vehicles such as guns from munition wagons, machine guns from field kitchens, [or] when they are on the march or in bivouac. The battle equipment of unmounted troops simplifies the process of getting an accurate count of the unit.
>
> Covering equipment with ground sheets is effective protection against observation only [when] covers blend in with the surrounding landscape–when they do not, such equipment is spotted more readily. In some circumstances, shooting at airplanes can be not only ineffective, but also actually betray troop positions. Higher headquarters set up in close quarters in the open make their presence known and invite being bombed. Setting up a headquarters next to an easily recognized landing field is not recommended for the same reason. The number of bivouacked, sheltered troops under observation can usually be determined by the number of parked vehicles in the vicinity. Observation is made more difficult by breaking up larger artillery and wagon parks into smaller elements and putting it under available cover in cultivated areas. This also applies to troops in bivouac. Whether and how accurately aerial

spotting of troops who are not moving and not in close formation can be carried out depends on many circumstances.[47]

Lighter-than-Air Reconnaissance

In August 1914, the German army had six airship battalions totaling seventeen companies. Each company had four officers, fourteen NCOs, 150 enlisted men, and about eight civilian airship specialists and mechanics. A company operated one or two airships and an airship hall. The total number of dirigibles initially committed in the west was, however, only five. Under direct command of the General HQ were the Zeppelin airships VII, VIII, IX, Hansa, Victoria Luise, and Sachsen, and the Parseval airship IV; and under the Army of the Meuse was ZVI. The intent was to use them early on long-range strategic reconnaissance. Once the opposing forces were heavily engaged, it was believed the dirigibles could best be used at night for offensive operations. Early on, these platforms were supposed to be the key to strategic reconnaissance because of the distances involved. These airships, it was argued, could travel immense distances and identify flanks and forces heretofore secure from discovery.

Fixed-Wing Aircraft

In the fixed-wing category, the modern amateur of German military aviation generally thinks there existed a reconnaissance plane called the Taube. While this is true, it tells only a small part of the story. The Germans entered the war in 1914 with two standard types of aircraft: the Taube monoplane and the tractor biplane. The monoplane was older and approaching obsolescence. Compared with the biplane, it was heavier, had a slower speed and rate of climb, and a very long takeoff run. It had its fans, however; Major Siegert of the flying troops considered the Taube a superbly stable airplane whose single wing would enable a free field of observation and fire. In total, the Germans were equipped with a wide variety of aircraft including both monoplanes (A-types), and biplanes (B-types). The biplane became the mainstay of the army due to its increased capabilities. Observers achieved better results with the biplanes because their wing size was smaller than the monoplane single wing. In 1912, the army purchased sixty monoplanes and seventy-nine biplanes. By 1913, those purchase numbers rose to 183 monoplanes and 278 biplanes. However, none of these aircraft were homogeneous: By February 1914, the War Ministry had purchased planes from eleven different manufacturers. Although there were other B-types, the aircraft produced by the firms of LVG, Aviatik and Albatros were by far the most numerous. Together, they formed the backbone of the aircraft in 1914, combining to make up nearly 75 percent of the German Air Service's inventory.[48]

At the time of mobilization, typical endurance for a German aircraft was three hours. Considering an average cruising speed of fifty-five to seventy miles per hour, each aircraft was roughly limited to a hundred-mile radius of its own airfield. Cruising altitude varied greatly depending upon the types of aircraft and mission. For long-range flights, B-type aircraft were expected to cruise at between six thousand and seven thousand feet, whereas A-types were to operate at around five thousand feet. Once an enemy column was sighted, however, German aviators typically dropped to around thirty-five hundred feet to better identify details of the enemy force. Prewar guidelines set one thousand meters (thirty-two hundred feet) as the minimum altitude allowed over enemy occupied territory. Tactical reconnaissance and artillery direction flights were therefore performed between three thousand and four thousand feet, although circumstances often compelled airmen to ignore the rule in order to provide better results. The radius was roughly one hundred miles (depending upon the aircraft type and wind conditions), which made the overall distance covered during a roundtrip about two hundred miles (320 kilometers). The flight path would not be "directly to point A" and then "turn 180 degrees" and travel straight back. Instead, the aircraft would travel in a wide loop in order to cover a broader area of territory.

Created in 1913, the five German aircraft battalions included one Bavarian battalion. Each active army corps had an aircraft company, a *Feld-Flieger Abteilung* (FFA)[49]; the reserve corps had none (except for the Guard Reserve Corps, which also had an aircraft company). The HQ for each numbered army had an assigned company with six aircraft; the same number was assigned to each active army corps.

These five aircraft battalions mobilized thirty-four flying companies for the field. In addition, they mobilized eight flying companies for the fortresses for a total of 232 manned aircraft.[50] After mobilization, each field aircraft company consisted of fifteen officers and 117 NCOs and enlisted men and operated six aircraft. There were twelve different types of aircraft, including Rumpler-Taube, Albatros, Aviatik, AEG, and Gotha models. In general, they had mostly hundred-horsepower Mercedes-Benz (or Argus) engines that allowed them to fly between eighty and one hundred kilometers per hour. With a ceiling of two thousand to twenty-four hundred meters, they would ideally operate at an altitude of eight hundred to one thousand meters, but this altitude left them exposed to infantry and machine-gun fire.[51] Planes were not armed; the pilots only carried pistols, the 08 Lugar or its long-barreled variant, and later their Mondragon or Mauser self-loading carbines. Only after Anthony Fokker invented a mechanism that allowed a machine gun to fire through the propeller blades did the Fokker E1 become the first truly efficient fighter plane.

Aviation Analysis

The biggest problem confronting aviation units in 1914 had nothing to do with the airmen's skill or their equipment, but was instead the lack of any centralized authority overseeing their employment. As Inspector of *Fliegertruppe*, Col. Walter von Eberhardt was forced to remain in Berlin where he was powerless to influence unit actions in the field. Even more problematic was the lack of an aviation staff officer at each army HQ. Thus, without any commander with authority over all flying sections in the field and without aviation staff officers, the flying companies each largely depended on their respective corps or army commander's orders. Aircraft were a new tool. Neither the commanders nor their staffs were experienced in detailing reconnaissance requirements to aviation companies. As a result, requests for information that originated with the OHL were seldom imparted to the flying companies. Operational orders for aviators often did not dictate the things that they should investigate. Unfortunately, this often resulted in the aviation company receiving no orders at all. If the company commanders did not get in touch with the higher unit HQ, then they would not even know the orientation of the front lines. Consequently, HQ initially did not expect much from aerial reconnaissance and often confirmed aviation reports by other reconnaissance means. Experience soon proved that the aviation reports were reliable when they gave positive observations; however, negative reports were a bit trickier because it was possible the observers overlooked the target or the target was concealed.[52]

Aviation assets should have been assigned to the same analyzing HQ as the cavalry reconnaissance. That way, there was only one clearinghouse for all the reconnaissance assets. Clearly, the authors of the cavalry memoirs expected this but it did not happen, and aviation reconnaissance and cavalry reconnaissance were kept separate and analyzed separately.

Communication Failures

In the German context of mission type orders, with its emphasis on initiative, it should not seem surprising that no system of communications was devised. For the most part, no direct communication of any sort existed between Moltke's HQ and the German right wing armies or among those armies themselves. No real effort was made to take advantage of the network of Belgian civilian telephone lines or to adapt or reconstruct the network for military use. The only means of direct communication among the various western army HQ and the OHL was by radio, then a new and unreliable technology. With no system of liaison officers and with such inadequate means of electronic communication, the German High Command frequently remained in the dark for twenty-four hours or more with no news at all from one or another of the numbered armies.[53]

Reconnaissance is an exercise in communication. It begins with the observer, who must describe what he has seen. Next comes transmitting the description to the proper authorities. This is followed by an analysis of the description by the intelligence staff. Finally, the staff informs the commander of their analysis and he makes a decision. At that point, the decision should be written into an order and then transmitted to the intended recipient. Then the recipient in turn must go through his decision cycle to execute the orders that were sent to him. This method has been used for a very long time and is most successful when completed quickly. Technology was supposed to increase the speed of these steps. Every single step in the exercise is subject to somebody making a mistake. The observer can do a poor job describing what he has seen. The transmission to higher authority can go awry. The analysis by the staff could simply be wrong. The commander might make the wrong decision—albeit this is usually determined in hindsight, when the results are evaluated. The order implementing that decision could be poorly constructed. The recipient of the order could make his own mistakes in his decision cycle. Technology could not only speed the process, but also cut down on mistakes as clarity was increased.

Communication between HQ had been practiced for centuries. Napoleon once said, "The whole secret of the art of war lies in making one's self master of the communications."[54] Napoleon did it by moving army corps along separate routes, maintaining coordination by messenger. In general, the process seems to have been efficient—most of the time. The inevitable delays were generated as armies grew larger and then organizationally more complex, however, increasing interest in the advantages of *Auftragstaktik*. Technology underscored the shift. Although telephones and telegraphs had been shown to be effective in the Russo-Japanese War, technology was still in its infancy. Technology was not understood nor was it trusted. Yet, there were many examples of handwritten notes and verbal communicating going wrong—remembering perhaps the charge of the light brigade in the battle of Balaclava when a single message carried by Captain Nolan triggered a synergy of disastrous events. That was the familiar way. And under stress, soldiers tend to revert to the familiar.

Unsurprisingly then, electronic communications were a glaring area of neglect in the German Army. Moltke the Younger had been content to conduct annual maneuvers and staff rides by each night handing out detailed plans and directives for the next day's assignments. Moltke the Elder had used this same method. Electronic communications had a very bad reputation despite a lack of concrete reasoning. Based on oral criticism as well as guidance written in textbooks, electronics were not trusted. The expectation was that electronic means would fail at the critical moment and that a messenger or courier would have to be used. The speed of the electronic communications was recognized but not considered a replacement for reliability. Think of how the reliable ease of cell phones and email has dominated modern communications.[55]

There were only two means of electronic communication in the German Army: telephone and radio. Telegraph communications were abandoned in 1910. By 1914, the intent was to provide each army corps with a company, and each numbered army with a battalion, of telephone specialists. At the beginning of the war, there were nine signal battalions.[56] While this might seem a robust system, many problems existed in the infancy of communications. There were radios but these were large and cumbersome, scarce, and had very limited range. In addition, the distribution of the radios was haphazard. The radio equipment was not the same at all HQ and was not always compatible. The Telefunken equipment was more modern and had a range of 250 to three hundred kilometers. There was also the older style Poulsen system that had a range of one hundred kilometers. These two different types of radio systems were not compatible and could not communicate with each other. Each of the numbered armies on the right flank therefore had two radios in its HQ, one of each kind. There was, however, only one radio at the OHL. This highest HQ had one large radio station that was motorized. There were also three fortresses on the Western front (Metz, Strassburg, and Köln) that had strong stationary radio sets capable of transmitting at ranges up to one thousand kilometers. Each numbered army had two large radios that were horse drawn. Army corps active or reserve did not have a radio; army corps only had a telephone detachment. In the cavalry, the corps-level HKK had no electronic communications at all—the cavalry division had two mobile Telefunken radios and a telephone squadron. These two radios consisted of one large one like the army-level radio and one smaller, more mobile, that had a range of only eighty kilometers.[57]

Unlike the modern-day standard practice, communication in the German Army of August 1914 was established from front to rear. Divisions had no communications troops. Messages among divisions and army corps were designed to be handled by dispatch rider or motorcar. Army and corps did have telephone equipment. It might not have all been standard, but it did function. What was needed for that to happen was for wire communications to be established between army and army corps HQ. The operative word is wire. Phone lines not only had to be constructed, but it required wire; lots and lots of wire. As the distances between units in August 1914 expanded, the length of wire required metastasized. The size of the army corps telephone detachments varied widely. Ninth Army Corps had five wire construction platoons and 160 kilometers of wire. Second Army Corps had only four platoons and 128 kilometers of wire. The Reserve Army Corps had a much smaller footprint, with only three construction platoons and 72 kilometers of wire.[58]

General Major Hans von Kuhl lamented extensively about the lack of communication. He characterized liaison between the OHL and the different numbered armies as defective. He claimed that the telephone sections were far too weak and insufficiently equipped with communication equipment. By using the telephone equipment in the rear area, he was able to make contact occasionally with the OHL. If the telephone connection did not work, the fallback plan was to use a motorcar. However, motorcars frequently arrived at an HQ to find a nonfunctional telephone line. Therefore, First Army relied almost entirely on radio to communicate. Of the two different kinds of available radio equipment, only one of the radios was compatible with the OHL radio. The second kind of radio could only communicate with adjacent armies in the hope that the message would be relayed all the way back to the OHL. Even in the best of conditions, the second method was employed with the understanding that there would be significant delays in the communication. In the first method, the expectation was a wait of several hours because of the processing of messages from the different armies at the OHL. Frequently, messages had to be sent some three or four times. Decoding required further delay when it was necessary. Even at critical times, delays of twenty-four hours were not uncommon. There was a tendency, especially for long messages, for the encrypting step to be skipped. Of course, this led to early radio intercepts such as that which was so important in Tannenberg.[59]

Other means of communication were haphazard. Signal lamps had been discontinued, but flag signals were used in both infantry and artillery operations. The army's stock of twenty-one thousand carrier pigeons was to offset this deficit.[60] However, the reality was that carrier pigeons were only used in fortresses at this point in the war. Some of the Jäger battalions assigned to the HKKs actually used message dogs. Air crews were trained in dropping messages to the ground, but results were unpredictable.[61]

3

Operational Issues

If people in Germany think I am the supreme commander, they are grossly mistaken. The General Staff tells me nothing and never asks my advice. I drink tea, go for walks, and saw wood.—Kaiser Wilhelm II[1]

Enemy Situation

With the 1839 Treaty of London securing its neutrality, the small nation of Belgium had little political will to increase the power of its military. Instead, most Belgians believed the treaty guarantees would somehow protect their territorial integrity. The dominant strategic concept was, upon invasion, to withdraw the army—what there was of it—into the fortress of Antwerp and wait for one of the guaranteeing powers to come to their rescue.

The fortress of Antwerp was built in 1868 despite strong political opposition. In 1880, King Leopold II decided, despite even more political opposition, on a defensive strategy to oppose an invasion by Germany or France with a series of fortresses along the River Meuse. The new forts were constructed from 1888 to 1892 on the latest German model, presumably capable of resisting high-angle artillery fire from long-range guns. As the political situation deteriorated, the king of Romania advised the Belgians in 1912 to watch the defense of all her frontiers.[2]

While many laymen might consider Belgium a flat country that would allow easy operations of infantry and cavalry, it is instructive to examine the specific terrain from the German border to the city of Liège. In 1914, there were 168,000 inhabitants in Liège. The city was thirty kilometers from the German border and fifteen kilometers from the Dutch border to the north. Three roads led directly to Liège from Aachen. One ran south to Verviers and then northwest down the Vesdre Valley; another straight across the open fields of eastern Wallonia to Visé, just below the Dutch border; still another ran between these two, dipping south from Aachen just inside the Belgian border and then running due west through Battice and Fléron. Another road led out of the Ardennes forest northward to Liège, from Malmédy over the Hautes Fagnes to Spa.[3] There are three rivers that intersect at Liège. The Meuse, flowing northwest, divides Liège. Ranging in width from one hundred to 160 meters, it was a formidable obstacle. Numerous bridges led across it, almost all of them within the firing range of the forts. The Meuse, Ourthe, and Vesdre merge at Liège and form very deep-cut valleys with steep slopes. The heights of the banks are disrupted by canyons. The view was considerably complicated, especially on the right bank of the Meuse, due to building development and forests. The forested and hilly Meuse Valley contained considerable dead ground that the forts could not completely cover. Large trees limited visibility. Ravines provided avenues of approach to some forts (Chaudefontaine, Embourg, Flémalle, and Barchon). On the other hand, the plateau in the north and west from Pontisse to Hollogne was completely open. Troops in closed formations mostly depended on the pathways.

Liège was a fortress but not the traditional kind with its center surrounded by a wall. The defenses constructed between 1888 and 1892 by the Belgian military engineer General Henri Brialmont consisted of twelve forts placed at regular intervals—six on the river's right or east bank and six on the left bank.[4] On the right bank of the Meuse, four fortresses were located between the lower stream of the Meuse and Vesdre and two fortresses or fortins (smaller forts) connecting to the south up to the upper stream of the Meuse. On the left bank of the Meuse were six fortins and fortresses. Fortins and fortresses had similar designs. They were surrounded by a dry trench. There, and on the glacis wire, obstacles were mounted. These were a series of detached concrete bunkers buried under mounds of earth. Piston-like gun turrets slid up and down cylindrical shafts. A network of underground chambers housed machinery to maneuver the guns; stored ammunition and supplies, electric generators, and ventilating fans; and provided living quarters for the garrison. Each fortress was equipped with eight heavy and four light cannons; the fortins with five heavy and three to four light. The facilities had on average 3.5-kilometer-wide gaps between them, which were not fortified during peace time. The 5.7-centimeter rapid-fire guns on gun carriages and flood lights, however, were present in the facilities, expected to cover in the spaces between the facilities. The range of the flat trajectory guns was up to 10,400 meters; the range of the high-angle guns up to 6,900 meters. The target-spotting fire control of the defenders in some cases was impaired by the obscuring terrain. Outside target observation was necessary; thus, interfering with the observers was important. The forts averaged about four miles from the city center and formed a defensive perimeter with a circumference of over thirty-two miles. However, the forts were isolated and unable to support each other. Perhaps not obvious, but when looking at communications, vital—the forts could not talk to one another. Therefore, there would be no mutual cooperation in thwarting German approaches. This tended to leave the rear approaches vulnerable, especially when following the normal supply routes in.

In August 1914, the fortresses and their garrison of approximately forty thousand men including mobile troops was placed under the orders of Gen. Gérard Leman, who performed the dual functions of Third Division Commander and Governor of Liège.

East of the city of Namur, and very similarly to Liège, the Meuse also flows between one hundred and 160 meters wide and two to six meters deep. The hills along its north bank are steeper and rockier than are those along the south bank. Some sixty-five kilometers upstream from Liège, Namur guarded the junction of the Meuse and Sambre Rivers. Its ancient citadel sat atop a triangular promontory overlooking the city and the two rivers. The city's defenses included five large and four small forts of the same design as those at Liège—six on the Meuse's left bank and three on the right bank.[5]

Whereas the fortresses at Liège and Namur were substantial, the ones at Huy were quite old and offered little opposition. North of Liège, the river and valley widened and the banks gradually flattened. A canal that paralleled the river was twenty meters wide and two meters deep.[6]

The turn of the century saw small adjustments in Belgium's military posture. Repair of the fortresses were begun in 1906. Conscription regulations were updated in 1909, eliminating the old system of drawing lots and establishing national service. The army budget was increased by 30 percent, but not until 1913. Previous systematic, serious budget shortfalls culminated in a complete lack of heavy artillery, a great deal of miscellaneous materials due from Germany at the war's outbreak, and a major shortage of rifles. Nonetheless, mobilization eventually brought 110,000 men into service, organized in six infantry divisions and one cavalry division. This field army was distributed with a division deployed facing Germany, France, and England, these intended as an advanced guard to absorb an initial shock. The remaining three divisions constituted a mass of maneuver whose movements depended on which nation violated national sovereignty.

This "defense in all directions" was a logical consequence of Belgium's loudly proclaimed neutrality; it meant however, that Belgium had no real plan—only ad hoc maneuvering in response to uncertain diplomatic situations. This deployment in three directions did not change during the initial German concentration of forces. The Belgian government was determined, right to the last minute, to maintain a neutral position. Not until August 4, 1914, was the army faced to the east to counter the German threat.[7]

Absent long-term planning about how to react to a violation of Belgian neutrality, the central questions revolved around how best to concentrate the forces against Germany. The king favored a forward defense along the River Meuse from Liège to Namur. Using those two fortresses as anchors, the army could have been a significant obstacle to any German invasion. Other options included defense of the Gette River, sending a division to the major fortresses, and an attack into Germany. After the war, Kluck said he feared that the king's plan would be implemented and create a significant delay.[8]

Railroad Blocking

The Belgians did have a railroad-blocking plan. They started discussing it in 1895 and adjusted it in 1907. Nevertheless, there was no unanimity about how it was to be executed or whether or not to destroy bridges and tunnels. The Belgian Supreme Headquarters (SHQ) initially decided to leave the tunnels and the railroad bridges intact, allowing a Belgian-Allied counteroffensive east of the Meuse River and into Germany.

Two main rail lines ran into Belgium from Germany and one from Luxembourg. One line ran from Aachen along the Dutch border, passed through a tunnel at Hombourg, and crossed the Meuse north of Liège. The second line came in from the direction of Eupen and ran along the Vesdre River past Verviers, where it connected with a line heading north along the Ourthe River. This line passed through the Nasproué Tunnel. The Luxembourg line ran along the Amblève River passed through a tunnel near Trois Ponts and connected with the Ourthe line. Another line from Malmedy ran through the Stavelot Tunnel before connecting with the Amblève line.

General Leman, in command of Liège, was not worried about the railroad bridges. Leman's programs concerned destroying railway tunnels but only blocking bridges. He sent Lieutenant van Billoen to Hombourg, Captain Baudry to Nasproué, Lieutenant Beaupain to Trois Ponts, and Lieutenant Dindal to Stavelot to ensure the tunnels were blocked. In addition, the viaducts along these railways were rigged for destruction.[9] According to this plan, both railway bridges would remain intact.

French Wishes

Belgium's neutrality had prevented even rudimentary joint planning on international levels before the war's outbreak. The French wanted the Belgians to advance, thinking the Belgians could either push their field army up to the Meuse in support of the projected French offensive in the Ardennes or could strike against the German right flank if it moved south of the Meuse. The French saw the Belgian Army as an adjunct to a grand alliance. The

3. Operational Issues

Belgians, on the other hand, were convinced they faced the main weight of the German Army and were bent on protecting Belgian territory. Whereas the French expected the Belgians to fall back south of Namur to extend the French line, the Belgian plan was to hold on the line of the River Gette and wait for the French to come to their relief. Failing that, the Belgians intended to retreat north to the stronghold of Antwerp.[10]

Garde Civique

Belgian men from ages twenty-one to forty-five years who were not inducted into the army were to be organized into the *Garde Civique* (National Guard), which was not subordinate to the War Minister but to the Minister of the Interior. This meant the Garde Civique mission and command arrangements were not at all clear. There were two organizations: an "active" and a "nonactive" Garde Civique. In towns with populations over ten thousand, the Garde Civique was active, which is to say it had a limited degree of leadership training. Actives wore full uniforms (which individual members were obliged to purchase) and drilled regularly. The role of the active Garde Civique in August 1914 varied considerably. A few units participated in the fighting. More typically, Garde members dug trenches and set up and then dismantled barricades. However they were employed, active Garde members

Garde Civique. With uniforms such as these, there is little doubt they could be confused for civilians.

were required to wear their uniforms. Most Garde detachments were disarmed and disbanded by August 18, 1914.

The nonactive Garde was expected to perform police functions during emergencies and only when activated by the king. It was to play no military role. In an inexplicable move that remains unexplained, before the invasion, the Belgian government called up about one hundred thousand nonactives but failed to mobilize the forty-six thousand active Garde members. The nonactive Garde Civique was inundated with applications during the first days of the war. New recruits, who normally wore a short blue tunic, were required as of August 5, 1914 to add an armband and cockade with the national colors and to bear their weapons openly. Three days later, a blue shirt was required as well. Some members guarded bridges, railroad lines, and other sites of strategic importance in the opening days of the war.[11]

Ultimate German Objective

"The ultimate objective ... was to disperse first the Belgian Army, then the British Expeditionary Force, and finally to fall on the French armies."[12]

The Germans had a slightly different military decision-making process in 1914 compared to today's, but several things are recurrent. The overall concept and mission is issued in the form of an order to the lower HQ, which then analyzes the mission it has been assigned. Because this is a very broad mission analysis, the identification of specific tasks is central. Some of the tasks are specified by the higher HQ in their order. Others are implied tasks. Implied tasks are derived from a detailed analysis of the higher HQ's order, the enemy situation and courses of action, and the terrain. Only those implied tasks that require allocation of resources should be considered. A higher-level organization task could easily be the entire mission for a lower subordinate organization. The challenge of a military plan is to identify *all* those tasks and the purpose of the task. That becomes infinitely more difficult facing an opponent with free will—the usual situation. After that is done, they identify troops to conduct or fulfill those tasks. It is often said that this sequence is obvious; however, it does require an identification of all the tasks—which may not be obvious. By then applying specific troops responsible for each task, they determine if they have the assets to perform all specified and implied tasks. This process is currently referred to as "troops-to-task."

During this analysis, facts are determined as well as assumptions. Fact: the river is 150 meters wide. Assumption: the river is not fordable. There is a broad spectrum of assumptions that can be made for most military operations. Assumptions are suppositions about the current or future situation that are assumed to be true in the absence of facts. Assumptions must have the probability of truth. If a known fact disproves the assumption, then it is an invalid assumption—not to be used for planning. "Assuming away" potential problems, such as weather or likely enemy options, would result in an invalid assumption.

Moltke and the GGS provided the overall vision:

> The main forces of the German Army are to advance through Belgium and Luxembourg into France. Their advance is to be regarded as a wheel pivoting on the area Thionville–Metz. Should Belgium offer resistance to the advance through its territory, Liège is to be taken by Second Army, so as to free the main roads which are covered by that fortress. For this purpose, Eleventh Infantry Brigade of Third Corps and Fourteenth Infantry Brigade of Fourth Corps (First Army) have been placed under the orders of the general commanding Tenth Corps. As soon as Ninth Corps, temporarily allotted to Second Army, has moved forward, First Army is to advance toward Aix-la-Chapelle [also known by the name *Aachen*]. When Liège has been taken and as soon as First and Second Army are in position on the roads of advance level with Liège, the general advance of the main forces will be ordered by the Supreme Command. Second Army will march with its right flank on Wavre, and First Army will receive orders to march on Brussels and to cover the right flank of the [numbered] armies. Its advance, together with that of Second Army, will regulate the pace of the general wheel.[13]
>
> It was essential to prevent the assembly of the Belgian, British, and French reinforcements as otherwise that could spoil the execution of the Supreme Army Commands [OHL] plan, which was to envelop the main French forces with the strong right wing.[14]

HKK 2, consisting of the Second, Fourth, and Ninth Cavalry Divisions, was at first placed under Second Army. Once the advance began, it was to come under the immediate orders of the Supreme Command and advance north of Namur toward the line Antwerp–Brussels–Charleroi in order to discover the position of the Belgian Army and to watch for any landing of British troops and the arrival of French forces in northern Belgium. HKK 2 was also tasked to keep First Army HQ supplied with information.[15]

Once the general advance was signaled, HKK 2 would report directly to the OHL. It was a formidable military shopping list. The order specified four individual tasks for HKK 2:

Task 1: Discover the position of the Belgian Army. Purpose: Although not specified, the purpose had to be keeping the Belgian Army in play until it was defeated by the much larger German armies in the field. The task did not specifically mention what to do with the Belgian Army, simply to find a position not to force it one way or the other. The absolute worst case would be to allow it to evacuate to Antwerp and perch on the flank of the German advance.

Task 2: Watch for any landing of British troops. Purpose: To keep the British from extending the French line or, preferably, to isolate them where they could be defeated in stride. This was a very ambitious long-range intent.

Task 3: Watch for the arrival of French forces in northern Belgium. Purpose: To identify the exposed left flank of the French Army, which was essential information if Second Army was to fix the French in place for First Army's flank attack.

Task 4: Keep First Army HQ supplied with information. Purpose: To allow First Army to maneuver independently and outflank the allies once their flank was discovered. This was perhaps HKK 2's most important task and it created a convoluted chain of command for the German forces. Initially the forces under Second Army would be directed toward Liège.

The staff work required for HKK 2 on these four divergent purposes would be large. The amount of work indeed seems overwhelming when applying a simple planner's tool of troops-to-task. Three divisions of cavalry were a far cry from the number Schlieffen envisioned. The next closest cavalry formation was HKK 1, which advanced in front of Third Army and consisted of only two divisions. Those two divisions, moreover, were far from the open fields of Belgium. In fact, HKK 1 was on Third Army's left flank, and HKK 2 was on its own. It was to surround Liège and ensure the Belgian Army would not escape intact into the fortress of Antwerp. HKK 2 was simultaneously to prepare for the general advance to follow by clearing the way, especially the roads. Initially, the scheme of maneuver was to send one division—Ninth Cavalry Division—directly against Liège south of the city, and two divisions north.

The plan included many *implied* tasks such as mobilization, moving to the assembly areas, crossing a major river (Meuse), holding or repairing bridges, and maintaining logistics built around railroads. A subsequent order was expected to provide more guidance on the advance, especially considering that other forces directly attached to the OHL were new and had not been fully tested. Further, airships were to be used for strategic reconnaissance from the start of the operation. One lower-level cavalry commander summed it up: "It was necessary [to go] as quickly as possible over the Meuse and get the stronghold Liège off with a punch at lightning speed. Then it was important to overrun Belgium, storming ahead to the sea, to make it a base for an attack of great magnitude and to advance according to the Schlieffen Plan in a favorable direction against the flank and back of the opponent."[16]

Disperse the Belgian Army

To fulfill Moltke's plan, certain tasks had to take place prior to the declaration of war. These included the invasion of Luxembourg and premobilization movement of forces in preparation for the attack on Liège. Belgium was to be handed an ultimatum upon mobilization. Should Belgium accept the ultimatum, then the German troops could transit Belgium and enter its forts, leaving infrastructure, including railroads, bridges, and tunnels, intact. The next step was to have the main body of the German Army meet and engage the main body of the Belgian field army. It was assumed, if not understood, that man for man, the Germans would overwhelm the Belgians. So, the object of the plan had to be to engage the Belgian field army and prevent its withdrawal into the national redoubt of Antwerp. The most dangerous result would be if the Belgians "got away." Therefore, the plan had to deny the Belgian field army any freedom of action and maneuver. And therefore, it was most important to stop the Belgians in place. Close to the invasion's start line would be optimal, but it really did not matter where the place was. The Belgians could even decide to withdraw prophylactically early on before the Germans could make contact. Once however, the Belgians decided—or were forced to—make a stand anywhere, the Germans had to keep them there and away from Antwerp. On paper, it seems like a simple plan. Freedom of maneuver would be denied the Belgian Army by decisively engaging the front of the Belgian force and then maneuvering to envelop its flank and force it away from Antwerp. But war, in Clausewitz's words, is the province of confusion—as the Germans were to discover.

Maastricht Appendix

The fastest and easiest way to make contact with the Belgian field army and to keep it away from Antwerp was to advance from Germany on a straight line to Antwerp (the direct approach). This would require two major river crossings. First would be crossing the Meuse River. The second crossing would be over the Démer River, somewhere around the towns of Halen or Diest. Crossing the appendix would be a relatively short movement, maybe forty miles in total. By crossing the Maastricht Appendix, the German First Army would be able to cut the route to Antwerp and concentrate on the heights between Moll–Quaedmechelen–Diest on the flanks of the Belgian positions expected to be establish on the Gette River. To prevent being cut off from the fortress at Antwerp, the Belgian Army would have to shift its position north. That would uncover Brussels and open the way for the advance of the Second German Army, in addition to moving the Belgians further away from any link up with their allies. The direct approach across Holland would have cut down the marching of First Army by between forty-two and forty-five kilometers. For the northern part of First Army, that would save three days marching and two days for the southernmost army corps. This is no small point given the vital nature of speed and the operational axioms of space and time. First and Second Army would advance abreast, instead of Second Army going first and then First Army following behind, as required by the operational funnel of Aachen.[17]

As mentioned, this militarily logical course of action had been discarded in 1908 because it violated Dutch neutrality. In a marginal note to the Schlieffen memorandum, Moltke avidly supported Schlieffen's speculation that it might be possible to come to some sort of working relationship with Holland to allow German troops to freely pass the Maastricht Appendix. It was not clear if crossing this little piece of terrain would cause the Dutch to enter the war. It was within the realm of possibility that this violation of neutrality would be allowed by the Dutch government—especially in the context of a short war and a German victory.[18] Schlieffen had good military reasons for invading Holland. Crossing Limburg made particular sense in operational terms, allowing the German armies to avoid the heavily defended fortifications at Liège and offering five more railway lines into Belgium.[19] It is important to note that almost none of the four-division Dutch army was stationed in Limburg. Holland's well known defensive posture put almost all its forces on the western side of the country in what was known as Fortress Holland. The fortress at Maastricht was quite old and not of any military use. A German invasion of the Netherlands through Limburg might precipitate an attack by Britain on the Schelde toward Antwerp, an option that was considered highly unlikely for Great Britain.[20]

Highlighting a difference of opinion in the short war–long war argument, Schlieffen wanted as short a war as possible while Moltke seems to have given much more credence to the possibility of a long war and the corresponding usefulness of a neutral Holland. He summed up his motives for avoiding the violation of Dutch neutrality in 1911:

> A hostile Holland at our back could have disastrous consequences for the advance of the German Army to the west, particularly if England should use the violation of Belgian neutrality as a pretext for entering the war against us. A neutral homeland security of our rear, because if England declared war on us for violating Belgian neutrality cannot herself violate Dutch neutrality. She cannot break the very law for whose sake she goes to war. Furthermore, it will be very important to have Holland a country whose neutrality allows us to have imports and supplies. She must be the windpipe that enables us to breathe.[21]

Keeping Holland neutral might be described as a political decision. However, the German Chancellor in 1899 said, "If the chief of staff, especially a strategic authority such as Schlieffen, believes such a measure to be necessary, then it is the obligation of diplomacy to adjust to it and prepare for in every possible way." There is no evidence that this position was abandoned or modified subsequently. To put it simply, politics had little if any impact on the shape of German war plans. This represented a total turnaround from the policy of Bismarck, who had let it be known in 1887 that it was an error to suppose that the conduct of German policy was subject to the views of the General Staff.[22]

After discarding this direct approach, the best the GGS could conceive was a huge detour, moving First Army south into an east–west oriented concentration area, moving sequentially through the city of Liège and then swinging north to get back in line before advancing. "When Liège has been taken and as soon as First and Second Army are in position on the roads of advance level with Liège, the general advance of the main forces will be ordered by the Supreme Command."[23] Operationally, the direct approach through Maastricht was abandoned in favor of this convoluted squeezing in order to enable First Army to fall on the left flank of the Belgians, as the strategic plan intended. This decision was made by the military staff for the purpose of keeping Holland out of the war. Moltke, in other words, balanced the considerable risks of using the southern (Liège) approach against the possible consequences of bringing Holland into the war. Why would he do this without the guidance and consent of the nation's political leaders? Abandoning the direct approach certainly increased the risk exponentially.

One study brings up an objection that incorporating the Netherlands into the theater of operations would have significantly weakened Germany's actual and projected force-to-space ratios. Acknowledging the point about force ratios, the Maastricht option did nevertheless avoid the restriction of Liège. It put the German First Army directly on the flank of the Belgian Army. A preemptive assault with early deployed forces, a *Handstreich* of the kind mounted against Liège, could most probably have taken this terrain while the Belgian field army was still concentrating.[24] As for the obstacles presented by the Dutch rivers, bridging rivers with pontoons was a normal task for the German infantry. There were bridge trains at divisional, as well as army corps, levels. These bridges could easily span a waterway of two hundred meters and, with a little reinforcing, could handle vehicle weights up to five tons. The slope of the bank and the speed of the river were important factors, but the Dutch locations offered flatter slopes than those further south.

The existence of a ford at Lixhe was a well-known stroke of good luck. This undefended route into the interior of Belgium was well known by the population as well as the military establishments of Belgium, Germany, and the Netherlands. It was commonly referred to as the "hole of Visé." Undefended is a strong word considering that the Belgians had stationed two policemen to defend the area. During the nineteenth century, General Henri Brialmont, the designer of the Meuse forts, recommended this area be fortified. Funding constraints found that no fortification was ever built. Between the world wars, in the 1930s, a fort named Eben-Emael was built in this location. The fort was considered impregnable by the Belgians but was neutralized by less than one hundred German glider troops in 1940.

Attack BEF

The Maastricht Appendix was a conundrum that had both operational and strategic elements. The challenge posed by the projected BEF was more operational. The only information about the British disembarkation was uncertain and contradictory. Reading information about the BEF in newspapers became the primary method of tracking its movement. As a result, the Germans never really knew where they were. Distance made location and movements difficult to ascertain; allowances had been made for this. Lighter-than-air reconnaissance was specifically designated for this unprecedented task. Its performance was vital for an operation based heavily on speed.

The dirigibles, however, were a complete and abject failure in the opening stages of the war. Prior to the German general advance, not a single strategic reconnaissance sortie was flown. The German official history makes a point of blaming this failure on the weather. Sadly, both Herwig and the author during an earlier book accepted this reason at face value. However, it is wrong. Looking at the weather, there were quite a few days when these airships could have been used. Given the distance involved, these were missions only airships could do. Yet not a single attempt was made, much less a systematic effort, despite the cost, force structure, and doctrinal arguments in favor. The first zeppelin sortie was a predictably unsuccessful bombing mission.

Fall on the French Armies

The strong German right wing was intended to flank the French. But was that to be a true envelopment or a breakthrough followed by a short, tactical flank attack? The latter seemed increasingly likely but would be much more difficult to accomplish, let alone conceptualize.[25] The chief of the General Staff amended and issued the war plan biannually. For example, theoretical planning for 1904–1905 was applied from April 1, 1904, to March 31, 1905. Broad guidance was issued to army commanders in a document known as the *Aufmarschanweisung* (deployment directive). This was an initial direction with no real stipulations about what to do after enemy contact. Upon mobilization, commanders of field armies and their chiefs of staff received sealed envelopes containing secret deployment orders. These orders would include the order of battle for their armies, deployment areas, and reporting lines and some general directives about railroad deployment and logistics, together with a concept of operations covering the first days of hostilities. During this planning process, the Railway Division put out a railway deployment schedule based on the Directives for Deployment, which were issued annually in November or December. These *Aufmarschpläne* (deployment plans) were allegedly destroyed at the end of the mobilization year in accordance with the great secrecy.[26] The plan known as *Aufmarsch 1914–1915* went into effect April 1, 1914, and was implemented as the actual war plan on August 2, 1914.

Due to the bombing of the Prussian archives during World War II, only fragmentary parts of this *Aufmarsch 1914–1915* remain, distributed in several different sources. The specific orders to the numbered armies, *Aufmarschanweisungen*, exist for only three of the western front's seven armies. Fifth, Sixth, and Seventh Army *Aufmarschanweisungen* still exist, so it is possible to get a view of the left wing. Unfortunately, this is not true of the all-important right wing. We can derive some concept of the operation from these three existing orders. We know each numbered army received its own mission statement. There was apparently no attempt to prescribe the detailed complete operation. Nor was there any indication that the annihilation of the French Army was the objective.[27] How this plan was to be accomplished was up to the individual army commanders.

This principle was inculcated in their military culture from the very start. In the Unification Wars between 1864 and 1871, the size of the army had outgrown the supreme commander's ability to exercise direct command of his deployed forces. To keep some form of control, it became important to develop a new concept that on one hand would enable some independence of action, while on the other hand preclude misguided action by lower-level leaders. Avoiding such misguidance would require uniformly trained and thinking military leaders on all levels—thus the need for general staff officers. The elder Moltke addressed the problem by developing a leadership doctrine, for the first time going beyond tactical drill manuals such as the *Exerzier-Reglement*. Moltke the Elder created an operational-level command between the tactical leadership in the firing line and the strategic leadership of the HQ with its multiple political implications. He also became the spiritual father of operational doctrines and principles, which then served as the basis for general officers' training. Thus, Moltke the Elder played a decisive role in developing *Auftragstaktik*.[28]

Particularly with poor communication lines, *Auftragstaktik* allowed the subordinate leader to pursue the given goals following the intent of his commander even if things developed differently under enemy fire. A core, at times overlooked, aspect of *Auftragstaktik* was a clear understanding of the goals and intent of the assigned mission. But *Auftragstaktik* was not a random process. Only with clear guidance during the issue of the order could the subordinate leader accomplish his mission given unexpected friction. When acting under mission-type command, the subordinate should never "wait for further advice," but independently attempt to troubleshoot and problem solve instead. Such independent action clearly risked violating other previously expressed constraints as a routine step to accomplishing the mission. Therefore, *Auftragstaktik* was seen as a leadership doctrine sustaining a particular type of innovative and independent leadership culture. Still today, this resulted in a leadership doctrine that teaches junior German army officers that when under fire, making a wrong decision is always better than making no decision and waiting for further direction.[29]

If *Auftragstaktik* was the first axiom of leadership, *Vernichtungsschlacht*—the battle of annihilation—was the second axiom. For the German Army around 1900, the offensive at all levels became increasingly central. Clausewitz considered the defensive as the stronger form of combat. Schlieffen inverted it into a dogma of the offensive—not only offensive but also annihilation—because for Schlieffen, a victory achieved over the enemy by frontal attack was only an "ordinary victory." Rather, he considered only total annihilation of the enemy force by envelopment acceptable. At that time, all European armies focused more on the offensive than on the defensive. However, before 1914, the German doctrine of the offensive had been transposed into a dogma of annihilating the enemy in one huge battle, usually by enveloping the enemy force from the flanks.[30] Clausewitz contradicted this concept. His maxim that defense was a stronger form of fighting than attack was certainly not easy to explain when looking at offense at all cost.[31]

In his series of Cannae writings, Schlieffen declared Hannibal's victory over the vastly superior Roman Army under the command of Consul Aemilius Paulus on August 2, 216 BCE as the role model for the operational leadership of the German Army.[32] Schlieffen, a student of military history, went so far as to slightly bend historical truth to fit his Cannae theories. His writings re-interpreted the wars of Frederick the Great and Napoleon and the Unification Wars in the focus of the Cannae-style battle.[33] Possibly the most famous quote from his works is, "The enemy's front is not the objective. The essential thing is to crush the enemy's flanks … and complete the extermination by attack upon his rear."[34]

Schlieffen deeply influenced the operative thinking of an entire generation of German military leaders who undertook general staff training. The handbook on tactical training at officers' schools also proclaimed a frontal breakthrough dangerous because the attacking forces breaking through could easily come under flank attack. This doctrine led German leaders to focus, perhaps obsessively, on trying to conduct outflanking operations and envelopments. Only Cannae–like attacks could lead to success; ordinary victories would damage but not annihilate enemy forces. In a diary entry for August 22, 1914, about the BEF, Gen. Wilhelm Groener wrote, "Just let them come! Our most ardent wish is to achieve no 'ordinary' victory against these scoundrels but rather one à la Schlieffen."[35]

Single Point of Failure: Staff Plans

The final German strategic plan allocated most of the army's resources to the west. This forced German planners to make all sorts of decisions during the July crisis in which military plans trumped civilian designs. In her 2003 book, *Helmuth von Moltke and the Origins of the First World War,* Annika Mombauer[36] masterfully analyzes that crisis. She strikes at the core of our understanding and makes it clear how Moltke alone understood the implications of military risk associated with the decision to go to war. Nobody else knew. Nobody else understood the risks. Everything was secret. The decision to go to war necessitated a preliminary attack against Luxembourg and a violation of Belgian neutrality. The entire plan hinged on a single means to an end—opening the gap at Liège. And nobody knew. The kaiser, the supreme warlord, was not enabled or made to understand the risks inherent in this military solution. Saying that nobody knew is quite a bold assertion, and it is contradicted by Herwig when he points out that in December 1912 both the Chancellor, Theobald von Bethmann Hollweg and the War Minister Josias von Heeringen were informed in writing that the broad contour of the empire's war plan was a major attack against France with a screen against Russia and that Belgian neutrality would have to be violated. Herwig concludes that the subsequently asserted innocence of German political elites was totally shattered; in fact, they understood the war plan and its general implications. We conclude instead that they may have known the broad context, but the top-level civilians in particular had no idea of how much risk was associated with implementing this plan. There is an essential difference between knowing, "We are going west" and being informed, "Oh by the way, this is a very very, risky operation."[37]

Nobody Knew but Moltke and the GGS

The kaiser did not know. The war minister did not know. The Chancellor of the empire did not know. The military cabinet that assigned the leaders did not know. Most importantly, the units and troops that had to execute this attack did not know. They could not train for it and could not know the objective. Only the General Staff knew. Even the general officers who had been involved in the planning knew only tangentially. "Talks with the senior political level on operational-strategic issues were also an exception. Under the constitution of the Reich, the operational-strategic plans should have been brought together in the person of the kaiser. This, however, was implemented only inadequately. No attempt was made in any quarter to scrutinize the plans of the Chief of his General Staff as to their inherent political risks."[38]

If the first attack did not open a gap at Liège quickly and decisively, then the entire plan would be in serious, potentially fatal, jeopardy. Moltke was the only one who understood this, which perhaps explains why he took the extremely unusual step of writing the ultimatum presented to Belgium—an action clearly out of his depth and official position. Perhaps he thought a properly worded ultimatum would cause Belgium to at least allow the Germans free passage. Moltke alone understood that trying to take the gap by force was at best a bad gamble. There is one more caveat as to why he did this. Herwig made it clear that each passing day diminished the chances of success. Moltke had long advocated war sooner rather than later. On July 29, 1914, he counseled Kaiser Wilhelm II that the Reich would "never hit it again so well as we do now with France's and Russia's expansion of their armies incomplete."[39]

Belgian Actions

The great unknown for the German planners was the status of Belgium. Would Belgium resist? What would the planners assume? France was mobilizing near its Belgian border, British intervention would extend the French deployment on the left of their line should the Allies advance into Belgium. If Belgium did not seriously resist, then the Belgian Army would be of little concern. Gaining territory rapidly would be the primary objective. Even then, Germany's armies would not be in position to advance until they completed mobilization. A screen or a covering force would be required to protect the vulnerable, still forming main armies from enemy action. What would comprise this covering force, given a military vacuum the size of Belgium and the necessary accompanying assumption that France would advance into that vacuum. What size should it be? How far would the German covering force advance? How far *could* it advance?

Certainly, the German cavalry could be the covering force. As conceived by Schlieffen, eight cavalry divisions would be on the right flank. They would enable peacetime-strength formations to follow up moving rapidly and taking terrain, and providing the covering forces to block any potential French incursion until the main German armies could deploy.

There seems, however, to have been no contingency plan, even in outline form, based on Belgium accepting the ultimatum. What would Germany do then? If indeed, for example, Belgium turned over the railroads that would have enabled significantly different German movement schedules. Should there not have been a branch of the plan based on the Belgians doing what Germany wanted them to do? Could there not have been a best-case scenario designating forward assembly areas in Belgium that First Army could reach by train? If Belgium had allowed free passage of the railroads, why should the main concentration area be around Aachen? But how realistic was the concept of completing mobilization within Belgium? Did this seem even remotely possible?

Schlieffen and Moltke both fully anticipated the worst-case contingency of Britain's appearance in the ranks of Germany's enemies. Schlieffen even predicted a British army some one hundred thousand strong would cooperate with the French on the left of their line. Both Schlieffen and Moltke believed the German right wing armies could execute their advance so rapidly that British intervention would be ineffective to save the French from destruction. On the other hand, neither Schlieffen nor Moltke appeared to have considered seriously the possibility of resolute resistance by the Belgian Army. That oversight would prove expensive.[40]

Secrecy and the General Staff

The German Army highly emphasized general staff officer training to ensure uniform ways of thinking and understanding the doctrine. Confronted with a particular tactical or operational problem, each general staff officer and higher commander—because higher commanders usually were also recruited from the pool of general staff officers—was expected to reach essentially the same assessment of the situation and finally come to the same decision on the situation. Given this uniformity in operative analysis and thinking, pursued to even the lower levels of company grade officers and even NCOs, detailed orders became obsolete. A very brief communication of mission, goals, and leader intention would be sufficient guidance to ensure subordinates accomplish the goals as intended.

The elder Moltke led his armies during the campaigns in 1866 and 1870–1871 by telegraph: sending short daily orders, usually using only a few words per army. Before taking Moltke's communication style during the Unification Wars as a role model, however, bear in mind that whenever possible, Moltke preferred face-to-face meetings with the king and with subordinate commanders. That legacy remained even as communications technology developed.

Before 1914, it was commonly said that Europe was home to five reputedly perfect institutions: The Roman Curia, the British Parliament, the Russian Ballet, the French Opera, and the Prussian General Staff. The GGS was the organizational center of the German Army.[41] In Berlin, the General Staff building at Königsplatz 6 was directly opposite the Reichstag building, yet it seemed invisible, covered by a veil of secrecy.[42]

In theory, the General Staff was subordinate to the War Ministry. In 1883, the chief of the General Staff gained immediate access to the kaiser.[43] Traditionally, however, the chief of General Staff could only execute his right of immediate access when the war minister and the chief of the military cabinet were also present. The General Staff neither appeared in public nor took a political role. Except for Alfred Waldersee, the chiefs of General Staff dedicated themselves to their military profession and did not develop political ambitions. Waldersee's efforts, moreover, achieved nothing significantly positive. His strict neutral political stance made Schlieffen appear an ideal chief of General Staff to follow Waldersee.

General Staff work was conducted under strict secrecy and behind literally closed doors. The public would only recognize General Staff work during the autumn maneuvers and the *Kaisermanöver* through publications of the General Staff itself[44] or publications of the departments for military history (*Kriegsgeschichtliche Abteilungen*).[45] Due to the high level of secrecy, hardly any enlisted men were assigned. Officers were required to do even the basic work of typing and filing because most issues were considered top secret and could be handled only by general staff officers. That resulted in a tendency to become absorbed in routine and nurtured serious inhibitors of the kind of organized thinking expected of general staff officers. Working tools were rare. For instance, until 1914, the Railroad Department had only one typewriter available to it.[46] Besides the telephone on the desk of the chief of the General Staff, only one additional telephone was available—and in a corridor used by all the other general staff officers. Some chiefs of the General Staff had personal idiosyncrasies. For example, Schlieffen—a widower who lived with his daughters after his young wife passed away—looking for company, sent a messenger to his direct subordinates, delivering a war game exercise to them on Christmas Eve afternoon. Accompanying it was an invitation to have coffee with him on Christmas afternoon for the presentation of results.[47]

The limitations of the General Staff's institutional responsibilities were as important as the tasks it performed. The General Staff was the kaiser's tool to lead the army. Its mission was to advise and prepare, not to command. Even after mobilization, the chief of General Staff, who changed his title to *Chef des Generalstabes des Feldheeres,* could only issue orders on behalf of the kaiser (*Seine Majestät befiehlt*). The staff had responsibility for neither the training nor the command of troops, nor the task of compiling field regulations. Instead, either the Ministry of War or the corps commanders accomplished these tasks.

In 1914, the staff consisted of 625 officers divided between the GGS in Berlin and the Troop General Staff that provided officers for corps and divisions.[48] There were three general staff officers per army corps staff and one per divisional staff. It is instructive to know that small unit commanders would go to the "General Staff Officer" to find out what was going on inside the division.[49]

The corps staffs eventually grew to four general staff officers known as the Ia, Ib, Ic, and Id, led by a *Chef des Stabes,* usually abbreviated as the "Chef," all of whom were known as *Truppengeneralstab*, headed by a colonel. Wartime army staffs also included the ordnance officers IIa, IIb, and so forth. The Chef had a direct reporting line to the GGS in Berlin. Divisions only had one Ia officer—roughly comparable to contemporary G3 (plans, operations, and training) NATO officers. Due to their direct line to the GGS, they often worked behind the backs of their own commanders.[50]

"Technical Problems"

In November 1914, Moltke summarized the consequences:

> Count Schlieffen even wanted to march the right wing of the German army through southern Holland. I changed this in order to avoid forcing the Netherlands also onto the side of our enemies, and preferred to take on the great technical difficulties which were caused by the fact that the right wing of our army had to squeeze through the narrow space between Aachen and the southern border of the province of Limburg.[51]

Squeeze Through Liège

The First and Second German Army alone amounted to 530,000 men that had to be squeezed through the gap at the city of Liège. The three major organizations involved were First Army, Second Army, and a cavalry force—HKK 2.

Actually, the numbers that had to squeeze through and make the approach march on the right flank remain subject to considerable debate. The Germans generally did not like to record headcounts; they preferably discussed the number of units. British sources, however, tended to seek a number. Figures from the British official history quoted German official accounts as: First Army, 320,000 and Second Army, 260,000.[52]

According to Volume 1 of the German official history,[53] First Army comprised 164 battalions, forty-one cavalry squadrons, 138 batteries with 796 guns and howitzers, and twenty-four engineer companies. Given that a battalion was roughly one thousand men strong in 1914, and given the relatively limited strength of the noncombatant rear echelons, it is clear the overall strength of First Army was unlikely to reach three hundred thousand at the start of hostilities. Further, the German official history (published in 1925) could not have sourced the British official history (published in 1922). According to the *Sanitaetsbericht ueber das Deutsche Heer III Band* page 36, the number was around 175,000. However, it was not clear which units this document counted; the number seemed low compared with our estimates that

First and Second Army would have had about 250,000 men each. So, it is not undisputedly clear exactly how many men and equipment had to be squeezed through the gap. But by any standards, their deployment would cover a large body of terrain.

The original order from the OHL covered only the start of the operation. Its intent was to enter Belgium and deploy the forces to advance. The OHL would order the advance. Task: Pass through the twenty-kilometer wide chokepoint of the fortress of Liège. Purpose: To align forces to continue the advance. Finding and gaining position on that flank had to be the operation's laser focus. If an advantageous position on the flank could be achieved, the German Army would be in position to roll up the Allied forces. Failure to execute that destruction did not bear thinking about or even planning for. Planning and force structure, therefore, had to focus on achieving that goal. Capturing Liège was a means to an end.

Railroads

The reason the Germans had to have Liège was neither because of the city nor the forts. Rather, it was the railroads and the roads. The Liège gap was the only place where substantial lines of communication extended from Germany around the Allies' projected left flank. All too often, accounts of the battle at Liège focus on the forts, but reducing the fortress was simply a means to an end—the end being securing undisrupted lines of communication. Logistics would be a function of railroads and railheads. Supplies would be moved forward from the German homeland along the railroads. Then they would eventually move to the west and could be accumulated at railheads. From there, supplies would be cross-loaded onto wagons and then taken by wagon and road to the combat units. Nothing, *nothing*, could be accomplished without the railroads being clear. But before the Germans could accomplish that, all Belgian forts that could shoot at the railroad had to be neutralized. Therefore, two elements were important in planning the operation. Success at Liège was an absolute necessity for future operations. And, to repeat an often-stated point, success would be determined and defined by speed.

Moltke said, "Liège and Namur are of no importance in themselves. They may be weakly garrisoned but they are strong places. They block the Meuse railway, whose use cannot therefore be counted upon. It is of the greatest importance to take at least Liège at an early stage, in order to have the railway in one's hands. The possession of Liège is the *sine qua non* of our advance."[54]

A subtle but major change occasioned by the Liège obstacle was that the zone of concentration of First Army was done along the roads east of Aachen

3. Operational Issues

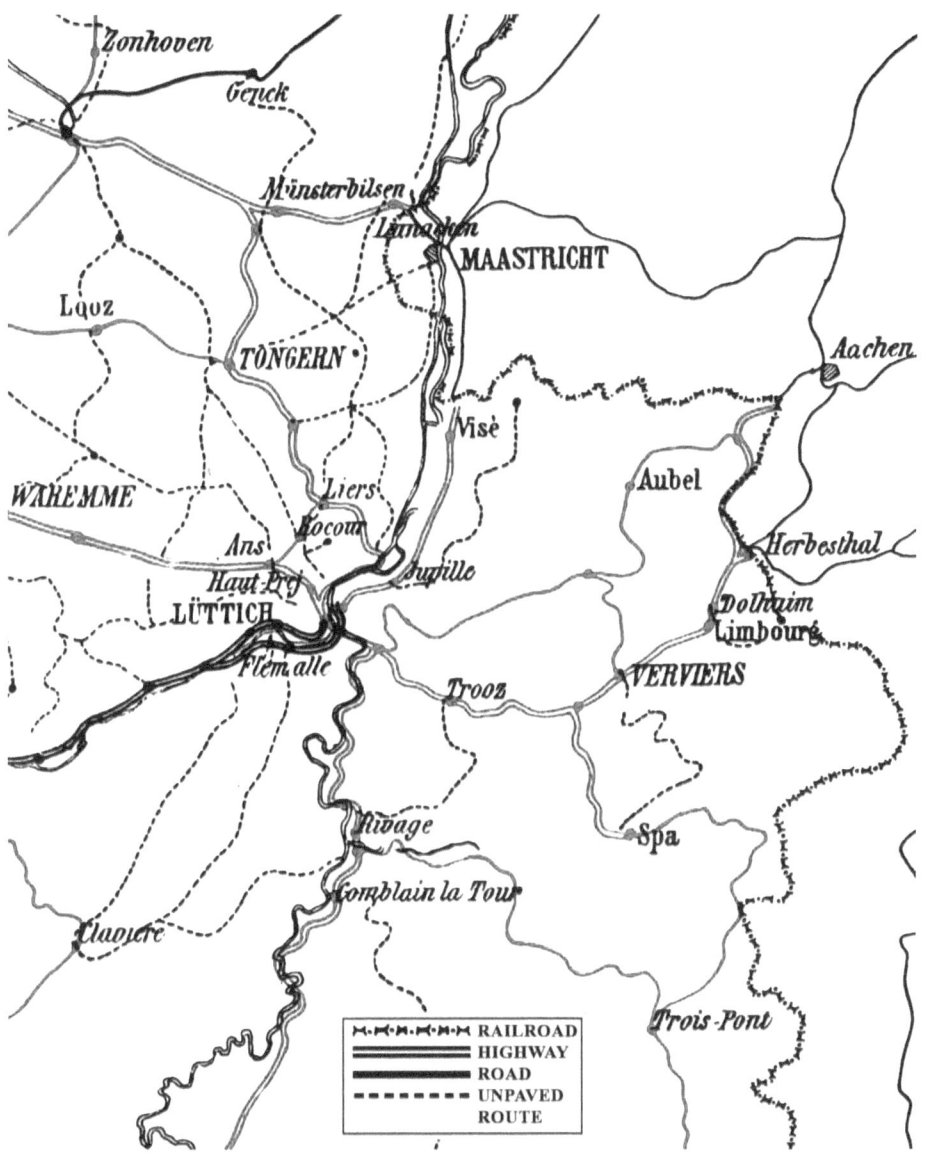

Railroads in 1912.

in an east–west manner. This was a small constricted zone that was called too small by Hew Strachan. Had the Germans maintained Schlieffen's direct approach across the Maastricht Appendix, this concentration area could have been north–south along the major rail hubs. For instance, First Army's subordinate corps could have been detrained at Kaldenkirchen, Dahlheim, and

Geilenkirchen. That would have put them between twenty-five and forty kilometers closer to the frontier. They would have been closer to Antwerp, to the Belgian Army, and to the left wing of the French Army projected to withdraw into Belgium. It would have been equivalent to an advance of about two days on the Allied forces. Two full days of marching fatigue that was inflicted upon the German Army. This would have also allowed the use of the large frontier rail stations at Baal and Dalheim, which though developed before the war as major transportation centers, in 1914 were only used as ancillary support.[55]

Bridges and Tunnels

A focus on railroads in turn calls attention to several very specific critical points: bridges and tunnels. Obviously, by damaging these, the defender could slow down the German advance—giving rise to the assumption the infrastructure would be defended logically and with plans made to replace or repair them as needed. This would be a very high priority.[56]

Highlighting the bridges from north to south along the River Meuse clarifies their importance. The first bridge was no bridge at all, but rather a ford located at Lixhe. Slightly further south at Visé was a somewhat substantial bridge that crossed the Meuse River and led to the heartland of Belgium. Further south at Argenteau, a smaller bridge was destroyed early and did not play a part in the battle. South of Argenteau, in the town of Herstal, a fairly significant bridge would later become center stage for a struggle between the Germans and the Belgians. Next, the city of Liège had five pedestrian bridges: Pont Maghin, Pont des Arches, Pont Neuf, Pont Roi Albert, and Pont Fragné. Almost adjacent to the southern pedestrian bridge was the railroad bridge named Val-Benoit.

Moving further upstream, there were bridges at the towns of Ougrée and Jemeppe-Seraing. Directly under the guns of Fort de Flemalle was a second railroad bridge, this one named Val-Saint-Lambert. Continuing along the river toward the city of Huy, there were other bridges at the towns of Egnis, Hermalle-sous-Huy, and Ombret.

In the rugged, hilly terrain between the German border and the city of Liège there were four railroad tunnels. So, before railroad bridges, the meandering railroad lines leading from Germany had to pass through tunnels. These could be easily sabotaged, choking off at least temporarily the movement of German supplies and troops. A U.S. Army study calculated, for example, that the destruction of the Meuse River railroad bridge, two tunnels, and a steep grade would have stopped the Germans cold from sending any trains across northern Belgium before September 7. If these rail lines had been compromised severely, there would have been no German movement enabling anything like the Battle of the Marne. If this had been the result,

Maghin Bridge

the railhead would have been one hundred miles away by the time of the battle of Mons.[57]

Nevertheless, the GGS gave excessive optimism about the success of keeping the rail lines intact. In war, luck is the residue of design. German General Groener called it "luck" that the tunnels remained intact. There is almost no evidence on how the GGS aimed to accomplish this task except by some undefined combination of surprise, speed, and Belgian irresolution. It is difficult to understand the GGS accepting so great a risk without some sort of underlying bias. The lesser military risk alternative of moving through Holland was deemed as prohibitive in perspective long-term cost. Remember, the ultimate objective was first to disperse the Belgian Army, not just seize Liège. Modern staffs call such a risky improbable course of action "the throwaway." It is added to the courses of action as a filler; one to be discarded to call the commander's attention to more feasible courses of action.

Handstreich

If Belgium refused the right of passage, then the following options were available for capturing Liège:

A. A surprise strike conducted by a reinforced corps with forces ready to march and positioned in advance. B. A surprise attack with stronger forces under the direct command of Second Army. C. A siege-like attack, set piece operation.

> For its action against Liège, Second Army will have all the roads south of the Dutch border at its disposal.... As soon as possible, Second Army will clear the march routes designated for First Army.... If Second Army fails to open the blocked advanced routes through Liège by the twelfth mobilization day, it will initiate the scheduled attack by reserve units against the fortification and bypass Liège in the south. In this case, First Army will advance through Dutch territory—but only upon explicit order of the supreme command [OHL].[58]

Looking at the 1913–1914 *Aufmarschplan*, the timing of these three options seems to have been the fourth mobilization day for the surprise attack, the tenth mobilization day for a force of three divisions, and the twelfth mobilization day for the set piece, respectively.[59]

These initiatives had been planned for several years. A separate force was to be organized from various army assets. This force was known alternately as Tenth Army Corps or the Army of the Meuse. Its elements would deploy in their peacetime strength. This force, eventually comprising thirteen infantry regiments, five light-infantry battalions, six cavalry squadrons, six artillery groups (plus two extra batteries), and five engineer companies preceded by three cavalry divisions, would be put to the test before mobilization was completed. Mobilization would be conducted on the fly. Although this led to a higher level of cohesion, it also shows the units would be close to half strength.

This plan to seize a contested Liège was developed in 1911, a requirement created by avoiding Holland. The plan was known as the *Handstreich*. The very existence of the *Handstreich* plan was a great secret, especially kept from the gossipy kaiser. Only the GGS knew of its existence. "Discovery learning" by those who had to execute the plan would be the norm.[60] Task: Second Army would utilize an ad hoc reinforced corps to take Liège. ("Army of the Meuse" was a grandiloquent overstatement.) Purpose: To free the main roads and railroads covered by that fortress. First Army was to follow the movement of Second Army, but the exact timing of the formers advance was not specified.

Examined in detail, the *Handstreich* seems to have been constructed on wishful thinking and hope rather than sober analysis of the most dangerous possibilities. "It might work." The guns of the northern Liège forts guarding the Meuse did not cover the entire 8.6 miles to the Dutch frontier. The tactical intention was for a strong, rapidly moving force was to seize Visé, the northernmost Belgian town on the Meuse. This force would penetrate the five-mile gap above the range of the Fort Pontisse guns and then swing south, attack the western forts, and invest Liège. With Visé taken and its bridges secured, cavalry could fan out across the plains of southern Limburg and

3. Operational Issues

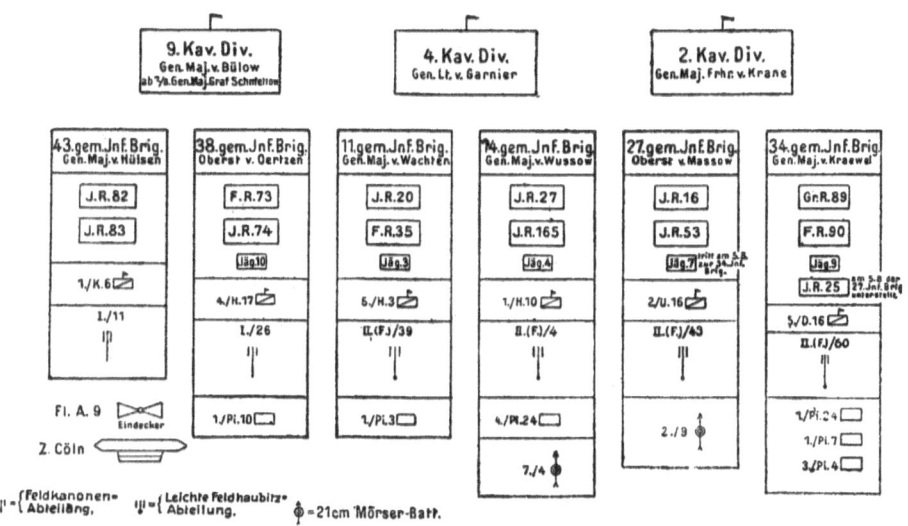

Original order of battle for the Handstreich. Note the change made to the Twenty-Fifth Infantry Regiment and the Seventh Jäger Battalion.

mask the movements of the invaders. Additional brigades were to attack the ring of forts from the south. They would cross the Vesdre at Verviers and proceed over the rolling hills between that river and the Ourthe. Waiting impatiently in and around Aachen would be Kluck's First Army and most of the remainder of Gen. Karl Ulrich von Bülow's Second Army.[61]

The most important objective in the attack had to be the railroad bridges. Thirty-Eighth and Forty-Third Infantry Brigades, reinforced by Tenth Jäger Battalion, were organized as a provisional division and were to secure them. Ninth Cavalry Division would precede this force certainly to provide flank security.

Infrastructure was also unpromising. A detailed order of battle chart shows that the German command for the *Handstreich* was not merely convoluted. It amounted to a "task force" system for an army that was unaccustomed to this kind of organization. Particularly given the German's comprehensive inexperience, it was the perfect recipe for an uncoordinated, wasteful attack in an operation demanding smooth and speedy execution.

At higher levels, Bülow commanded Second Army and was directly subordinate to Moltke. One of Bülow's army corps commanders was Gen. der Infanterie Otto von Emmich. In addition to his own Tenth Corps, Emmich

Although this photograph shows General Emmich as the victor of Liège, it was actually taken from a prewar picture where the much taller King of Belgium is riding on his right side.

also commanded the ad hoc force that would conduct the *Handstreich*. It had to begin operations immediately before mobilization, and its components were at peacetime strength: roughly half the wartime complement. A major omission from the task organization that would stagger modern-day planners but seemed unimportant to those of the time was the complete lack of signal troops.

The organic brigades of Emmich's Tenth Army Corps were Thirty-Seventh, Thirty-Eighth, Thirty-Ninth, and Fortieth. For the *Handstreich* operations, only Thirty-Eighth Infantry Brigade was assigned organically. Emmich had five more directly under his command: the Eleventh, Fourteenth, Twenty-Seventh, Thirty-Fourth, and Forty-Third. Eleventh Infantry Brigade was assigned from Third Army Corps; the Fourteenth from Fourth Army Corps; the Twenty-seventh from Seventh Army Corps; the Thirty-Fourth from Ninth Army Corps; and the Forty-Third from Eleventh Army Corps.

That kind of mixed bag meant all sorts of command stress. The Eleventh and Fourteenth Infantry Brigades were cross-attached from corps outside Second Army. Instead, it was organic to First Army. Although a superior–subordinate relationship existed between these two armies, they had no clean interface of logistical support. Troops and the supplies for those brigades had to come from First Army. But command and control proceeded to get far worse. The *Handstreich* order provided the detail of the plan. In theory, all Emmich needed to do was execute it. But he created a further mid-level chain of command, probably because of the before-mentioned lack of communication capability. He had an army corps staff that was in the middle of mobilization and suddenly had as well these six brigades, three cavalry divisions, and all sorts of other new unit responsibilities. Emmich's solution, which is not well documented, is that he created two subcommands—once again, ad hoc organizations. Maintaining direct command of the center brigades, he assigned the two southern brigades to the senior of the two commanders, Major General von Hülsen. Although the Thirty-Eighth and Forty-Third Infantry Brigades would operate as one, they came from different numbered armies. Emmich assigned the command over the northern group to Lieutenant General von der Marwitz. The northern group consisted of Thirty-Fourth Infantry Brigade, reinforced by Twenty-Fifth Infantry Regiment and a light field howitzer unit. This northern group was supposed to attack in four columns after overcoming the river barrier. The central point of the attack was on the three regiments intended to cross the Meuse north of Liège between Visé and the Dutch border and carry out the thrust from the north and the northwest. Marwitz remained responsible for HKK 2 and Second and Fourth Cavalry Divisions in the north.[62]

If that were not convoluted enough, Forty-Third Infantry Brigade was organic to Eleventh Army Corps, a part of Third Army. Making it more difficult,

Third Army was commanded by and ostensibly Saxon. Although this brigade had regiments from Prussia, regional differences provided another point of friction.

Then there was the small issue of Twenty-Fifth Infantry Regiment. This regiment came from Eighth Army Corps—which was part of Fourth Army!— and joined Thirty-Fourth Infantry Brigade a part of Second Army. It seems as though the regiment was included because its home base was in Aachen, along the path Thirty-Fourth Brigade would take.

These brigades came from no fewer than seven different army corps. That might not seem a significant issue, but it must be understood that their training was very much army-corps-specific. Training differences resulted from everything from interpretation of how to harness modern technology to the martial spirit forms fostered by institutional bias and regimental history—and could lead to serious brands as a subset of the annual maneuvers. Each major combat arm had traditional examples of martial spirit that occurred during the Franco-Prussian War. For infantry, the greatest example was the attack of the Guard at St. Privat; for the cavalry, the desperate charge of von Bredow's cavalry brigade at Mars-la-Tour; and for the artillery, the successful shelling at Sedan. During forty-three years of peace, the branches achieved no firm consensus on the application of the doctrine.[63] Doctrine had not kept pace with technology, as Col. Charles Repington, military correspondent for the *London Times*, concluded after observing the 1911 maneuvers: "No other modern army displays such a profound contempt for the effect of modern fire."[64]

Theoretically, the German manuals after 1900 used all the experience of contemporary wars and kept pace with technical developments such as the introduction of magazine-fed repeating rifles and machine guns. However, many traditional officers tried to keep infantry tactics at the level of the Franco-Prussian war. Starting in the fall of 1906, the Third and Fifth Army Corps commanders demonstrated the use of the new manual in their autumn maneuvers. However, the Sixth Army Corps commander did just the opposite, using massed infantry assaults and cavalry attacks without artillery. In 1907, both Seventh and Tenth Army Corps showed similar techniques.[65] The chief of the General Staff criticized the 1911 maneuvers as having skirmish lines too tightly packed. By 1912, infantry was once again advancing shoulder-to-shoulder in maneuvers. The kaiser himself identified the differences: "When I'm in East Prussia, I find one tactic; when in Metz, another—and when I go to Hanover, I find something else entirely—which is itself different from Silesia."[66]

The *Handstreich*, as mentioned, was a very closely guarded secret of the GGS. The officers who had to execute it were not advised of it in advance. To help smooth its execution, Second Army was assigned a deputy chief of staff, Gen. Erich Ludendorff. Ostensibly, his job was to liaise between the *Handstreich* and the higher HQ, Second Army. According to Ludendorff, he was placed in this assignment because of his knowledge of the plan. His energy, ambition, and talent were also contributing factors.

Moltke initially approved the *Handstreich* in 1911. In the plan as developed, twenty-five thousand soldiers would defeat a Belgian garrison estimated at six thousand soldiers and three thousand Garde Civique. The *Handstreich* would be executed starting on the first day of mobilization, moving troops toward the Belgian border in trains before war had been declared on Belgium. Again, as mentioned, the Grand Duchy of Luxembourg had to be invaded and occupied prior to declaring war on Belgium. These two actions had to occur at the same time the ultimatum was given to Belgium. That meant the *Handstreich* would move forward regardless of Belgium's answer. The Germans assumed that the Belgian Army would be south of Brussels or at Namur. Its operational capability within the first days of the mobilization was rated low; its intervention in Liège was considered unlikely. But it was expected that in case of a threat to the fortress, elements of the peacetime garrisons would stay there. It was estimated that these garrisons, which in peacetime consisted of two infantry brigades, one cavalry and one field artillery battalion, one engineer battalion, and twelve-foot artillery batteries, had a total strength of six thousand men. In contrast, the garrison in the case of war was estimated to be nineteen thousand men including reserves. It was assumed impossible that the wartime garrison would be completely present within the first days of the mobilization.[67]

No plan should assume away the enemy. That, however, is exactly what the GGS did. They assumed there would be an obliging enemy, making the right mistakes at the right time—a risky and invalid assumption! A planner should present both the most probable and the most dangerous courses of action to the commander. In this case, the commander was Moltke. The total failure of a reasonable plan was his responsibility. He assumed away the problem. And then he decided it was an approved plan anyway. Why would he make such a fundamental blunder consciously and deliberately? An obvious shortcoming of the plan was that, in addition to the six thousand standing garrison, the Belgian Third Infantry Division had Liège as a mobilization station. These had already been given the order to mobilize, and the Germans knew it. The Germans would have to destroy these elements before the Belgian division could finish their mobilization

Given the convoluted chain of command and the lack of experience in working together, discussed before, the operation's tactics impelled simplicity. Orders called for the Germans to advance down the roads: "Every column goes straight ahead to the city, unless it is confronted by resistance or is not able to break it. Every resistance is to be thrown back by the use of the bayonet, the guns were not loaded. Thinking that the defenders could only offer fierce resistance in one section, all delays had to be avoided. Careful advancing is too time consuming and only an advantage for the defender."[68]

The details of the "Structure and goals of the attack columns" were attached to the instructions about the breakthrough. It stated that the six reinforced infantry brigades were supposed to break through between the forts in eleven columns. Seven officers who were working in the GGS were provided as guides for the most important routes. Using a night attack (something the Germans almost never practiced), they would advance on the ground between the forts (which they expected to be undefended). The concept expected several forts to surrender outright and "hoped" the others would follow.[69]

Night attacks are by nature difficult, high-risk operations. Darkness amplifies the many things that can go wrong in any attack. Just identifying unfamiliar figures is difficult (consider the fate of Stonewall Jackson at Chancellorsville). The objective of a night attack was surprise—to surprise the Belgians—an achievable benefit when the approach to the attack position is recognized and marked during daylight. Troops always tend to bunch up in the dark, but the plan made no allowance for a holding area (attack position) to reorganize the formation for the attack. Rather, the brigades would march down the road four abreast in column of route, limiting their land navigation problems.

For the continuation of the operation, it was determined that the corps commander of Tenth Army Corps had to set up Liège for defense after accomplishing the *Handstreich* successfully. If the *Handstreich* failed, he was supposed to hold his ground with the troops subordinated to him.

Considered in retrospect, this *Handstreich* plan was structurally unworkable. It was incredibly complex and convoluted: a night attack conducted by badly cross-attached troops who had never seen an engagement against a much stronger defense than originally surmised. The attacking troops were for the most part recruits and had never been in contact previously. Had the attack instead been delayed, mobilization could have been completed, the chain of command greatly simplified with full-strength organizations, bridging, and heavy artillery moved into place. Strachan stated, "Much of the urgency with which Moltke pressed mobilization by July 30 derived from the necessity, dictated by his own war plan, to attack Liège by the third day of mobilization." In other words, it was a bad plan executed simply because there was a plan.[70] Group think? Who failed to tell the emperor that he had no clothes? And which emperor did not see this: Moltke, Bülow, or Emmich? The only advantage that seems to have been gained by declaring war and entering Belgium for the *Handstreich* was gaining more time to work on repairing the rail lines and tunnels. And that was antithetical to the speed, shock, and awe at the core of the German war plan in 1914.

Number of Cavalry Divisions

Strachan explained: "Even had he wished to do so, Moltke could not have added additional personnel to the German right wing. His chosen deployment area was too small to allow any greater initial concentration." However, this restriction could have been solved from an operational perspective. This analysis is a matter of the tail wagging the dog. The assembly area is not fixed in the planning process; the troop assignments get finalized first. If the assembly area is too small, make it bigger or move it. Moving the First Army concentration areas further east would create more space for additional force structure. The east–west concentration area meant First Army elements had to march through Aachen one at a time to get to their ready positions. Any unit added meant it was just a matter of marching further and starting to march earlier. The main concern would be the location of railheads in the concentration area. It was not, however, a constraint.[71] Remember that marching through the Maastricht Appendix would allow the concentration area of First Army to be oriented north–south and start all the forces abreast of Second Army.

The German Army's fundamental problem was one of overfocusing: making things work because they had to. It would characterize its conduct in two world wars. Mission tactics did not necessarily imply flexible operations. In his writings about the Battle of Cannae, Schlieffen talked about the weak infantry center while cavalry and light infantry moved around the flanks to the Roman rear.[72] Delbrück, who also wrote about Cannae, said the decisive factor was the attack on the rear of the formation by the Carthaginian cavalry.[73] According to this model, even with only the German right wing involved, there could be no better use of cavalry troops than on the far-right flank. However, of the four cavalry commands available to the German Army,

Generalleutnant von der Marwitz, Commander of HKK 2.

only one HKK was employed on the right flank. It is almost as though the other three were assigned to numbered armies on a fair-share basis, as opposed to the basic tenet of troops applied to tasks. But why?

> The General Staff had underestimated the interdependence between the time pressures at the operational-strategic level and the mobility of the troops required for the execution of operations. They thus failed to recognize that mobility was not only the most important, but the decisive factor in the conduct of operations. In rapid mobile warfare conducted under time pressure over large areas, the army that is supposed to inflict a crushing defeat on an enemy must have not only well-trained and -equipped units, but especially highly mobile ones.[74]

Why did the Germans put large numbers of cavalry in front of troops that were not involved in the turning movement? The situation in 1914 would seem to be a clear case for the use of three HKKs on the right flank. It is unlikely that any planner would leave this right wing short of cavalry forces. However, the actual deployment instead amounted to three cavalry divisions in front of First and Second Army. There were four cavalry divisions in front of Third and Fourth Army and three cavalry divisions on the left flank, in the forests and mountains of Alsace-Lorraine and southeastern France. Cavalry in very difficult terrain. Why would the staff put them there instead of the open plains of Belgium?

If indeed the GGS was considered one of the quintessential organizations of its time, then how could it have made such an error? That the higher cavalry organizations were at best ad hoc compounded this mistake. The HKK commanders were not on the same level as infantry corps commanders. Their logistics were a disaster. Training of already improvised formations was seriously lacking. And, if that were not enough, it seems the HKKs were positioned in the wrong place. Why? In his review of the operation, Gen. Walter Friedrich Adolf von Bergman, who was responsible for logistics in First Army, clearly stated the cavalry divisions could have been readily spared from other points of the front. He wrote, "It would have been possible to withdraw from the southern wing and from the remainder of the line at least four army corps and several cavalry divisions for transfer to the northern wing, where the decision was sought."[75] Poseck was similarly damning. He pointed out that Schlieffen had placed eight of Germany's eleven cavalry divisions on the right wing in his one-front scenario. Moltke put ten cavalry divisions on the western front, but only HKK 2's three divisions could be considered truly on the right flank. The two HKK 1 divisions were at best marginally available. "This would have left, besides the divisions of HKK 1 and HKK 2, another HKK of three divisions for the extreme swinging wing where the decisive battle was to be expected."[76]

In the Moltke Plan, there simply was not enough cavalry on the right flank to accomplish all the missions expected of HKK 2. Three cavalry divisions could not simultaneously cover the right flank, the landing of the BEF, and the denial of Antwerp to the Belgian Army. A simple calculation of troops-to-task would raise any planner's eyebrows: The Germans needed either more troops or fewer tasks; and HKK 2 Commander Marwitz either did not realize it or did not do enough to prevent it. Perhaps he was in no position to prevent it.

4

Preparation for War

Subordinating the political point of view to the military would be absurd, for it is policy that has created war. Policy is the guiding intelligence and war only the instrument, not vice versa. No other possibility exists, then, than to subordinate the military point of view to the political.—Clausewitz[1]

The GGS was a purely planning organization in peacetime. In wartime, the planning had to continue but suddenly also had to command and control an army numbering in the millions. This is an entirely different skill set. The physical act of command and control is far different than planning a potential operation. The GGS failed to develop a methodology for command and control especially while lacking sufficient means of communications. Centralized command and control of an operation of this kind that Schlieffen had envisioned was inconsistent with the system of leadership by directives used by the Germans at the operational level.[2]

July 29

As first published in special edition newspapers on July 29, 1914, the "official" text of the Austro-Hungarian declaration of war read:

> The Royal Government of Serbia, not having replied in a satisfactory manner to the note which had been given to it by the minister of Austria-Hungary at Belgrade on the date of July 23, 1914, the Imperial and Royal Government finds itself with the necessity of safeguarding its rights and interests and to have recourse, to this effect, to the force of arms. Austria-Hungary considers itself, therefore, from this moment, to be in a state of war with Serbia.[3]

Another newspaper report:

> Brussels, July 29: The partial measures of mobilization which had been suspended are

definitively restarted. The forts of the Meuse are mobilized. The classes of 1909, 1910, [and] 1911 have been recalled, and tomorrow morning every man will receive the order to rejoin his unit. The surveillance of the frontiers is operating normally. The demolition chambers on the bridges have been loaded.[4]

July 30

The Intelligence Department of the GGS identified the Belgian mobilization: they had begun arming the fortresses, digging field fortifications in the intervals between the forts, and preparing bridges and railway lines for demolition.[5]

July 31

Belgium fully mobilized its army on July 31, 1914. General Leman sent detachments of army engineers to place explosive charges in the railway tunnels along the lines coming in from the east.[6] Belgium's mobilization gave its Third Infantry Division almost a week to prepare for the German attack—and to organize more than nine thousand defenders. The mobilization date of the Belgian Army was not a secret. Before the *Handstreich* even started, the planners knew Liège contained many more defenders than in the German calculation. One reason for going through with the operation despite enhanced risk was arrogance: the Germans were so arrogant they expected the Belgians to mount no more than token resistance. Another explanation is momentum. Once set in motion, halting the process became literally unthinkable.

According to the German General Staff, a memorandum about the *Handstreich* was passed on to the general in command of Tenth Army Corps in Hannover and at the same time to the subordinate units assigned to the assault. The exact degree of the dissemination is uncertain. Clearly it went down far enough to disseminate general awareness of early initial movements. But it is not clear exactly how much information was provided, nor how low the information went—no one was keeping those kinds of records in the context of a major war's initiation. A legitimate speculation based on one author's experience is that the *Handstreich* was so secret that even at this late stage most participants did not have any knowledge of it as a whole. Commanders at brigade level and below did not know what they were about to do. The *Handstreich* memorandum went to Emmich as well as the staff of Tenth Army Corps. There was no special staff for this operation. Tenth Corps was fully engaged in enacting its own mobilization. In other words, the command structure was structurally overloaded, especially with its complete inexperience of actual war.[7]

At about 1400 hours, Imperial Germany declared the premobilization "period of imminent danger of war." The chief of operations executed the most recent deployment plan. The Telegraph Section instructed three hundred thousand telegraph employees and operators at post offices across Germany to send news of the declaration to the 106 infantry brigades scattered throughout the empire. Several preparatory steps were taken, including recalling soldiers on leave and instituting guard missions on railroads and depots. An even more labor-intensive step was to release cadres used to establish the reserve and Landwehr units. Because this requirement varied by army corps, the net result was that each active unit allocated different numbers of officers and NCOs as cadres. Therefore, the units participating in the *Handstreich* were at peacetime strength (about one-half) but not homogeneously among companies. It was anticipated that full strength for the *Handstreich* units would be achieved by August 11. By then, Liège must surely be firmly in German hands. This was a purely "come as you are" operation—for good and ill.

The General Staff's Railroad Section requisitioned thirty thousand locomotives, sixty-five thousand passenger coaches, and eight hundred freight cars. The empty mobilization transports started moving immediately.[8] A number of high-priority early mobilization trains had to be scheduled to ship the six reinforced infantry brigades from different army corps allocated for the planned *coup de main* against the fortress of Liège.[9] All these formations were still at peacetime strength when shipped to their assembly areas. Mobilization would continue even during the assault on Liège—disorder from the rear exacerbating the disorder at the front.

As a footnote, Italy backed out of the Triple Alliance on July 31, stating that it considered Vienna's attack on Serbia to be an act of aggression and hence did not bind Italy to act on behalf of the Triple Alliance. The two Italian cavalry divisions certainly would have bolstered the left wing of the German Army.[10]

August 1

One of the first things for the Germans to do when mobilization was announced was occupy Luxembourg. This was done as a prophylactic: seizing the major railroads in that country was considered needed for the German mobilization. The Germans used the fig leaf justification the French were planning to explain their preemption. In political circles, debate raged as to whether Sixteenth Infantry Division, the vanguard of the Moltke Plan in the west, should immediately cross into Luxembourg. Moltke insisted the occupation go forward to prevent the French from seizing Luxembourg's vital rail-marshaling points. Conversely, Bethmann Hollweg demanded the troops be held back to allow time to seal a deal with Britain to stay neutral. Kaiser Wilhelm II first ordered the Sixteenth to stand down. "When Gerhard Tappen, Chief of Operations, presented him with the order to keep Sixteenth [Infantry Division] on German soil, Moltke refused to sign the document. Later that night, the kaiser changed his mind and Moltke was allowed to let them go."[11] The familiar question of who really reigned in Berlin, the kaiser or the chief of staff, was by no means resolved!

A truly bizarre event took place at the village of Troisvierges. In what can be considered the very first invasion of Luxembourg, elements of Sixty-Ninth Infantry Regiment entered neutral Luxembourg. They were recalled twenty minutes later. This might have been explained as a mistake. However, all the political back-and-forth raised two key points to consider. First, Germany was clearly willing to violate Luxembourg's neutrality to seize its key rail connections. Those connections were so important to the German plan that the invasion had to be complete before the trains started moving—and the GGS would direct this deployment across political boundaries prior to any declaration of war. From a staff perspective, this showed that the actions of the staff in directing operational and tactical military plans operated essentially divorced from their political and strategic framework. Second, if this was a "fog and friction" kind of mistake in execution, somehow based on somebody getting the wrong word or no word, it made no sense at all. The invading detachment destroyed 150 meters of railroad track. A mistake to seize the railheads could perhaps be understood, but not a mistake to tear up the needed railroad.

French mobilization was ordered on August 1, anticipating its army would become combat ready on the tenth day of mobilization, one day ahead of the German mobilization timetable. The French actually attacked into Lorraine on August 14—another example of fog and friction, this one from across the battle line.

Germany also declared war on Russia.

August 2

Germany gave its ultimatum to Belgium. Claiming to have "reliable information" regarding French preparations to invade Belgium on the way to invade Germany, this ultimatum announced that German troops were about to advance into Belgium preemptively. It urged the Belgians to adopt "benevolent neutrality," permitting the German Army to pass through the kingdom unhindered. In return, Germany promised to guarantee the country's "integrity and independence," to purchase all supplies in cash, and to make good any damages caused by troops. If Belgium resisted, the Germans would regard the kingdom as an enemy.

The Germans demanded the Belgian response by 0700 hours, only twelve hours after they presented their demands. The ultimatum, moreover, was written in German, in hopes the Belgians would spend at least one of the allotted hours translating the note—not all that different from the Japanese in December 1941.[12] The concept of the ultimatum as detailed in the mobilization plan had a few twists. The Belgians were not only to open the forts immediately to the Germans, but to defend the fortress at Namur against a possible French raid. They were supposed as well to prevent English landings.[13]

Belgium had mobilized its army on July 31, 1914, but was not yet fully ready to resist when it received Germany's ultimatum on August 2. The Crown Council met that night, needing to make a decision. Belgium had three courses of action. It could give in to the demands of the ultimatum, withdraw their army and keep it intact for a withdrawal to Antwerp, or position all their forces along the River Meuse and try to hold off the Germans.

Some Belgian Crown Council members actually pushed for a fourth option—to abandon these three courses of action and attack Germany before the German mobilization was complete. While the reply to the ultimatum was polished, Belgium's military situation was again discussed. When it was proposed to blow up the Meuse bridges, the army's impulsive second-in-command Gen. Louis de Ryckel protested: "We need to drive the Germans back to where they came from."[14] Clearly, in his reasoning, Belgium had started mobilizing days before Germany had and would be more prepared. In accordance with this concept, the Belgians could not blow up the railroad bridges over the rivers because they would need the bridges for an attack on Germany. There was no unanimity as to the Germans intent. Would they cross the River Meuse? Would they try to advance south of the river toward France? Preemption might be Belgium's most promising course.[15]

Belgian Chief of Staff Gen. Antonin de Selliers de Moranville successfully convinced the entire group. He was unwilling to risk Belgium's entire mobile army in one stroke against Germany because a defeat would bring into question the army's ability to retreat to the fortifications of Antwerp. Moranville instead urged concentrating the main body of the army behind the River Gette, midway between the Meuse and Brussels. There the Belgians could await French and British reinforcements. King Albert I reluctantly acquiesced, insisting however that two divisions (Third Infantry, Fourth Infantry) and one brigade (Fifteenth) from the mobile army be sent to reinforce the garrisons of Liège and Namur. They would defend en masse along the Namur–Gette River–Diest–Antwerp line.[16]

Faced with a foe of overwhelming size, the Belgians had few choices. If they proposed to remain neutral, feigning a three-way defense would make it quite difficult for the Belgian Army to defend Liège with its entire force. Logically, Belgium hoped its army could join with that of France and England to stop the German onslaught. To that end, however, the Belgian Army had to stay in existence. It could not allow itself to be trapped or destroyed; it had to remain a "force in being." If Belgium fought on its own, the advantages of timing and position Clausewitz claimed would accrue to the defender would not be enough to stop the German juggernaut, let alone repel it. Therefore, keeping the army intact had to be the Belgians' major plan. King Albert I decided the army would eventually withdraw from its forward locations to the relative security of the forts surrounding the city of Antwerp if the Allies did not arrive in time. From there, the Belgians could stage a sortie to threaten the flank or rear of any German advance through Belgium. The Germans could not ignore an army in Antwerp.

On the German side of the line, from the first day of mobilization, August 2, 1914,[17] the entire country automatically became subject to a state of siege. This was a legal concept authorized in Article 68 of the Imperial Constitution:

> Should the public safety of the federal territory be threatened, the kaiser may declare any part of the same under martial law. Up to the publication of an imperial law regulating the occasions, the form of announcement, and the effects of such a declaration, the provisions of the Prussian Law of 4 June 1851 (*Gesetzes-Sammlung für 1851*, p. 451), shall be valid in such case.[18]

In fact, an imperial law was never enacted; therefore, the Prussian Law of 1851 continued in force. The 1851 law did not specify in detail how this state of siege was to be executed, how long it was to endure,—or indeed what it was. This lack of specificity gave considerable leeway to the army corps commanders on how to implement it. Some commanders only introduced a dusk-to-dawn curfew and restrictive police regulations. Others included press censorship, prohibition of political assemblies, and price control for foodstuffs. Still more used or abused the state of siege to systematically act against socialist politicians, union leaders, and the press—even beyond the requirements of military censorship. The effect was to make the military legally dominant over the rest of the civilian administration, but the intention was for a limited period: another example of the short-war illusion that so compelled initial German planning and policy. In fact, the law was used primarily against liberal elements of the Reich's left wing. Interesting to note, a major demand of the 1918 mutiny in Kiel that helped end the Great War was elimination of this power.[19]

Upon mobilization, the army corps and their divisions and brigades were assembled and dispatched to their assigned frontline position. Back home, a wartime organization assumed their roles: thus, a *stellvertretende Infanterie-Brigade* (best translated as "being in place of") replaced each infantry brigade command. The *stellvertretende Brigadekommando* took the role of the active brigade commands in regard to personnel replacements. In the same way that *stellvertretende Generalkommandos* replaced the active army corps, a *stellvertretende Generalstab* was created in Berlin after the OHL departed for Koblenz.

Once the mobilization was started, the chief of the GGS called to his office the newly appointed army commanders, together with their chiefs of general staff, army by army, to explain and discuss further details of the deployment order and goals of the coming operations. Based on these briefings, the commanders and their chiefs returned to their respective HQ, whether existing or newly created, to draw up initial operations plans while their troops were mobilized and transported to the deployment areas.[20]

The first conference of the First Army commander with Generalmajor von Kuhl took place. Formerly employed as Quartermaster General in the "western section" of the GGS at Berlin, Kuhl had been appointed Kluck's chief of staff.[21]

> The preliminary conferences between the chief of staff and the deputy chief of staff with regard to the general work of the First Army staff concluded with complete unanimity. As the right flank of the German armies in the west, First Army had a most important part to play in executing a wide movement, probably of an enormous wheel through Belgium and Artois and perhaps into Picardy. It became evident that large tracts of country must be traversed with heavy fighting and many obstacles overcome. Rapidity of movement would be the primary condition of success in attaining the ultimate objective, which was to disperse first the Belgian Army, then the BEF, and finally to fall on the French armies.[22]

German mobilization planning was conducted in annual cycles known as mobilization years. Each mobilization year (*Mobilmachungsjahr*) commenced April 1 and lasted until March 31. The General Staff prepared their mobilization orders for the army corps, army inspections, and railroad line commanders (among others) for the mobilization year 1914–1915 in March 1914. The corps chiefs of staff and Ia officers had to implement changes based on these orders in turn into their own mobilization calendar (*Mobilmachungskalender*). This large amount of work further increased after the large expansion of the German Army in the mobilization years 1913–1914 and 1914–1915. All new reserve formations and reservists in active formations had to be staffed with reserve personnel in cooperation with the *Bezirks-Kommandos*. Then, they had to be fed, accommodated, armed, outfitted with uniforms, and finally moved by train to their assembly areas.

The assembly areas also required preparation. Each needed sufficient accommodations—usually one family house or small farmhouse per squad was assumed adequate. This meant about three to four houses per platoon or about ten or twelve per company were required. Medical officers checked hygiene standards of the villages; farmhouses, water wells, and so forth in the assembly areas. Further, hundreds of thousands of men in often very remote countryside along the western border had to be fed. If assembly areas were changed, railroad connections had to be changed and, if necessary, new railroad head stations built. This would explain why small Eifel villages had such extensive track layouts and unloading ramps.

Train transportation had to be arranged. The mobilization railroad timetable overruled the civilian timetable during the mobilization. The planners had to take into account the capacity and speed of the mobilization trains. Because the trains moved at slow speeds, food, water, and coffee had to be prepared at many railroad stations to feed the soldiers coming through. The sheer quantity of planning in a pre-electronic age seems overwhelming. To cover the twenty days of initial mobilization, 20,800 trains of fifty cars each were planned down to the minute; they transported 2.07 million men, 118,000 horses, and four hundred thousand tons of assorted supplies.[23] All of these preparations required considerable detailed planning work, particularly for the Ia officers. Because the mobilization calendar was top secret, there were strict limitations on its handling. In practice, this meant the Ia did all the work himself; he could not delegate it to NCOs or enlisted men.

The *Militärfahrplan* was based on the standard military train with 110 axles and six-hundred-ton capacity, made up of both passenger cars and freight cars.[24] The freight cars were used for the ordinary men or horses, with up to forty men or eight horses in one car. A certain number of freight cars were turned into flatbeds to transport wagons by removing the cars' side walls and roofs. A G3/BR 53 steam engine or one comparable usually pulled the standard military trains. The trains traveled at a comparatively slow average speed of thirty kilometers per hour on major lines or twenty-five kilometers per hours on narrow-gauge lines. This slow speed was chosen to create enough slack in case of technical problems or other delays. In autumn 1913, the Railroad Department started calculating a new *Militärfahrplan* based upon an average speed of forty kilometers an hour to speed up mobilization, but this was not ready for use during the 1914 mobilization.

On dual-tracked lines, trains could be dispatched every twenty minutes. However, on single-tracked lines, the frequency was halved to one train every forty minutes in order to allow for return journeys. Beginning in 1912, the *Militärfahrplan* also scheduled local trains for civilian traffic, to supply essential goods to civilians in urban areas during the mobilization and for the initial deployment of the army (*Militärlokalzüge*).[25] The *Militärfahrplan* distinguished between mobilization (*Mobilmachungstransporte*) and war transports (*Kriegstransporte*). The purpose of mobilization transports was to bring all military formations and fortresses up to war strength. The purpose of war transports was to deploy operationally ready formations into their assembly areas as per the operations plan.

The main railway line from the German assembly areas designated for the right wing ran from Aachen to Liège and Namur, then to Brussels or to Charleroi. From Brussels, the line moved southwest toward Lille, and from Charleroi south toward the French border area. Much of the German Army would be fighting at the end of this rail line. Therefore, as the army advanced, the further away it moved from its supplies.

> In the tradition of Friedrich II, the logistics and transportation elements of German operational planning were designed for warfare close to the borders, a function of the central position of the German Reich. Neither in the west nor in the east had the prewar operational plans extended beyond a depth of approximately four hundred kilometres from the German borders.[26]

Units participating in the *Handstreich* left their home stations and moved to assembly areas without a clear explanation of their destination or mission. Instead, an officer of the General Staff met them and provided secret orders that detailed their roles. These instructions had the brigades bivouac on the night of the August 3, cross the border, move to an assembly area on the night of the fourth, and continue moving to a further assembly area on the night of the fifth. The officers with the instructions were also charged to be brigade guides for the most important routes because they allegedly had reconnoitered the route. According to the GGS, these officers reported for duty in Aachen on August 3. General von Emmich left Hannover for Aachen with a small staff in the evening. He arrived in the morning of August 3.[27]

Thus far, so good. At the same time, German forces crossed into neutral Luxembourg again without a declaration of war. This was the second invasion of Luxembourg after the abortive or mistaken attempt from the day before. Luxembourg was nonmilitarized with no possible defenses; this was an occupation. However, it seems the German troops that executed the occupation early in the morning of August 2 were administrative rather than operational, as they did not have adequate planning for food or lodging. The following messages were sent from Berlin:

> The military measures which we have taken in Luxembourg do not constitute a hostile act against Luxembourg but simply measures destined to ensure the safety and security of the railways which we exploit and to forestall an attack by France. Luxembourg will be indemnified for any damage. Please assure the government, Bethmann-Hollweg.[28]
>
> The military measures have, to our great regret, become inevitable because we have certain news according to which French forces are marching on Luxembourg. We had to take measures for the security of our army and the protection of the railways. An act of hostility against a friendly Luxembourg has never been envisaged by

us. The pressing danger has not, unfortunately, given us the time to discuss this with the Luxembourg Government beforehand. The Imperial Government assures Luxembourg that it will be fully compensated for all damages caused by us. Jagow.[29]

August 3

Germany declared war on France. The OHL began operations in Berlin. Britain ordered the army mobilized. Belgium rejected the German ultimatum.

The Belgian SHQ issued *Instructions for the Concentration of the Army*. The Belgian field army would deploy between the Gette and Dyle Rivers: First Infantry at Tirlemont, Second Infantry at Louvain, Fifth Infantry at Perwez, and Sixth Infantry at Wavre. The cavalry division would concentrate at Gembloux. Third Infantry was to concentrate at Liège and defend. Fourth Infantry had the same mission at Namur. Neither division was given a mission statement or an operations order.[30]

The German intelligence estimate reported that the garrison of Liège had been substantially reinforced.[31]

At 1500 hours, General von Emmich gave his first order. He ordered that the Belgian border was to be crossed only on a written order. They could begin their advance across the border on the August 4 at 0900 hours:

- The HKK 2 with Thirty-Fourth Infantry Brigade via Gemmenich, Hombourg to Visé had to capture the Meuse Bridge at Visé as well as the canal crossings west and northwest of this place on August 4.
- Twenty-Seventh Infantry Brigade from La Maison Blanche (two kilometers northeast of Henri Chapelle) via Henri Chapelle, Station Audel up to the road Berneau–Julemont–Battice.
- Fourteenth Infantry Brigade from eastward Prussian Moresnet via Henri Chapelle, following Twenty-Seventh Infantry Brigade up to there, then via Battice to Hervé.
- Eleventh Infantry Brigade from Eupen via Limburg, Verviers up to the area of Soiron.
- Thirty-Eighth Infantry Brigade from Malmedy via Spa up to the area of Theux, Louveigne.
- Forty-Third Infantry Brigade from Stavelot to the area of Stoumont, La Gleize.
- Ninth Cavalry Division from the area of Baugnez (southward Malmedy) on the same road as Thirty-Eighth Infantry Brigade via Malmedy, Francorchamps, Spa, Theux, Louveigne and Poulseur. It was supposed to capture the Ourthe crossings there and to gather intelligence in direction of Namur and Givet.

The headquarters of the commander of Tenth Army Corps was supposed to be in Hervé from August 4, 1400 hours.[32]

Belgian forces in turn conducted early demolitions based on news of German preparations around Aachen, Eupen, and Malmedy, including the rail tunnels leading from Germany. As part of this blocking plan, engineers were sent to Argenteau and Visé to prepare explosives to blow up the bridges. At 2200 hours on August 3, the explosives were set off. They damaged but failed to destroy the bridges. New charges were placed later that night. On August 4, the Visé Bridge finally collapsed at 0400 hours, and then the Argenteau Bridge at 0500 hours.

A bit later, the bridge at Pont de Arches was destroyed. The bridge at Herstal and all five pedestrian bridges in Liège remained intact. The railroad bridges Val-Benoit and Val-Saint-Lambert were also left intact, but the southern area bridge at Jemeppe-Seraing was destroyed. In addition, the roads to Liège were blocked with fallen trees and rubble. After the Germans crossed the border, the Belgians destroyed three more road bridges upstream from Liège—the bridges of Hermalle-sous-Huy, Ombret, Engis—and affected a derailment on the railway bridge of Val Saint-Lambert.[33]

On the evening and night of August 2–3: German Seventh Jäger Battalion left Bückeburg in two train transports. Destination: Railroad Station Aachen-West.

During the next day, the transports arrived in Aachen. The battalion immediately marched via Waldschenke toward Hergenrath. While this quotation makes no mention of "opening-night jitters," there it was—a false alarm pre-invasion.

> August 3–4, Hergenrath: Accommodated in halls, schools, the church. That night the battalion was alarmed. A Belgian attack was expected. This did not happen. Distant detonations could be heard as concluded later from the demolition of the bridges by Belgian troops.[34]

Visé Bridge

Colonel Dujardin recalled in 1956, "The organization of the platoon of Engineers Cyclists I commanded on August 12 as a Captain-Commandant was zero. We got old, foldable bicycles and out-of-date material handed over by the cyclists. We had been equipped with 'material' from the Antwerp Engineer Depot."[35] The dynamite used on these tunnels and bridges was like that used later on bridges in Halen by the Belgians—it seemed to have lost its strength due to age and improper storage. Later, it was said it had only one-quarter of its power. It took two attempts to destroy the main bridge at Visé, and then only the spans, not the supports.

4. Preparation for War

Van het Oorlogsterrein in België. — De opgeblazen brug bij Visé. — Op den voorgrond Duitsche soldaten, bezig met voorbereidingen de brug te herstellen.

The all-important bridge at Visé.

Each of the four rail line demolitions had different significance. Two (Stavelot and Trois-Ponts) were on the same single-track line in the southern portion of the zone. This was not the major rail line. One tunnel (Hombourg) was on the northern single-line track, also a bypass. Although all rail lines were impeded, the most important was the double-track line between Aachen and Verviers blocked at Nasproue.[36]

Hombourg Tunnel

General Leman gave the order to blow the tunnel on August 3 at 2000 hours (or maybe 2130). In his report, Leman said the destruction plan provided two breaks of about twenty meters: one in the western mouth at the Liège side and the other in the middle of the tunnel. The charge in the center section failed. The one in the western tunnel mouth functioned only in part, causing an obstruction of about fifteen meters. Leman wrote, "The first train was able to use the tunnel again on August 18 at 0200 hours."

The German report more accurately talks about an interruption of forty meters due to the collapse: "Fortunately, thirty-five caissons, twenty-five kilograms of black powder each, and a large number of charges of dynamite have not exploded." Otherwise, the clearance would have lasted much longer. According the German, the railway track re-opened on August 21.[37]

Stavelot Tunnel

Leman wrote, "Although intended to cause a destruction of fifty meters of rail line at 185 meters from the tunnel entrance, a single charge [out of seven or eight] did explode. Damage was low; the first machines were able to pass after four days of clearing on August 8." The Germans were again more precise. "Unexploded charges were defused; a wooden structure was put in place to support the wall. The first train passed the morning of August 8, direction Trois-Ponts."³⁸

Trois-Ponts Tunnel

The plan for the Trois-Ponts Tunnel was to create an obstacle in its middle. Six of the eight charges detonated caused an obstruction such that on August 11 the Germans started constructing a bypass track. They finished on August 30. Meanwhile, trains stopped on one side of the tunnel, and their cargo transshipped. German accounts said that on August 11 the line was cleared up to the tunnel of Trois-Ponts but with a break of forty-two meters in the middle of the tunnel (six charges had exploded, two others had not) and it would take months to reopen. In consequence, the Germans then opted for a 1.75-kilometer bypass to span the River Salm, building a 120-meter long and twelve-meter high wooden bridge. That work lasted until August 28.

The tunnel repair was entrusted to a private German company, Grün und Bilinger, which started work on August 30 and cleared the passage on one track by November 26. In early 1915, the Germans decided to rebuild the tunnel for two tracks while maintaining traffic on a single track. That work ended in December 1915.³⁹

The tunnel at Trois-Ponts. This was the only tunnel that was truly blocked and had to be bypassed.

Nasproue Tunnel

The order to demolish the Nasproue Tunnel was given on August 3 at 2000 hours. Ten chambers had been prepared in the middle of the tunnel, each holding 470 kilograms of powder. Only one of the ten charges exploded. Once again, old dynamite and other explosives had lost their once powerful explosive nature—a perfect example of the fog and friction of war explained by Clausewitz. When things can go wrong, they will, especially at the beginning of an operation. It seems incredible that the detail of the power of the explosives would be overlooked on such a vital set of missions. As a result, Leman issued the order to crash seventeen locomotives in the tunnel. Clearance work began on August 4 and was completed on August 15. Apart from the Trois-Ponts Tunnel and the bridge over the Ourthe at Melreux, which required major renovation works, acts of sabotage on the Belgian railway infrastructure were minimal, and it did not take long to bring the network back into an operational state.[40]

5

Handstreich

The success of a coup de main depends absolutely upon luck rather than judgment.—Napoleon[1]

August 4

After Belgium refused its ultimatum, Germany formally declared war. The Army of the Meuse crossed the border into Belgium on a forty-kilometer front: six brigades of infantry and all of HKK 2—approximately twenty-five thousand soldiers and eight thousand horsemen supported by 124 guns and four 21-centimeter mortars. At Emmich's direction, this proclamation was read in every Belgian town. Parenthetically, the fact that in peacetime no proclamation was prepared but had to be prepared by the staff of General von Emmich is an indicator that the chief of the General Staff thought—or hoped—that the invasion would end peacefully. Characterized by token resistance; this could be more of an occupation than a combat operation.[2]

> It is with the greatest regret that the German troops find themselves forced to cross the frontier of Belgium. They are impelled by inevitable necessity, the neutrality of Belgium having already been violated by French officers who in disguise crossed Belgium in a motor car to enter Germany. Belgians! It is our greatest wish that there may yet be found a way of avoiding a combat between two nations who have hitherto been friendly and at one time even allies. Remember the glorious day of Waterloo, when the German armies helped to found and establish the independence and prosperity of your country. But we must have a free road. The destruction of bridges, tunnels, and railways will be regarded as hostile acts. Belgians! It is for you to choose. I therefore trust that the Army of the Meuse will not be compelled to fight you. All we wish is to have a free road to attack the enemy who wanted to attack us. I give a formal guarantee to the Belgian people that they will not suffer from the horrors of war; that we will pay in money for the provisions that must be taken in the country; that our soldiers will show themselves good friends of a people for whom we feel the utmost esteem and greatest sympathy. It depends on your discretion and wisely conceived patriotism to save your country from the horrors of war.[3]

The advance of August 4, the first day of the war between Germany and Belgium.

Most of the Belgian reserve units initially deployed at Liège were sent specifically to help secure the rail bridges. Although some sources question this decision, it made perfect sense. If the Germans recognized the rail bridges as the most important objective within Liège, certainly the Belgians would likely do the same. As a rule, studies about Liège focus on the forts instead of the lines of communication. Without the railroad bridge, there would be a risky delay in advancing the logistics of the invasion force. The purpose of forcing the gap was after all, to set the conditions for the advance. But neutralizing the forts was essential in order to clear and secure the communication lines.

It became a question of priorities, and the bridge at Visé was key. Unlike the rail bridges that would take more time to become primarily important, the need for this bridge was immediate. If the Germans did not have this bridge, they could not put their troops on the other bank of the Meuse River swiftly. If the troops could not cross the river, they could not get into position for the essential execution of the *Handstreich*. Here the German Thirty-fourth Infantry Brigade had three infantry regiments instead of the standard two, with two entire cavalry divisions behind it and ready to cross. The German force was predictably tactical in structure in order to capture the bridge quickly. In this dual mission context, information about what was happening was essential as rapid correction was not possible without it. However, as related earlier, the bridge was destroyed on August 3, a day before war was even declared. The Germans never had a chance to capture the bridge intact.

The hastily mobilized FFA 9, *Luftschiff* "ZVI," and the field airship battalion Second *Feld-Luftschiffer Abteilung* (FLA) were put at Emmich's disposal.[4] As Emmich's troops started moving, the first airplane of FFA 9 took off from Flugplatz Aachen. The FFA 9 had to reconnoiter alone around Liège until August 10 because FLA 2 had not been able to complete its mobilization in time. FFA 9 (which was normally assigned as part of Fourth Army Corps from First Army) had to reconnoiter to the north at Visé and in a wide curve northwest and west of the fortress against roads and railroads to protect the German attack against surprise by the Belgian field army. Furthermore, FFA 9 had to report about the fortress and the belt of forts. As early as August 4, Emmich received the partially false *Fliegermeldung* report that the roads leading to the Meuse from Visé, Argenteau, and Hervé were free, and the false report that the Meuse bridges—except for the one near Argenteau—were intact.

Up to Tongeren-St. Truiden and Waremme, neither troop concentrations nor specific railroad traffic had been observed. According to the pilots' reports, the Liège forts showed weak armament. North of Fort de Liers down to Fort Barchon, no expansion of field fortifications was observed in the terrain between the forts. In the east, however, two infantry strongpoints between Forts Evegnée and Fléron were seen. Similarly, three infantry strongpoints were spotted in the south at the mouth of the Ourthe River in the

Meuse near Sart Tilman, between Forts Boncelles and Embourg. Each stronghold was estimated for one battalion group. The Meuse bridges down to Huy were intact. During their sorties, the pilots also dropped pamphlets above Liège with Emmich's call for calm and assurance of financial compensation for all army requisitions.[5]

These very first pilot reports provided the command of the assault force an insight on the enemy situation. While there seem to be reasonably accurate reports about new construction of defenses between the forts, reporting on the status of the bridges continued to be faulty:

The Belgian field army—then assembling in the region Tienen–Mechelen–Perwez–Wavre—did not seem to be intervening at this stage. On the eastern and southern fronts of Liège, the fortresses were prepared and fortified between the forts.

In other words, the Army of the Meuse was preparing to execute an attack although the staff knew for five days that the Belgian Third Infantry Division had mobilized to defend the area between the forts. They knew on July 31. There were thousands more defenders than the Germans plan anticipated. The original tactical concept of the operation was to advance between the forts through areas supposedly undefended, then attack at night, surprising undeployed forces. Instead, the Germans faced superior forces in reasonably well-prepared positions. This was an attack that objectively had no or very little chance of success.

Second and Fourth Cavalry Divisions (Garnier)

Implementing the German plans also overtaxed HKK 2. There were four tasks assigned to the three divisions and not one of them had anything to do with the *Handstreich*. The cavalry's primary mission lay beyond Liège, in locating the Belgian Army. However, in the initial stage, HKK 2 was assigned to the Army of the Marne. The commander, Marwitz, had also been tasked to lead the crucial northern element in the attack on Liège. The cavalry advance started on August 4. The intent was for the German cavalry to precede the main advance and accomplish three things: ensure the Belgian Army did not escape to the northwest and flee into Antwerp, clear the way for the advance, and perform reconnaissance.[6] Cavalry elements of HKK 2 would arrive by train until August 8. The Fourth German Cavalry Division crossed the Belgian frontier at Gemmenich at 0800 hours on August 4, 1914. It was not able, however, to cross the Meuse River.[7]

With the Fourth Squadron of Fifteenth Hussars in the lead, Second Cavalry Division headed off to secure the bridges that crossed the Meuse River and the adjacent canal around Visé.[8] The bridge at Visé was particularly tricky because it could come under fire from Fort Pontisse in Liège. Possibly the

Visé. Writing on the card in pencil translates as, "In enemy country.... Yesterday we were in Ratzenberg [the Jäger garrison]; today, we are in enemy territory in front of Liège. Practically incomprehensible, but nevertheless quite true."[9]

most important task in the *Handstreich* was to seize the bridge at Visé intact. This would allow Thirty-Fourth Infantry Brigade and HKK 2 to cross the River Meuse rapidly and free the cavalry in the north to encircle Liège and fulfill the numerous tasks that it had been saddled with in the initial order. Approaching the bridge, they found it destroyed. There would be no easy passage across the wide river.[10]

Called the Flying Column, the Bicycle Company of Ninth Jäger Battalion and the truck-mounted First Company Ninth Jäger Battalion with a platoon of engineers headed off to seize the bridge at Visé at about 1130 hours. They were supposed to link up with a group of requisitioned trucks in Aachen. Various sources dispute whether the trucks appeared. Others told tales of roadblocks delaying the motorized advance. In any case, the Bicycle Company continued forward toward the bridge. It was not clear exactly when they arrived at the bridge but, upon reaching it, they found the bridge blown up and the opposite bank defended.[11] The river was three hundred meters wide at this point, and sixty-five meters of the bridge had been destroyed.[12]

Restoration of the bridge at Visé was not practicable because it was under fire from Fort Pontisse. The bridge at Argenteau had been destroyed, and that at Herstal was in Belgian possession.

5. Handstreich

The German plan had considered this possibility. There was a ford further north, near the Dutch border at Lixhe. However, it seemed not so easy to cross the ford as it had on paper. Two bridge transports would not arrive until the next morning south of Liège. They then had a day's march just to get to the bridge. Until their arrival, only a few cavalry pontoon bridge wagons, some fishing boats, and timber stacks were available for bridge construction but none sufficient on the wide, fast-flowing river. This was an unwelcome realization. According to the Moltke Plan, attacking infantry and parts of the cavalry divisions were supposed to be west of the Meuse on August 5. If these troops did not reach their starting positions in the course of that day, then the attack—intended as simultaneous and to be mounted from all sides of Liège—would be thrown off schedule and objectives.[13]

A quick crossing was impossible without a fixed bridge. After the crossing, the troops still needed to march twenty to thirty kilometers to reach the attacks assigned starting points. The guides who supposedly knew the region had not shown up. Bridge Transports Thirteen and Fourteen did not arrive until the afternoon of August 5. Finally, the mission of the cavalry divisions according to the plan *Handstreich* expanded for the next day. After their arrival north of Liège, they were to take part in the attack as far as circumstances allowed. Now, all of that was impossible.[14]

The Belgian defenders of Visé withdrew to the center of Liège, leaving the Belgian commander no reliable reconnaissance source for what was happening in the north. Instead, erroneous reports of several German cavalry regiments with artillery on the west bank of the Meuse were forwarded to the Belgian General HQ in Leuven. Thus, on the evening of August 4, neither side knew what the next day would bring.

Cavalry near Lixhe. Actually in Moelingen on the east side of the Meuse River.[15]

The manuscript of an individual cavalry soldier from Third Squadron of Kürassier-Regiment "Königin," Pommersches 2, part of the German Fourth Cavalry Division, had less posturing than did most regimental histories. This soldier, Arthur Brühe, was captured on August 13. He simply provided his thoughts on things that mattered to him, writing about how he was out in the rain and totally drenched. He observed German foot units marching by with their field kitchen cooking away, lamenting his hunger and the fact that the cavalry had no such field kitchens. His only consolation for his hunger was that he did not have to walk. The supply wagons could not catch up, and there was no normal nighttime bivouac. Instead, the soldiers slept beside their horses with their coats as blankets.[16]

Thirty-Fourth Infantry Brigade

The German Thirty-Fourth Infantry Brigade was the *Handstreich*'s northernmost column. It moved from Aachen to Visé intending to cross the Meuse River and attack the main city from the north. Ninth Jäger Battalion crossed the border first. After them, Eighty-Ninth Grenadier Regiment led the brigade, followed by the artillery, and then Ninetieth Fusilier Regiment. Unable to cross the river since the bridge at Visé had been blown up, the brigade bivouacked near Warsage. What followed was a night of frayed nerves and fratricide. Both regiments were involved in firefights and assaults trying to flush out an enemy that was never found or was not there. Nine fatalities and thirty-one wounded were reported. An interesting note in the Ninetieth Fusilier Regimental history was that allegedly each company commander was given two thousand marks each to pay for items requisitioned from the locals. It is not clear if or when they used this.[17]

Twenty-Seventh Infantry Brigade

Twenty-Seventh Infantry Brigade was to focus on the fort of Barchon. At 0700 hours, its march began from Hergenrath along the Belgian border toward Weisshaus. There the forces of Colonel von Massow (Twenty-Seventh Infantry Brigade) assembled, composed of the Sixteenth and Fifty-Third Regiments; one squadron of Sixteenth Ulanen Regiment; a battery of Forty-Third Feld Artillery Regiment; and Seventh Jäger Battalion. Emmich was reported there as well as with Fourteenth Infantry Brigade. The Jäger battalion formed the vanguard of this detachment. They crossed the Belgian border at 1130 hours and made a short march to bivouac at Mortroux and partially Julemont at 1530 hours. They were delayed by barricades of all kinds.[18] The wildest rumors circulated in Sixteenth Infantry Regiment, such as several French corps were marching on Aachen. These rumors, of course, turned out false but cost a night's sleep from frayed nerves and constant alerts.[19]

Fourteenth Infantry Brigade

Fourteenth Infantry Brigade on the main road from Aachen traversed past several villages to get to the fort of Fléron that guarded the eastern approach to Liège. Major General von Wussow ordered at 0845 hours to advance across the border. After a thirty-kilometer march, the brigade bivouacked between 1600 hours and 1700 hours near Hervé or Battice,[20] towns fifteen kilometers east of Liège. Jäger Battalion Four, driving ahead, chased away hostile cavalry patrols. At about 1600 hours, the German spearhead reached the marching goal Hervé. The majority of the brigade rested in this place and parts of it in Battice. Second Battalion Infantry Regiment 165 took over the protection of the roads from Battice to Barchon, and from Hervé to Micheroux and Soumagne. Emmich and his staff accompanied the brigade. Sniper fire from unknown sources was reported often, and one soldier was allegedly shot in Battice.

Eleventh Infantry Brigade

Eleventh Infantry Brigade rode the train to Eupen, arriving after midnight on the night of August 3–4. Leaving the town at 0900 hours on August 4, the brigade was given an order at the railroad station to advance toward the forts of Chaudfontaine and Embourg southeast of Liège. The intent of the advance—the *mission*—was not included in the order, nor were the company and battalion commanders briefed on the attack on Liège.[21] Eleventh Infantry Brigade crossed the border at 0940 hours with Third Jäger Battalion in the lead. They encountered the blocked railroad tunnel at Nasproue and eventually established a bivouac around Soiron.[22]

Thirty-Eighth and Forty-Third Infantry Brigades

The Thirty-Eighth and Forty-Third Infantry Brigades composed the southern left-flank column moving from Malmedy toward Fort Boncelles south of Liège. Forty-Third Brigade Commander General von Hülsen took command of a provisional "division" composed of the Thirty-Eighth and Forty-Third Brigades. The Eighty-Third Infantry Regiment Commander, Colonel von Moltke, became Forty-Third Brigade Commander.[23]

Fourth Squadron Hussar Regiment Seventeen, with the Bicycle Company of Tenth Jäger attached, attempted to prevent the destruction of the Belgian railroad tunnels on the Stavelot rail line—unsuccessfully, as the tunnels had been destroyed the previous day. Thirty-Eighth Infantry Brigade marched thirty-five to forty kilometers—a forced march by any peacetime standards—and bivouacked between Theux and Louveigné, reporting roadblocks and felled trees along the road.[24]

Ninth Cavalry Division

Ninth Cavalry Division preceded Thirty-Eighth Infantry Brigade and established a bivouac around Poulseur. Perhaps because of the lack of different roads, the plan ordered Thirty-Eighth Infantry Brigade and Ninth Cavalry Division to use the same marching road from Francorchamps to Louveigne. As a result, the infantry brigade did not arrive at its assembly area until late at night. Nor did Ninth Cavalry Division reach its marching goal of Poulseur. Just one squadron that was sent ahead occupied the bridge over the Ourthe River there.

On the next day, it proved impossible for Ninth Cavalry Division south of the fortress to cross the Meuse between Liège and Huy without bridge materials because the large bridge west of Ombret-Rausa had been destroyed. This division was supposed to gather intelligence on both banks of the Meuse toward Namur and Givet, but now it could do so just south of the river.[25]

HQ at Hervé

As part of the dictated *Handstreich* plan, Hervé was foreseen as HQ for this operation until further notice. Operation *Handstreich* allowed so little allowance for communication—a peacetime pattern that did not allow for fog and friction—that the HQ could be cut off for long intervals of time. The First General Staff Officer, von Stülpnagel wrote about this in 1938: "We were without any means of communication. There were neither radio departments nor telephone units, even no cars." He could also have added: "No balloons, no optical light contact, not even motor cycles."[26] A liaison officer of the OHL returned to Aachen in order to get in contact with the general staff, and in the late evening of August 4 the operational department in Berlin was informed about the course of August 4 by telephone. Berlin was further informed that it had not been possible to capture the Meuse and canal bridges at Visé, and the majority of Ninth Cavalry Division on the south wing had fallen considerably short of reaching its goals, too. By now, Emmich considered the entire operation extremely risky even though he had the will to carry out the *Handstreich* as ordered. The brigade commanders that had no knowledge about the operation in peace time were apprehensive about its accomplishment. Berlin considered delaying the operation for one or two days based on this report. During this time, the columns on the sides could advance further, the troops could be prepared better for the operation and perhaps reinforced by heavy artillery. This idea was, however, abandoned. We don't know why it was abandoned but we can speculate that perhaps it was arrogance, an unwillingness to change what the GGS had put together.[27]

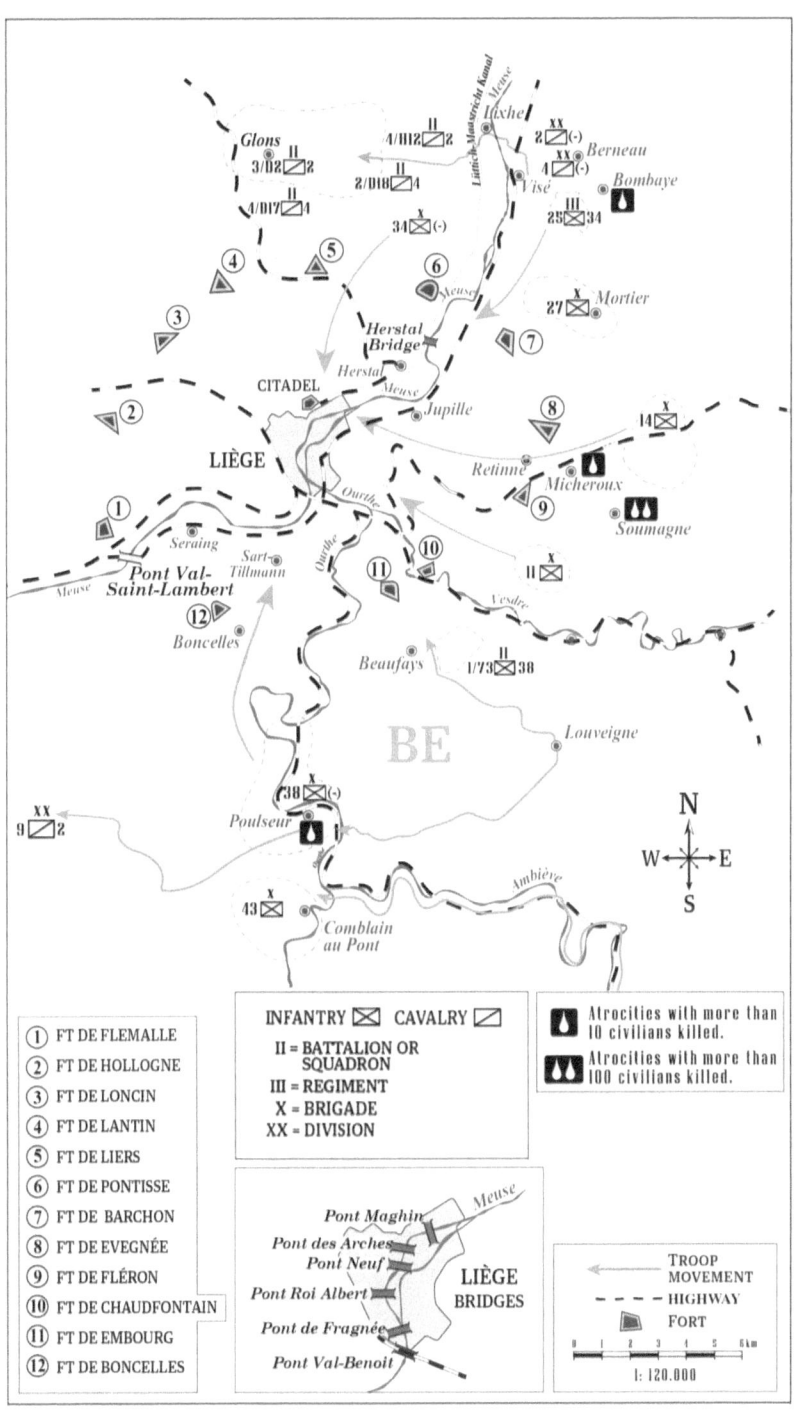

German advance of August 5, showing the biggest atrocities.

August 5

When the Germans sent an emissary to ask for their surrender, the Belgians responded, "Force your way through the gap."[28]

The actual fight for the city and fortress of Liège started the night of August 5. What resulted was a massacre of the strike force. The initial assault on the Liège fortresses (August 5–6) cost not only time, but also fifty-three hundred German casualties—for zero gain.[29] A Belgian officer commenting about the initial infantry attacks stated, "They made no attempt at deploying but came on line after line, almost shoulder to shoulder, until we shot them down; the fallen were heaped on top of each other in an awful barricade of dead and wounded."[30] Clearly, the Germans had fallen back on traditional doctrine and practice and disregarded any need to disperse per the 1906 regulations. One clue concerning the lack of dispersal is that Third Battalion Eighty-Ninth Infantry Regiment lost their battalion colors and First Battalion Ninetieth Infantry Regiment buried their colors near one of the forts. What were flags doing in a night attack when the inspirational value would approximate zero?

Second and Fourth Cavalry Divisions (Garnier)

Instructions from the General Staff for the fourth day of mobilization, August 5, stated that HKK 2 with the available parts of Second and Fourth Cavalry Divisions were supposed to cross the Meuse before daybreak. If they had not gotten to the other shore on the third day of mobilization, then they

Van het oorlogsterrein aan de Belgische grenzen. — *Op den voorgrond Duitsche Ulanen-officieren ; op den achtergrond het Duitsche legerkamp.*

Cavalry near Lixhe. Actually in Moelingen on the east side of the Meuse River. The building in the background is still standing and can be seen on Google maps.[31]

5. *Handstreich* 99

Cavalry patrol swimming over a river.

would gather intelligence toward Antwerp–Brussels–Charleroi, as well as protect the attack troops focusing on Liège and against Belgian field troops from the direction of Antwerp, Brussels, and Namur and, as far as possible, take part in the attack against Liège.[32]

With the bridges across the Meuse destroyed, there was no way to move artillery and wagons across the river to support HKK 2. The result was a bifurcated reconnaissance scenario. Four reconnaissance squadrons pressed forward across the ford at Lixhe, but the bulk of the divisions were kept on the eastern shore of the Meuse—making, parenthetically, a bad logistical situation far worse. From these squadrons, patrols were sent out with specific orders to disrupt the railway connections at St. Trond and Landen.[33] The banks were quite steep on both sides and the current was so strong that the horses were dragged away in many cases. Ostensibly, the forward patrols of those reconnaissance squadrons went to the following locations: near Hasselt, south of St. Trond, northeast of Waremme, between Faismes and Horion, and near Ombret-Rausa and Huy.[34] The German cavalry, however, was operating behind Liège in an area thirty kilometers broad and twenty kilometers deep. The reconnaissance squadrons could continue to push forward but had no way to call for support should they need it. Logistically, moreover, these reconnaissance squadrons had no support or supply elements to rely on, contrary to how they had been trained and therefore what they expected.

Thirty-Fourth Infantry Brigade

Thirty-Fourth Infantry Brigade had to move to its starting positions across the river and arrive there somewhere in the daylight hours of August 5. Its attack was to start on the evening of August 5 from the west side of the Meuse River. Instead of the normal two regiments, this brigade had five separate maneuver elements: Eighty-Ninth Grenadier Regiment, Ninetieth Infantry Regiment, Twenty-Fifth Infantry Regiment, Ninth Jäger Battalion, and joining them for this mission, Seventh Jäger Battalion. This was a particularly significant stretch of command structure since brigade HQ were small and tactically oriented. In the very early morning of August 5, Ninth Jäger Battalion received the order to move through Berneau to Lixhe, cross the Meuse on ferries and pontoons, clear the other side, and hold the crossing over the Liège–Maastricht canal. Based on the start time, the troops must have been tired. They moved forward a little bit, went back to rest along the Visé–Berneau Road until 0920 hours, and reached the village of Mouland at 1430 hours—with Seventh Jäger Battalion right behind them. However, it was decided that Eighty-Ninth Grenadier Regiment and Ninetieth Infantry Regiment would cross first.

The assault troops would also clearly not reach their initial positions for the attack in time. Support by the light field howitzer unit was also excluded because there was no way to bring it over the Meuse. The attack would have to be carried out without any artillery support. The ferrying of just two infantry regiments and the Jäger battalions were all that could be accomplished in the time allowed. The absence of two expected guides from the general staff had a further disconcerting impact. There was also a complaint about the low stockpile of maps. This compounded friction made an attack from the northwest impossible in any case.[35]

Twenty-Fifth Infantry Regiment would not cross the river that day. Instead, it was subordinated to Twenty-Seventh Infantry Brigade in exchange for Seventh Jäger Battalion but for no recorded reason. Speculation suggests this reflected the fact that Twenty-Fifth Infantry Regiment was an anomaly. It was actually part of Eighth Army Corps and part of the Fourth Army. Its garrison at Aachen seems to have been the major reason for their inclusion. It was not organic to any of the other participating units. As an independent unit, Seventh Jäger Battalion was practiced in joining other brigades. Exchanging them might have been more natural for the commander of Thirty-Fourth Brigade. So, on the fly, the order of battle was changed and Twenty-Fifth Infantry Regiment exchanged command and control with Seventh Jäger Battalion—without calculating the contribution to an already confused situation:

The morning of August 5, we [Seventh Jäger Battalion] marched to Berneau, where

5. Handstreich 101

we met up with Ninth Jäger Battalion. There we came under the command of Thirty-Fourth Infantry Brigade with Eighty-Ninth and Ninetieth Grenadier Regiments. During that night, in Berneau civilians had fired upon the resting Thirty-Fourth Brigade. It had come to fierce fights. [On] August 5 at about 2200 hours, the battalion was now at the left bank of the Meuse and advanced toward Hermée. North of Hermée, the detachment assembled in marching order: Thirty-Fourth Infantry Brigade, Ninth Jäger Battalion, Seventh Jäger Battalion. All Machinengewehr-Komp [machine gun companies] and Radfahrer-Komp [bicyclist infantrymen companies] were positioned at the rear.[36]

Generalleutnant von der Marwitz commanded the entire northern column, including HKK 2. Organic to the cavalry regiments were small pontoon bridges capable of only crossing minor impediments. Using those pontoons along with other gathered materials, Thirty-Fourth Brigade began crossing the Marne at 1430 hours. The northern German forces constructed improvised boats of two connected pontoons. It took three hours alone for Ninetieth Infantry Regiment to cross. The vehicles had to be left behind; no artillery could cross. The two divisional bridge trains did not arrive until 1645 hours, too late to assist the crossing. Some equipment taken across included battalion colors—indicating a major effort and an accepted policy to cross the river with the flags.

Cavalry on a pontoon boat crossing a river.

As luck would have it, while waiting for the infantry battalions to cross, a very heavy thunderstorm broke out. The two infantry regiments crossed first, and so the Jäger battalions did not start crossing until 2030 hours. They did not complete the task until 2330 hours. The brigade had already moved out. Ninth and Seventh Jäger caught up just south of Hermée, but the thunderstorm turned the route to mud. The troops were exhausted and the mounted officers walked their horses to stay awake.

Twenty-Seventh Infantry Brigade

Some significant daylight maneuvers in the northeast around the fort of Barchon led to action and reaction by both armies on August 5. The daylight advance was conducted by Fifty-Third and Sixteenth Infantry Regiments, ordered to get between Fort Barchon and Fort de Evegnée. Sixteenth Infantry Regiment eventually got as close as three hundred meters. The regiment's history described the regiment's formations as being very deep—again, a reflex recourse to sheer mass.

While the Belgian forts started shelling in the morning by 0700 hours—and, predictably in a first battle, seem to have flailed a great deal—it is not clear whether the Germans did much preparation besides small scale artillery preparation and infantry patrolling. Two heavy mortar batteries opened fire against the two fortresses from positions west of Mortroux and at Bolland. The brigade pushed forward into the line Argenteau–Trois Fontaines. There were reports in the German Official History (GOH) of Fifty-Third Infantry Regiment storming Barchon and sustaining substantial casualties in the daylight, but the casualty figures do not support this. When the third battalion arrived at the wire obstacles directly in front of Fort Barchon around 1030 hours, they were surprised that the mortar fire had not driven the garrison away. The battalion quickly withdrew. Thus, there are significant discrepancies between the accounts of the two sides.[37] As darkness fell, the brigade met with Fifty-Third Infantry Regiment on the road at Argenteau and with Sixteenth Infantry Regiment at Blegny for the advance toward Liège.[38]

One thing is certain. As Twenty-Fifth Infantry Regiment started moving south, it came under heavy rifle fire allegedly with "terrorists" in several significant incidents. The first, in the town of Berneau, found the Germans marching in a dense column through the dark night when suddenly the entire column started shooting wildly and randomly, predictable in the context of a night march and a first engagement. Action was stopped only by the use of bugle calls. After this incident, in which thirty men were severely wounded, all weapons were unloaded to prevent a repeat display. This unloading certainly indicates that the leaders on the spot realized the shooting started from soldier nervousness and not civilian involvement. The regiment continued onward, marching in column with battalion flags waving, until another incident in the narrow village street of Chératt.[39]

Fourteenth Infantry Brigade

Fourteenth Infantry Brigade moved out of their bivouac and approached the town of Micheroux at about 0300 hours. Both the Twenty-Seventh and the 165th Infantry Regiments reported significant involvement with *francs-tireurs*. The brigade commander, Major General von Wussow, and the commander of the Twenty-Seventh were still mounted when they ran into an artillery battery and were both killed. This was—and still is—a universal conundrum of combat command. On horseback, officers were targets. Dismounted, they were invisible and immobile. Besides, it was a question of setting an example, of behaving honorably. Fourth Jäger Battalion enveloped the position of the Belgian battery and took the crossroads of Liéry. Fourth Infantry Regiment 27 was sent to Ayeneux to establish a connection with Eleventh Infantry Brigade but was taken for the enemy and hit by friendly fire. Heavy losses resulted: dead—one officer and thirteen NCOs and soldiers; wounded—two officers and 69 NCOs and soldiers.[40]

Eleventh Infantry Brigade

Starting its advance around 0330 hours, Eleventh Infantry Brigade continued toward Forêt, where they rested until about midday. During the course of the afternoon, the brigade commander, Major General von Wachter, led his troops to the road La Neuville, Ayeneux as ordered. At nightfall, the brigade was ready for the thrust against Liège. More and more troops assembled on the road in double-marching column, Twentieth Infantry Regiment next to Third Jäger.[41]

The attack was designed to penetrate between Fort de Fléron and Fort de Chaudefontaine, with Twentieth Infantry Regiment deployed on the left of the Olnye–St. Hadelin road and Thirty-Fifth Infantry Regiment on the right. Twentieth Infantry Regiment entered Forêt at 1000 hours and took the town. Between 1000 hours and 1100 hours, Thirty-Fifth Infantry Regiment reached Ayeneux without contact and continued the march to St. Hadelin.

At 2350 hours, the brigade moved out again for the night attack, their objective the town of Magnée. The General Staff had attached an officer as a guide. The brigade was soon in single file, but the guide lost his orientation, backtracked, changed direction, and returned. In the dark, the result was disorder, increasing intermixing of the units. Arriving at Romsée, the commanders of the Twentieth and Thirty-Fifth Infantry Regiments were killed. The time is not clear—the sources disagree with each other on what exactly occurred—but the result was decapitation and confusion. German regiments had no second-in-command or executive officer; command evolved on the senior battalion commander. But finding that officer under fire in the dark was no easy task.

Both regiments came under heavy fire. The troops in the brigade main body were tired, hungry, and strung out along the road. When they took fire from Romsée as well as from numerous snipers, the squads and platoons scattered in all directions. With visibility only fifty to one hundred meters, the brigade became completely confused.

Thirty-Eighth and Forty-Third Infantry Brigades

At 0640 hours, Thirty-Eighth Brigade continued the march southwest to Sprimont and Poulseur with Seventy-Third Infantry Regiment continuing to bivouac at Esneux and contacting Belgian cavalry patrols at Fort de Boncelles. It was reported that Seventy-Fourth Infantry Regiment troops and supply vehicles while advancing to contact, were fired upon from houses and trees on both sides of the road, and several Belgian civilians were taken prisoner. By 1100 hours, after a twenty-kilometer march, Seventy-Fourth Infantry Regiment bivouacked in Poulseur. The Seventy-Fourth's commander immediately convened a field courts martial to try two Belgian civilians accused of firing on the supply wagons. One was released for lack of evidence; the other, convicted by eyewitness testimony, was ordered to be executed. The brigade commander confirmed the sentence.[42]

Thirty-Eighth Brigade had been given the mission of infiltrating between Fort Boncelles and the Ourthe River and taking the rail junction and rail bridges at the confluence of the Ourthe and Meuse by dawn. Forty-Third Brigade was to take the towns of Ougrée and Seraing and the Meuse Bridge, while the Seventy-Third would move independently to demonstrate against Fort d'Embourg. The troops would unload their weapons, fix bayonets, and wear white armbands.

Moving forward at approximately 2000 hours, Thirty-Eighth Infantry Brigade marched and countermarched almost aimlessly around the town of Plainevaux. In addition to the difficulty of a night attack, a massive thunderstorm drenched the soldiers and added to the confusion. Darkness and shelling from Fort Boncelles added to the issues.

The Germans had anticipated no Belgian troops in prepared positions between the forts. Instead, they found networks of field fortifications, improvised but disconcertingly effective. The German plan was predicated on an unopposed walk through the vacant area between the forts. Now they were opposed, in close formations appropriate for maintaining momentum and cohesion in darkness—but highly vulnerable as well. The brigade ran into a wire entanglement, and command and control fell apart. One story relates that the provisional divisional commander was wounded by an accidental fratricide bayonet in the back. Seventy-Fourth Infantry Regiment determined they could do nothing except wait for daylight. All the confusion led to time delays, and time delays led to mission failure. It is not clear whether the troops ever achieved the penetration reported on the maps for the *Handstreich*. A map in the history of the Seventy-Fourth Infantry Regiment rather clearly showed that nobody made it past the town of Sart-Tilman.[43]

One significant issue came from the of the Seventy-Fourth Infantry Regimental History. A company commander reported that as he was rallying some of the forces lost in the night, he had one hundred soldiers and two of the battalion colors with him. Again, the fact that they carried battalion flags onto the battlefield makes one wonder how well this specific regiment had embraced the tactical changes necessary on a modern, firepower-based battlefield. The Commander of Seventy-Fourth Infantry Regiment, Colonel Prince Wilhelm of Lippe, was killed in this engagement when he ordered "the flag" be raised. Although the report does not specify "the flag" to be the regimental colors, what other could it be? Was this a signal for a rally point? This seems in any case an example of regression under stress—a pattern that contributed significantly to German casualty counts and Belgian reports of German forces moving literally shoulder to shoulder. Perhaps some of this shoulder bumping can be explained away as well by a natural tendency to bunch up under fire. The German experience reflected the fact that humans are not nocturnal. Neither their vision nor their nervous systems are significantly adapted to nighttime activity. This can be compensated for, but compensation cannot be assured—as the Germans discovered. In addition, there was a serious loss of officers and NCOs.[44]

Ninth Cavalry Division

Ninth Cavalry Division, south of the fortress, continued its advance to the west and approached the River Meuse—then discovered no available bridge crossings between Liège and Huy. The main bridge was destroyed at Ombret-Rausa. Unable to cross, this division was to explore other crossings between Namur and Givet.[45]

The suicide case of German Gen. Karl Ulrich von Bülow, the commanding general of Ninth Cavalry Division, is of interest in this context. He was the younger brother of Prince Bernhard von Bülow, Chancellor of Germany. The general was once military attaché in Vienna, where the German ambassador was then the enormously influential imperial intimate Philipp Graf zu Eulenburg, who was surrounded by homosexual rumors. As commander of Ninth Cavalry Division, Bülow presided over a retaliatory strike on the town of Lincé on August 5. He organized a court-martial, subsequently executing many Belgians and burning the town on August 6. On the next day, investigation found the entire incident that led to the retaliation could not be substantiated and was probably false. But the massacre and senseless devastation of Lincé were real. Bülow had let his most rabid officers have a free hand. He shot himself in the evening of August 7. Whatever Bülow's motives and emotions, his suicide was another destabilizing factor in an HKK already overtaxed.

Francs-Tireurs and Atrocities

The *Handstreich* initiated a second crisis as well. In addition to conventional forces, the Germans fully expected the sort of irregular warfare (*francs-tireurs*) common throughout the Franco-Prussian War. For four decades, German citizens retold and embellished abundant stories about how *francs-tireurs* had ambushed, mutilated, and poisoned German forces during that war. The advancing armies in 1914 expected to encounter *francs-tireurs* whether they existed there or not.[46] Fully they expected irregulars to be a major consideration to be dealt with should it arise.

Who exactly were *francs-tireurs*? One army corps deputy commander tried to define them as any citizen of a combatant nation not in uniform who in any way disrupted German operations, communications, or supply. They had been a major concern to the Germans in the Franco-Prussian War. The French considered them partisans and the Germans regarded them as terrorists. If caught by German troops, the *francs-tireurs* could be shot out of hand (if in the act) or set before a one-officer court-martial with the power to hand out death sentences. Residents of Alsace-Lorraine found with weapons could be shot as traitors and those suspected of being *francs-tireurs* would be handed over to a formal court-martial.[47]

This "*francs-tireurs* doctrine" really dealt with applying the rules of war. As such, it has fed atrocity discussions for decades. There certainly were atrocities. There were standing orders to shoot resisting civilians. A view of the inevitability of civilian involvement in combat and an "appropriate" military response permeated the German military. There was an anti–French feeling against the "people's war" or *levée en masse*, which was legal but reprehensible. Noted theorist Julius von Hartmann wrote, "Where the people's war breaks out, terrorism becomes a principle of military necessity."[48] Senior commanders in their sixties and seventies during the invasion of 1914 had been young officers during the Franco-Prussian War and had distinct views based on their experiences with *francs-tireurs*.

The Hague conventions of 1899 and 1907 internationally endeavored to define the laws of war more tightly. The intent was to make warfare more civilized, less barbarous. Because of the first convention, the German General Staff developed a "war book" to offer some guidance. It required prisoners of war be conditionally identified if some proof existed that they were operating as enemy soldiers. The negotiations involved a seesaw battle between smaller countries that wanted the ability to have a mass "people's war" and Imperial Germany, which emphatically did not. In 1908, the German Army issued the *Felddienstordnung*.[49] It advised that preventive security measures were justified when there were possible attacks by enemy civilians. This guidance included threatening the inhabitants with penalties, taking hostages, and burning streets. This rule was in direct conflict with the previous endorsement of the Hague Convention, which was published as an appendix to the *Felddienstordnung* in 1911.[50]

Despite this conflict, the language of the *Felddienstordnung* remained unchanged. Imperial German officers were trained to expect civilian resistance and to treat it as a criminal act. Specifically, the *Kriegs-Akademie* taught that Article 2 of the convention did not comply with the German viewpoint. The noted theorist and writer Colmar von der Goltz dismissed the 1907 Hague Convention as hypocrisy because none of the signatories intended to abide by it.[51]

Again, the Germans saw *francs-tireurs* as terrorists. The Belgians viewed the German reaction as unnecessary, unprovoked violence and random atrocities. The tension was not helped by the mobilization assignments of the Belgian Garde Civique. Most Germans were not even aware of the organization's existence. The Garde Civique's inactive element in particular caused much confusion. Members of the inactive element were not uniformed. For the most part, they were not even aware of the need under the existing legal agreements to wear uniforms. They had no training. The Belgian Interior Minister did not even publish guidance on their use until August 5, 1914. Clearly, these members could easily be mistaken as illegal combatants and reported as *francs-tireurs*.[52]

The German reaction to whatever they considered as *francs-tireurs* was swift and harsh. Operationally, purported irregulars often became the focus of unit actions. Constant company and regimental alerts not only fed fear but added to the attacking soldiers' stress. Dealing with alleged atrocities and the other real or imagined involvements of the Belgian population against the German Army not only fulfilled German expectations but also became an all-consuming, self-fulfilling prophecy. Cavalry patrols expecting popular resistance found it whether it was there or not. As result, patrols increasingly spent their attention looking over their shoulders, focused on the local populace instead of conducting operational reconnaissance. No unit escaped the dilemma, and there were examples of serious operational impacts on units assigned to the alternate mission of retaliation. Across Belgium, German troops looted and burned homes, murdered the inhabitants, and shot hostages singularly and in groups. Standard accounts describe up to six thousand civilians executed in the course of the month. The worst of the carnage took place during the eight-day period between August 19 and August 26, 1914. Although most problems with civilians—real or imagined—were covered with a certain amount of veneer and euphemism to justify the German actions, some German regimental histories from this action were blunt. "The male inhabitants were shot. Women and children led away. The houses set ablaze."[53]

The real issue with the atrocities was that they absorbed German attention, which should have been fully focused on the mission. While a self-fulfilled prophecy, the sheer volume of atrocities was staggering. The following discussion addresses only individual atrocities that killed ten or more and highlights those that killed more than one hundred civilians. Of course, the Germans also took casualties. However, most were attributed to friendly fire incidents where panic and sometimes alcohol contributed. Although the panic might be understandable, it is more difficult to explain incidents where civilians were used as human shields to protect German forces.

The first major incident was recorded on August 5. The highly frustrated Thirty-Fourth Infantry Brigade burned a large part of the town of Berneau. The ten civilian deaths and eighty houses burned were no doubt in reprisal for the friendly fire incident of the night before, in which several German casualties were recorded. Fourteenth Infantry Brigade moved forward with a vengeance, killing eleven in Micheroux. Worse, just south of that location in Soumagne, they killed 118, burned over one hundred buildings, and used civilians as human shields.[54]

On August 6, Fourteenth Infantry Brigade pushed forward behind another human shield at Retinn, killing forty civilians. Also in their rear area, they burned the town of Battice, setting ablaze 147 houses and killing thirty-three civilians. In the far south, the Thirty-Eighth and Forty-Third Infantry Brigades killed thirteen civilians in Poulseur.

The Mecklenburgers in the far north, Thirty-Fourth Infantry Brigade and their two Jäger battalions (Seventh and Ninth), burned 149 houses and killed eleven civilians in Hermée. The town of Warsage, quite far from the front lines, saw fourteen killed. As this brigade withdrew to the river crossing, it also killed twenty-seven civilians in the bridge town of Herstal and when they arrived at Lixhe, killed eleven more. Eleventh Infantry Brigade killed twenty-seven civilians in its advance to Romsée. Along the way, it killed seventeen at Magnée and another sixty-four at St. Hadelin, where it also used a human shield.

In the south, at the end of an unsuccessful attack, the Thirty-Eighth and Forty-Third Infantry Brigades seem to have taken their fear and suspicions out on the town of Spirmont, killing forty civilians and burning sixty houses. A similar fate came to Louveigné, where Seventy-Third Infantry Regiment killed twenty-eight and burned seventy-seven houses. On the way into the attack, the town of Esneux saw twenty civilians killed. Not to be left out, Sixteenth Infantry Regiment of Twenty-Seventh Infantry Brigade not only killed nineteen civilians at Blegney, but was also implicated heavily in burning all Battice.

On August 8, Fourteenth Infantry Brigade kept up the pace of atrocities. The town of Melen near Fort Barachon saw 108 of its citizens killed. In addition to thirty-eight civilian deaths, three hundred buildings were destroyed in Hervé, far behind the front lines. Eleventh Infantry Brigade retaliated against the town of Baelen, almost all the way back to the German border, killing sixteen. The same could be claimed in the town of Francorchamps, where Seventy-Fourth Infantry Regiment killed fourteen near Malmedy, almost at the German border.[55]

We can draw several conclusions from this. It looks as though almost all units on the German side around Liège participated in the atrocities. The German regimental histories, in general, tell tales of Germans enduring treachery and terrorism. However, the subsequent evaluations and investigations come down squarely on the side of demonstrating unnecessary atrocities. The frontline troops were not the only ones involved, and indeed towns far behind the front lines were regularly targeted. The use of human shields by Fourteenth Infantry Brigade certainly casts a shadow on their advance.

Seraing Bridge.

However, these atrocities should not be contextualized with those committed twenty-five years later by a different regime. In the Nazi regime, some three million Poles and three million Polish Jews lost their lives between 1939 and 1945. The Germans conscripted around 120,000 Belgian workers after October 1916, a move long resisted by the German Governor Gen. Moritz von Bissing. Some twelve to fifteen million slave laborers worked the mines, factories, and fields of the Third Reich. The Germans in 1914 had more scruples than they would twenty-five years later.[56]

In the long run, its *francs-tireurs* policies did not turn out well for Imperial Germany. Germany not only sustained a propaganda defeat, but also used a tremendous amount of energy chasing reported sightings in 1914. Inexperienced soldiers overreacted in fear—sometimes fueled by alcohol and a lifetime of horror stories—in many cases shooting at the "bogeyman" and taking revenge on entire cities for the actions of a real or imagined few. The German literature may have tried, but the atrocities certainly could not be justified under the extant Hague Convention or stand up in the court of international opinion.

French Cavalry Corps Sordet

The word exhausted has been almost universally used to describe the French Cavalry Corps Sordet. Operating on the French left flank, this organization did not start out with anything but the best of the best. Its elements received orders on July 31 to mobilize. All the officers were from the regular army. Of the thirty-six mounts per platoon, they were all considered magnificent, with an average age of six: prime of life for a troop horse. The men and animals were about as ideal as could be. "The scene of these magnificent regiments, composed of vigorous young men, newly equipped, mounted on horses in superb condition, provoked confidence and admiration." From August 4 to August 19, the entire corps covered three hundred miles. Reports clarify that this was double the regulation expectations. Most of the regiments covered more than 155 miles in the first five days of marching. The corps reconnaissance platoons did significantly more, averaging more than fifty-six miles a day. They were sent to the Belgian border with a very vague mission to determine the enemy advance on the Belgian frontier, delay the march of the enemy columns, and clear the region of enemy cavalry.[57]

Not entirely ignorant of the events around Liège, the French command ordered Corps Sordet to cross the Belgian border. It patrolled as far north as Laroche and made extensive use of the existing telephone system for reporting. The French troopers, however, were still far south of Liège and on the eastern side of the River Meuse. Prisoners taken by the French confirmed that they had made contact with a brigade of the German Ninth Cavalry Division.

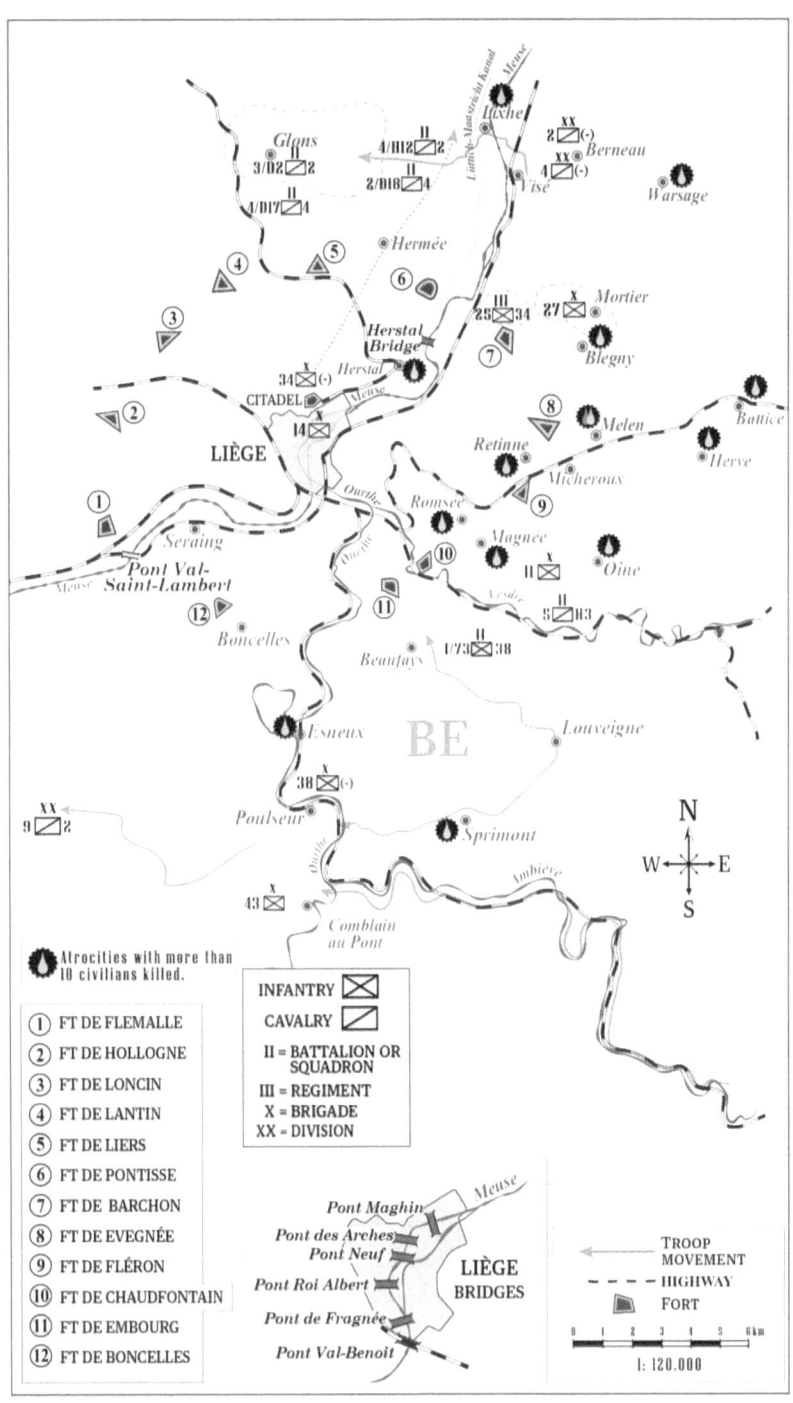

Major German atrocities on August 6, 7, and 8—just the Handstreich.

French analysis based on the interrogation of a single prisoner was that twelve army corps had unloaded around Aachen. This prisoner also declared that thirty-nine army corps had been concentrated in Alsace-Lorraine. This disconcerting information reached the French Cavalry Corps on August 9.[58]

August 6

The OHL ordered support of the ground forces by Luftschiff ZVI. Under the command of Hauptmann Kleinschmidt, the airship departed Cologne at 2200 hours on the night of August 5. By 0300 hours on August 6, it was over Liège. There, the crew dropped a load of 15- and 21-centimeter shells onto the Belgian fortifications. However, artillery fire struck the airship, and she began losing gas. Heading for home, she eventually made a forced landing in a forest at Walberburg and was damaged beyond repair. The crash eliminated the Army of the Meuse's lighter-than-air capability. This element conducted no long-range reconnaissance, and now that entire capability was completely and drastically removed. FFA 9 was not tasked for any missions.[59]

The British Cabinet decided to send a smaller BEF than originally intended and dispatched four infantry divisions and one cavalry division to the Continent.

Pont de Arches bridge destroyed.

The Belgians destroyed the central Liège bridges of Maghin and Arches at 1105 hours and 1130 hours, respectively.[60] By now the Belgian Army was in position, with four divisions behind the Gette, one division at Namur, and one division at Liège for a total of about 117,000 troops. The Army regarded itself as the vanguard of its French, and now British, allies. "Here the Belgian Army was to wait until the military forces of the guaranteeing powers occupied the intermediate space between the Gette and Namur.... At the same time, liaison could be maintained with the base of operations, Antwerp, from which in no circumstances should the Army let itself be cut off."[61]

Second and Fourth Cavalry Divisions (Garnier)

An unheralded combat occurred near the Belgian market town of Waremme and led the Belgians to capture many prisoners. This action significantly affected the forces available for the two German regiments involved—Fourth German Cavalry Division lost the equivalent of half of a cavalry regiment out of only six. The German official history was silent on this matter, as was Poseck.[62] However, the destruction presented at Waremme was a precursor to the events at Halen. Yet, like the later battle of Halen, almost all sources ignore the events at Waremme.

As mentioned, four reconnaissance squadrons went forward on August 5. (One reconnaissance squadron came from Twelfth Hussar Regiment (IV) under the command of Cavalry Captain Kleffel, one from Second Dragoner Regiment (III) under the command of Cavalry Captain Baron von Yorck, one from Seventeenth Dragoner Regiment (IV) under the command of Cavalry Captain von Troschke, and one from Eighteenth Dragoner Regiment (II) under the command of Cavalry Captain von Boehm-Bezing.) The two squadrons from the Fourth German Cavalry Division (Seventeenth Dragoner IV and Eighteenth Dragoner II) operated as one. They were at about half-strength each because they had been assigned to the Liège strike force and had not received their allocated share of reservists. The results of their reconnaissance produced two reports, but neither the reports nor the dispatch riders ever arrived at division HQ.

Both squadrons initially moved in the direction of Celles and Les Waleffes. They met enemy riflemen who immediately opened fire. The squadrons thought the enemy had surrounded them, so they charged—only to crash into a network of hedges, wires, and fences before they even reached the Belgians. The enemy fire produced casualties. Some horses tumbled while galloping through wheat fields as the ripe wheat wound around the horses' legs. The senior officer ordered the signal *Apell*, "roll call," sounded to reassemble his squadron. The trumpet call was not heard in the turmoil of the fight. Only three *Unteroffiziere* (NCOs) and two troopers reported to the Rittmeister.

The rest of the squadron under Lieutenant Unger tried to break through but came under heavy rifle and machine-gun fire near Waremme. It suffered casualties and the greater part was captured.[63] Unger and a few of his men were able to save themselves and joined part of the no less roughly handled squadron of Seventeenth Dragoner Regiment. Blundering around during the night of the August 6, the cavalrymen veered near the Liège forts and were nearly captured a second time. On the morning of August 7, Unger encountered Yorck's squadron—Third Squadron Second Dragoner Regiment, with whom he stayed until August 11. Only then was he able to return to the regiment with his few troopers, already listed as lost.

Some of the proud German cavalry surrendered. A single sergeant in the Belgian Carabineer Cyclist Battalion, twenty-year-old Georges van Espen, bravely led a five-man detachment in an attack that ended by taking thirty-eight prisoners, including an officer, along with accounting for ten Germans wounded and four killed. The Belgian Cavalry Division had spent the morning massed near Hannut waiting for a German division that allegedly had been near St. Truiden. Cyclist patrols, which were extremely effective in this terrain, eventually discovered the Germans. Van Espen's detachment quickly captured one rider and identified Seventeenth Dragoner Regiment. The sergeant then shot at the squadron and pursued it into the town of Waremme with his few men. Advised by the civilian population, the detachment located the Germans in the garden of a judge's house.

Van Espen's words describe the situation: "I continued going on. I was surprised to see a white flag floating at the tip of a lance! I have to admit that I was not proud at that moment. I found myself all alone on the street, asking myself whether this could be a trick to ambush me." Still running, he slung his rifle across his back, firing a revolver. After entering the open gate of the garden fence, he pointed the revolver at the officer's head, shouting, "Do not move." Imagine this young sergeant alone in the middle of forty heavily armed German troopers, summoning them to surrender! The German officer responded in French and surrendered his sword to a detachment of five cyclists.[64]

The losses of Second Squadron Eighteenth Dragoner were severe. Six dragoners fell; three officers and sixty-nine troopers were captured. Second Squadron was so reduced that the regiment dissolved it and assigned its men and horses to other squadrons. Fourth Squadron Seventeenth Dragoner was reduced to just one platoon, which was made the guard for the regimental colors. Thus, two squadron-sized formations were eliminated from the order of battle. By later standards, these losses would be insignificant. However, removing these two small counters from the map just two days after the start

5. Handstreich

Luitenant Sanden, ordonnans-officier, begeeft zich per auto van het oorlogsterrein naar het hoofdkwartier. — Men ziet duidelijk dat de blinkende helmen der hem vergezellende kurassiers met grijze stof zijn overtrokken. — Officier en manschappen rijden met den vinger aan den trekker door de vijandelijke omgeving.

A group of Dutch civilians gawking at a German liaison officer near Lixhe.[65]

of the war encourage closer examination of the reconnaissance. Considering that cavalry allocation had been weak from the start, the Germans could ill afford the loss of these two squadrons—about half of a regiment for no reason or gain.[66]

One source mentioned that Seventeenth Dragoner Regiment had a very hard time managing the lances in combat.

> The place was crowded with very agitated civilians, a part of them hiding behind barricades, firing at us with shotguns. At a sharp curve in the road, a few dragoners that had pushed forward in the wildest gallop had tumbled at the slippery cobblestone pavement and some of them had impaled one another with their lances. The civilians now fired into this tangle. My horse jumped over this wild cluster of humans and animal bodies.[67]

The "lance question" had been part of the cavalry's discourse for a century. Only in the German army were they a universal weapon. There, effective use in combat had been stipulated, not demonstrated. Experience teaches hard lessons!

Thirty-Fourth Infantry Brigade

The brigade reached Hermée at midnight. In the confusion, it seems Ninetieth Infantry Regiment ended up going first, followed by Eighty-Ninth

Infantry Regiment, directly into contact with Fort Pontisse. A report stated that a battalion flag from Eighty-Ninth Infantry Regiment was buried to save it from capture. More alarming, it was reported that the brigade commander gathered the field grade officers at the village of Hermée and gave them their orders for the first time. Allegedly, the officers were not aware their objective was the Citadel in Liège until that early hour. If the report were true, there must have been a little doubt that during a few hours at night the regiments could find their way over the large amounts of ground required to reach their assigned objectives. Once again, it seems as if the progress arrows shown in the official *Handstreich* history were pure fiction.[68] "Still at dark the infantry storm troops advanced without any artillery support with unloaded guns and fixed bayonets, among them many recruits who never experienced a night battle. The thrust was carried out from an unfavorable direction toward an invisible enemy and unknown obstacles."[69]

It is not clear why exactly this change was made. The brigade commander next ordered Seventh Jäger to become the brigade advance guard and continue the march due south to Liège. Now, however, instead of having the entire Thirty-Fourth Brigade behind it, Seventh Jäger was followed by only Ninth Jäger. Seventh Jäger moved along the road and slipped into a gap between Forts Pontisse and Liers, as imagined in the original plan. Without making any contact whatsoever, the battalion had broken through and was behind Belgian lines. This success occurred at night by a unit only just assigned to the brigade. At dawn, Seventh Jäger reached the Quartier du Nord in Liège—and stopped. The battalion arrived unaware in front of the house of the Military Commander of Liège, General Leman. Leman and his staff were completely surprised by the advance and progress of the Prussian troops. Staff members evacuated Leman, but this led to a collapse of the Belgian command-and-control system at a critical time. Ninth Jäger Battalion took Haute Préalle, though the battalion history gave no details. Seventh Jäger Battalion remained unsupported.

Out of contact with the rest of the brigade, Seventh Jäger commander Major Donalies therefore decided to withdraw. By 0900 hours, the return march toward Vottem began. Patrols, however, returned reporting they had not made contact with the brigade. That information led Donalies to believe that the brigade indeed had occupied Liège without the Seventh's presence. Disconcerted at least, probably embarrassed, he decided to turn back to Liège at 1600 hours. Before getting very far, however, the bulk of the battalion, exhausted, unfed, and disoriented, was either captured or scattered. At the end of the day, Seventh Jäger Battalion could only muster fewer than two companies.[70]

As for the rest of the brigade, the Eighty-Ninth and Ninetieth Infantry Regiments, receiving fire from Forts Pontisse and Liers, arrived at the railroad embankment. The shaft of the Ninetieth Infantry Regiment's standard was leaned against the slope as a marker and a challenge; the men climbed up the two- to three-meter high embankment. A wild fight between the German infantry and the fort's Belgian defenders ensued, much of it featuring bayonets. Many German and Belgian officers were killed setting examples. Eventually, the attack stalled three hundred meters from Fort Liers. The commander's conclusion was that it could not continue without artillery support and, of course, that artillery could not cross the river. A mixed column from Ninetieth Infantry Regiment and Third Battalion Infantry Regiment 89 under Major Arnim had pushed into Herstal.

By dawn, Thirty-Fourth Infantry Brigade was scattered haphazardly across the terrain behind Fort Liers and Fort Pontisse. In front, elements of Ninth Jäger were in Préalle and Seventh Jäger on the north side of Liège. In the middle was Eighty-Ninth Infantry Regiment II with elements of I and III at the churchyard of Rhées. About six hundred soldiers from different units were east of Rhées. Most of what was left of Ninetieth Infantry Regiment managed to consolidate on the high ground north of Rhées by approximately 0700 hours but stood in place.

The Ninetieth regimental commander ordered a withdrawal to Hermée

German pontoon bridge

at about 1030 hours on August 6. The brigade commander followed suit at 1045 hours. The remnants assembled at Lixhe, but still took disruptive artillery fire. During the night of August 5–6, the new bridge at Lixhe was completed. As HKK 2 prepared to move to Tongres, their way was blocked by the retreating brigade. Finally, a desperate request for help arrived at HKK 2 "in order to save the brigade from total destruction."[71] In the evening, the rest of the brigade was withdrawn over the Meuse River to bivouac east of Mouland.[72] Many German officers and soldiers from Thirty-Fourth Infantry Brigade had been taken prisoner.[73]

Twenty-Seventh Infantry Brigade

In this brigade's zone of advance, a thunderstorm developed. In the darkness, the assigned guide from the general staff concluded a breakthrough was not possible. The commander of the leading regiment, the Sixteenth Infantry, therefore decided only to demonstrate in front of the forts. Instead, he turned his attention to the citizens of Blegny, thought to be shooting at the Germans. The brigade's regiments returned to the start point. Further unfavorable intelligence from Fifty-Third Infantry Regiment about its own similar failed thrust and subsequent withdrawal compelled Oberst Bober of Sixteenth Infantry Regiment to withdraw all the way back to Battice.[74]

At dawn, Twenty-Fifth Infantry Regiment launched a bayonet attack just west of Fort Barchon. Although not mentioned in the history, most of the commissioned and noncommissioned leaders and many soldiers were killed or wounded in a charge that certainly resonates of a traditional bayonet charge:

> A high price had to be paid for this great success. In the assault on the enemy fortifications Hauptmann von Wellmann, Oberleutnant Egon Pax, Leutnant Viebeg, Freiherr von Godin, and Leutnant der Reserve Gräfenhan together with seventy-eight brave Unteroffiziere and men died the heroes' death. Oberst von Strantz, Major Kutzbach, Hauptmann Schell von Lehenner, Oberleutnant von Collani, Leutnant Werner-Ehrenfeucht, Stroedicke, Leutnant der Reserve Ruoff, Fähnrich Werner-Ehrenfeucht, and 313 Unteroffiziere and men were wounded.[75]

Fourteenth Infantry Brigade

General Ludendorff, accompanying the rear of the brigade's column, pushed forward. He took command of an unspecified force, probably elements of Twenty-Seventh Infantry Regiment, and continued the battle, pushing on into and then withdrawing from the town of Retinne. About 0300 hours, the Germans commenced an attack on Queue-du-Bois. Ludendorff was quite visible while leading some of the artillery into position. The coop-

6. August 1914. Die 14. Inf.-Brigade bei den Kämpfen um Lüttich

Artist rendition of the Fourteenth Infantry Brigade on August 6, showing General Ludendorff.

eration of the infantry and artillery and the personal leadership exerted on the spot enabled the Germans to capture Queue-du-Bois by about 0630 hours. Fourteenth Infantry Brigade was to pass successfully between the two forts and, by daylight on August 6, held positions on the high ground sloping down toward Liège.[76]

By 0630 hours, the Belgians were retreating through Bellaire all the way to Jupille. The Germans in pursuit entered Bellaire at about 0730 hours. Once the Germans took Queue-du-Bois, they had penetrated between the forts and into a dead zone the forts' fire could not reach. Leman had already committed all his reserves to Sart-Tilman. When Leman heard the Germans were at Queue-du-Bois, he immediately ordered the Belgian troops in the sector to withdraw. This withdrawal threatened the rear of the Belgian troops at Sart-Tilman, who also were forced to withdraw. At 0930 hours, the troops at Jupille received the order for the general withdrawal of the Belgian Third Infantry Division. At 1100 hours, German Twenty-Seventh Infantry Regiment took control of Jupille.[77]

Obviously, this part of the *Handstreich* had worked. The brigade was beyond the forts and overlooking Liège. Patrols were sent out to find the neighboring brigades, but Eleventh Infantry Brigade was not at Beyne-

Heusay, nor Twenty-Seventh Infantry Brigade at Wandre. Similarly, at 2200 hours, two Jäger companies were sent to secure four of the bridges, but Belgian engineers had destroyed the bridge at Pont du Arches to halt the German advance.

Eleventh Infantry Brigade

The brigade commander finally restored order by daylight. At this point, Eleventh Infantry Brigade had broken through Fléron and Chaudefontaine and was behind the line of forts, but troops had to maneuver to avoid artillery fire from those forts. By 1400 hours, elements of Thirty-Fifth Infantry Regiment entered Beyne-Heusay. The troops were by then exhausted, and the brigade faced the built-up area east of Liège; fighting would be street to street and house to house. The commander therefore withdrew the brigade to bivouac west of Magnée, but at 1800 hours, artillery fire from Fort Fléron forced them to move to a ravine southeast of Magnée. Their casualties were quite light compared with those of other brigades.

August 7

Handstreich Postmortem

There was no allowance for signal troops of any kind to be assigned to establish and maintain communication between Emmich and his higher HQ. As the commander of Second Army became anxious about the lack of information, he sent forward a liaison officer, Captain von Fouque. This resulted in a report on August 7 that Fourteenth, Twenty-Seventh, and Thirty-Fourth brigades were still outside of the fortifications and there was no idea where General von Emmich was. The captain sent another report around noon on the seventh that Liège had still not been taken. And yet another report at 1800 hours relayed that intelligence officers in Koblenz were questioning whether the HQ of General von Emmich still existed. Wild rumors abounded. One assessment was that the command had been annihilated. Another rumor was that Emmich had committed suicide. Generalleutnant von der Marwitz, the commander of HKK 2, thought he had to take command of the Army of the Meuse because of the absence of Emmich. Based on rumors and lack of information, both the OHL and the Second Army HQ believed the attack had failed.[78]

Official German sources gave German losses for August 4–6 as 169 officers and 3,279 men. The *Handstreich* had indeed failed. But what were the key lessons concerning the preliminary reconnaissance? The battle of Liège provided an early example of German officers disregarding any sort of doctrinal innovation that differed from the glory days of the Franco-Prussian War. St. Privat had been forty years earlier. Perhaps they were literally "reverting under stress." Reconnaissance squadron commanders Kleffel, Troschke, and Boehm lost two-thirds of their men. Few riders came back from the remote patrols. Of the four patrols led by officers in Seventeenth Dragoner Regiment, just one returned.[79]

The Germans used no deep aviation reconnaissance. The location and intent of the Belgian field army had not been determined. At least two squadrons of German cavalry had been destroyed. The crossing over the Meuse River had been destroyed at Visé. The presence of the battalion colors gives a major clue as to the training of the different army corps. A flag waving at the front of an attack gives a strong hint of a traditionalist parent organization.

These brigades were products of peacetime training of six separate army corps: Third, Fourth, Seventh, Ninth, Tenth, and Eleventh. Going from north to south, Thirty-Fourth Infantry Brigade was assigned from Ninth Army Corps. There is no question that Eighty-Ninth and Ninetieth Regiments advanced with their colors aloft and performed poorly. Seventh Jäger Battalion was also shown to have its flag flying while assigned to Thirty-fourth Brigade, even though it was originally trained in Seventh Corps.

Twenty-Fifth Infantry Regiment also attacked shoulder to shoulder with its flags flying, according to the unit history. This regiment was from Eight Army Corps. The rest of Twenty-Seventh Infantry Brigade was assigned from Seventh Army Corps and, while the authors did not find direct evidence of its using traditional tactics, Seventh Jäger Battalion was also from Seventh Corps and it did use traditional tactics.

Unit histories showed clear evidence that Fourteenth Infantry Brigade assigned from Fourth Army Corps and Eleventh Infantry Brigade from Third Army Corps followed a more contemporary pattern when it came to march and attack formations, while Thirty-Eighth Infantry Brigade from Tenth Corps and Forty-Third Infantry Brigade from Eleventh Army Corps lined up behind the traditionalists. By logic, correspondingly, that puts Third, Fourth, and perhaps Seventh Army Corps in the reformist camp, and Ninth, Tenth, and Eleventh in the traditionalist camp. This indicates some serious institutional disconnects, however persuasive its specific reasons in each case.

Another telling tale is that German senior officer losses were extremely high: The commanders of the Twentieth, Seventy-Fourth, and Twenty-Seventh Infantry Regiments; a battalion commander in the Thirty-Fifth, Twenty-Fifth, Eighty-Ninth, Fifty-Third, Seventy-Third, and Eighty-Second Infantry Regiments; and two battalion commanders in the Eighty-Third and Ninetieth Regiments were killed. The commanding general of Fourteenth

Infantry Brigade and the commanders of Seventh and Ninth Jäger battalions rounded out a significant loss of leadership in the infantry. The loss of so many senior leaders in such a short period certainly indicates both traditionalist training, as officers were supposed to be in the lead of any attack, and levels of confusion demanding senior officer involvement despite the risks.

Belgian Withdrawal

Leman's original HQ was attacked at 0445 hours on August 6, and he relocated by 0700 hours. Reports prior to the attack were troubling, and then for two hours the Belgian general was out of contact. At 0715 hours, he was informed that in the area of Chaudefontaine-Fléron, the Belgian forces had been defeated and forced to withdraw. At 0732 hours, Leman ordered the withdrawal of his field forces to the west side of Liège among the forts between Hollogne and Lantin. Finally, he decided to withdraw both Third Infantry Division and Fifteenth Brigade to join the field army, leaving only the fortress troops. Leman informed the Belgian SHQ that the division would be withdrawn because it was completely exhausted.

The *Handstreich* as conceived had obviously failed, but Belgian actions caused it to become a partial success. Leman was not only commander of Third Infantry Division, but also governor of Fortress Liège. As mentioned, one of the few successes in the *Handstreich* was that of the Seventh Jäger Battalion attack on the Belgian Third Infantry Division HQ, where the general was located. As Leman evacuated to Fort Loncin, command and control of the Belgian forces fell into complete confusion. Reports were contradictory, and the general did not understand the situation. He was of the opinion that four full German army corps—instead of multiple separate brigades—were attacking. With reports of penetrations throughout the perimeter of Liège, he believed he was facing a catastrophe and that the Belgian Third Infantry Division could be caught in a mousetrap. He heard excited reports of strong German cavalry to his west and as many as five thousand more German cavalry around Warreme. Because the Belgian troops had been withdrawn from the Visé area, Leman had no idea exactly how much German cavalry had crossed the Meuse River. Estimates were wildly different, but two cavalry divisions were known to be north of Liège and should have wanted to cross. Thus, the Belgians worried the German cavalry would not only trap the Belgian divisions, but also turn the flank of the field army. Our examination of the German side shows only a few reconnaissance squadrons present and that some of them did not fare well.

The Belgian decision to withdraw rather than counterattack is interesting. Originally, the Belgians had no prewar plans to defend the intervals between the forts. Leman succeeded in convincing the king to do so, over the head of the Belgian chief of staff, just days before the war broke out. It is not clear how many casualties the Third Infantry Division suffered as a result. The withdrawal in any case turned into a disorganized route march. When it arrived at Hannut on August 7, the previously strong division needed to be reorganized: the five brigades that had started the battle were consolidated into three. Further information on the convoluted German order of battle also worked to the German advantage by leading the Belgian SHQ to continue believing they faced elements of Ninth, Seventh, Tenth, Fourth, and Eleventh German Army Corps (rather than brigades). The SHQ also understood the forts still held out but that Leman had stayed in Liège and abandoned his division.

As the Belgian Army withdrew, it needed a pause to allow Third Infantry Division to catch up with the main body. Two main east–west roads also had to be guarded: the central road that ran from Liège to Tienen and a more northerly road that ran between Hasselt and Diest. These two roads were vitally important in planning movement of the German infantry and follow-on supply organizations, and the Germans would have to clear the roads to allow that movement. The Belgian Army could address both problems by resting at a naturally strong position halfway between Liège and Antwerp along the River Gette.

The Germans pushed into the city of Liège against little organized resistance. Fire from the forts was sporadic and not coordinated because each fort was by now isolated. Movement between the forts became easier for the attackers, and even many German staff cars seem to have found their way through. Ludendorff made his well-known capture of the Citadel. The mobile Belgian forces withdrew. Some units joined the retreat while others capitulated. As Fourteenth and Eleventh Infantry Brigades entered the city, it continued to rain. At 1300 hours, an officer of the General Staff brought the directive: "Lüttich is in our hands. The troops that stand near Julémont have to advance immediately!" Sixteenth Infantry Regiment was promptly put back in motion despite receiving shrapnel fire as it passed about three hundred meters from the fully occupied Fort Barchon. The advance to Liège from the direction of Jupille continued unhampered with flags flying in heavy rain.[80]

Announced Great Victory at Liège

By the end of the day on August 7, the Germans had in Liège two infantry brigades and an infantry regiment and had effectively secured the city center. The first authentic news to relieve the suspense in Second Army came toward the close of the day when Bülow's HQ intercepted a private telegram from Emmich to his wife. The information it contained was quite scant, reading only, "Hurrah, at Liège." Two hours later, formal word arrived from the Second Army's liaison officer: "General von Emmich entered Liège on August 7 at 0745 hours. The Governor in flight. The Bishop a prisoner. Liège evacuated by Belgian troops. Citadel of Liège occupied by our troops. As yet not known which forts have been taken."[81]

This report completely overturned and reversed the initial impression that the attack had failed. Now it was generally accepted by Second Army and the German High Command as an announcement that the struggle was over. The communiqué from Berlin proclaimed the capture of the fortress. The German press hailed the victory. Throughout Germany, the public received the news with smug satisfaction. And because of this impression, Bülow entrained his HQ on the night of August 7 for Montjoie, in the zone of concentration. The invasion, he was sure, could now proceed on schedule—more or less.

This left the Germans in a paradox situation. They controlled the city of Liège but not the surrounding forts, which could still interdict the lines of communication through the city. There was no direct contact or communication between Emmich in the city center and Bülow outside. At 1900 hours, therefore, Ludendorff left Liège to report to Bülow in person.

The Germans announced a great victory: Liège has been captured! Reality was more mundane. In a tactical context, it was not such a great victory. It was almost as though the Germans owned the center of a doughnut hole. Despite all the celebration and back slaps, there was still a great deal of work to be done just to open the railroad. The one rail line going into the heartland of Belgium was still blocked. With the tunnels blocked, there was no quick solution—no solution at all—except to clear the tunnels. The unbelievably good news for the Germans, however, was that neither of the railway bridges had been destroyed! There were only two railroad bridges and they were both intact. By clearing the rail blockages, these two bridges could be used without delay.

Reconnaissance

For their use to be optimized, the cavalry had to show the way and lead it. There lay an emerging rub. The Germans do not seem to have been overly proud of the events at Waremme. The engagement received no mention in the GOH, which published instead, the following entry:

> Right from the beginning of hostilities, elements of HKK 2 of Generalleutnant [von der] Marwitz were involved in the operation against the Liège stronghold. Additionally, he was responsible for the strategic reconnaissance of the Antwerp–Brussels–Charleroi Line. Up until August 7, the assigned reconnaissance squadrons had found

the region up to the Diest line "free of the enemy." The HKK had been held up due to the events before Liège and the delay at the crossing of the River Meuse.[82]

This entry was completely astonishing and equally false. The OHL considered HKK 2 responsible for the strategic reconnaissance of the line Antwerp–Brussels–Charleroi but clearly the formation had not reached that far. It was not even clear whether HKK 2 *could* have gotten that far even in the absence of any resistance. There was, moreover, the small problem of a Belgian Army willing and able to fight effectively on a limited scale but sufficient to bloody the cavalry's nose embarrassingly.

The reconnaissance squadrons so roughly handled at Waremme limped back to the main body. Rittmeister Boehm first met the patrols of Lieutenant von Goszler and Vizewachtmeister Klawikowski from Second Dragoner Regiment. Both had lost contact with their squadron. Then another five horsemen, stragglers from Seventeenth Dragoner Regiment, showed up. Boehm now had one officer and thirty-three troopers from three different regiments. He decided to try to return to the division rather than continue the mission, itself not an unreasonable or timid action under the circumstances—and eventually joined the main body on August 8. This was nevertheless hardly the aggressive strategic reconnaissance of the kind needed in the German invasion plan.[83] In the same time frame, Seventh Jäger Battalion entered Lixhe, where it came under the command of Fourth Cavalry Division. The battalion's Third Company, machine guns, and Cyclist Company, however, stayed under command of General von Kraewel, Thirty-Fourth Brigade—a significant diminution of the battalion's fighting power.

Despite repeated efforts, FFA 9 was not tasked for any missions again. Its commander was separated from his unit due to his dual role on Emmich's staff. Given the uncertainty of the outcome of the *Handstreich*, the OHL had also tasked Festungs-Flieger-Abteilung 3, based in Köln for aerial reconnaissance of the combat situation on August 6 and August 8. This unit failed in its mission despite long hours of operational flights—a paradigm for German strategic reconnaissance when and where it was most needed.[84]

6

Reducing Liège

It is the same with strategy as with the siege of a fortress—concentrate fire on a single point.—Napoleon[1]

August 8

Artillery Reduction

On the ground, the Liège operation seemed to be falling into place. Developing the original attacks, the 21-centimeter mortars from the Twenty-Seventh and Fourteenth Brigades together shelled Fort Barchon. The guns of the forts, all of mid–1880s vintage, were flat-trajectory weapons. The Germans brought thirty-two 21-centimeter mortars, four battalions, a generation newer and far more accurate than the high-angle weapons Liège was originally designed to face.[2] When Sixteenth Infantry Regiment received the order to storm Barchon, the German artillery continued to shell the fort. A summons to surrender was successful by 1700 hours.[3] An investigation after the war concluded that Fort Barchon could have held out much longer and that a German infantry assault was not possible. This was the first real break the Germans had experienced in Liège.

At the higher levels of command, however, confusion still seems to have reigned supreme. The German intelligence estimate speculated the BEF might be located as far forward as Brussels![4] When Second Army HQ arrived west of Aachen, the situation was believed to be critical; it discovered that the OHL had ordered the newly arriving corps to send units forward to support the Liège attack, assuming Liège had fallen. Ninth Army Corps was ordered to send a brigade, a regiment at the minimum, plus artillery to Visé. Seventh Army Corps was to send a similar force southeast of Liège, and Tenth Army Corps another south of Liège. Finally, as well, telephonic communication was established with the liaison officer, who was able to relay the situation report that had been given to him by Ludendorff.[5]

There was still no communication with Emmich, but Second Army HQ did learn that Fort Fléron was still in enemy hands. During its move, Second Army HQ did not have a radio station and thus was without connection to the outside world for hours. What were passed to the commander were rumors and not even verifiable random news. These said that not only had none of the other assault brigades advanced, but the Thirty-Fourth Infantry Brigade that was supposed to lead the decisive strike west of the River Meuse had been almost annihilated. Furthermore, not even one fortress had been taken.[6]

On the morning of August 8, Ludendorff reported in person to the commander of Second Army. He had not been able to get inside any of the fortifications. He reported that all communication with General von Emmich had been severed and assumed that the Belgians, along with some help from the French, had reoccupied the forts and that the Germans had been forced to retreat.[7] This nourished a fear in the German command that the guns of the forts maintained so accurate a fire and such a vigilant watch that they still commanded every road leading to the city. An overwhelming assumption seems to have developed at Second Army's HQ that the Belgians, possibly reinforced by significant French elements, had defeated the German troops in Liège. The three brigades still outside Liège were of little help in clarifying the situation inside the city. The High Command was also trying to direct the operation bypassing Second Army HQ. Bülow, suffering the agonies of apprehension, understood that the prestige of the German Army and the future of his own career depended upon the fate of the brigade trapped inside Liège and on his ability to make good the victory that had already been publically announced. Twenty-four hours passed without any significant change in the situation, while every effort to reach Emmich failed.[8]

Astonished and disappointed, Bülow initiated another improvised fall-back plan. This one consisted essentially of bringing up super-heavy artillery and smashing the belligerent Belgian fortresses into submission. He also complicated the chain of command even more. With Emmich out of contact, Bülow created yet another level that would be responsible for all forces in the siege of Liège. The unexpectedly strong resistance of the fortification belt required the reinforcement of the attack force. Ninth, Seventh, and Tenth Army Corps each dispatched one mixed brigade for this purpose. As they arrived, these elements and the heavy artillery would be at Bülow's disposal, while Emmich would stay in command of the Eleventh, Fourteenth, and Twenty-Seventh Brigades in the city.

The position of the reinforcement commander, the commanding general of Seventh Army Corps, was much like that of Emmich, an ad hoc appointment.

General der Kavallerie Karl von Einem now occupied a position between Emmich and Bülow in Second Army. Both Einem and Emmich were army corps commanders, but Einem was senior and had once been War Minister. He was now in charge of elements of four different army corps, but it is not clear exactly what his orders were. Unlike the misbegotten command of Emmich, Einem's was not a corps HQ trying to coordinate unrelated infantry brigades. Its position was arguably worse: a corps HQ now *responsible* for several separate brigades from different army corps, plus an HKK deficient in communication troops and staff. Einem's command was put together by fiat and expected to perform effectively. Moreover, rather than enable Einem's use of the staff and communication capabilities of Second Army, Bülow avoided blame by making coordination Einem's responsibility; a probable case of plausible deniability. Thirty-Fourth Brigade would continue to hold near Visé in the north, while Twenty-Eighth Brigade was to move toward Fort Fléron and d'Evegnée. On its left, Thirty-Eighth Brigade would secure to the north of Fraipont on the Vesdre and Forty-Third Brigade to the south of it. To their rear, Fortieth Brigade of Tenth Corps was to move on Pepinster. Ninth Army Corps would unload at Aachen, Seventh at Eupen, and Tenth at Malmedy, then all advance to Einem's support.[9]

Meanwhile German consolidation within Liège continued. Sixteenth Infantry Regiment reported these as rather pleasant times, extremely unusual with the Germans controlling the city center and the forts overwhelmingly intact. Movement of German reservists into the city to complete their parent brigade's mobilization and replace their casualties demonstrated the ineffectiveness of the forts in completely blocking the roads. Slow logistical trains, however, remained a vulnerable target of opportunity. In response, artillery was brought into position outside of the city to facilitate destruction of the forts.

As described earlier, Fort Barchon fell to the fire of six 21-centimeter mortars. It was 21-centimeter mortars that were solely responsible for the surrender of nine of the twelve Liège forts. Almost any history concerning Liège credits the 42-centimeter super-heavy German guns (also known as *Dicke Berthas*) in reducing the fortresses, but this was basically untrue. The Krupp monsters were not yet ready when war broke out. The chief technical difficulty to be overcome was how to make the guns mobile. The original 1909 model had to be transported by rail and, due to its powerful recoil, embedded in concrete before it was fired. A road model was tested in February 1914 and the Krupp plant managed to convert two *Dicke Berthas* into road-transportable models, but the howitzers would not be ready until August 10.[10]

The pontoon bridge across the Meuse at Lixhe was completed on August 8. A German infantry company crossed to hold the bridgehead, followed by

Another ad hoc commander, General der Kavallerie von Einem.

Second and Fourth Cavalry Divisions. They initially penetrated quite far into Belgium. The cavalry not only crossed the river, but also set up bivouac positions near Looz and Cortessem. Pausing at these locations, the cavalry divisions were able to consolidate their forces and limited heavy equipment while continuing to patrol forward. The patrols reported that no enemy forces were approaching Liège either from the northwest or from the west. On the contrary, the Belgian troops from Liège had flooded back in great confusion. The situation in the south, from where French troops were allegedly approaching, was still unclear. Consequently, Emmich bypassed the HKK 2 commander and ordered Ninth Cavalry Division to do everything in order to determine the strength and the marching route of the French and to hold them up if possible. This took the division far away from its original mission west of the River Meuse—where it was urgently needed to provide reconnaissance for the main advance. It is instructive to note that the division's radio stations finally joined up with the division after detraining. This meant no radio contact earlier among the patrols, the division, and Second Army. The only way to inform anybody of any contacts made by the Ninth Cavalry Division would have been through messenger. On the positive side, the Stavelot Tunnel was entirely repaired and the first German train could use that line of track.[11]

Traffic congestion of HKK 2 on the east side of the Meuse River at Lixhe.

Lack of Structural Integration

At this point in time, memoirs started complaining about the force structure of the cavalry divisions. Remember that Moltke fixed the strength of the army cavalry on the decisive wing at three, instead of the originally projected five to eight, cavalry divisions. Because Ninth Cavalry Division had been unexpectedly assigned a different task in the south by General von Emmich, Second and Fourth Cavalry Divisions had to perform the reconnaissance unaided on an excessively extended front. Over the next week, the structural issue of failing to integrate cavalry and aviation reconnaissance came to a sore point. HKK 2 was trying to provide information to those formations advancing behind it, but strongly lamented the lack of aviation. HKK 2 was expected to divert away from Antwerp stronger Belgian forces than those HKK 2 possessed. The cavalry regiments did not have organic machine guns to increase their mobile firepower. "Planes were not available to Higher Cavalry Command 2, as the aviation assets assigned to General von Emmich stayed in Liège. It would have been obvious as well to reinforce this severely weakened army cavalry at least with other weapons from the beginning. These were available."[12]

While the fighting for the forts went on, the attention of aerial reconnaissance focused increasingly to the southwest against possible French or Belgian relief attempts from the direction of Namur and Dinant. As it turned out, there was no indication of such an operation. An FFA 9 airplane managed to land on the Liège airfield and establish liaison with the troops inside the fortress.[13]

There certainly was a brief time when Emmich was out of contact, during which Marwitz thought he had to assume control of the entire Liège operation. This misconception was corrected when Emmich came back into contact. So from the night of August 5 until the aircraft liaison on August 8, there was no contact with Emmich. Troschke related:

> Apart from this, the general [Marwitz] was bearing the responsibility for the storming of the three infantry regiments that attacked north of Liège, and then he finally had to take the temporary lead over the entire operation against Liège. The commander of Thirty-Fourth Infantry Brigade, Major General von Kräwel, would have been the given leader[ship] of these three regiments, troops that were subordinated to the command of Lieutenant General von der Marwitz for the attack on Liège.[14]

A day of rest due to the horses being overfatigued was ordered for HKK 1(Richthofen). The Guard Division's report reads:

> March from Bitburg in the Eiffel to Diekirch was very exhausting on account of the steep mountains, new to horses. Roads were spoiled by every rain. Our two sick regiments with influenza were badly exhausted. The artillery was in a bad way. Its light munitions columns had been equipped with poor horses, mainly coldbloods

unaccustomed to rapid traveling. Four horses were dead of overstrain and many more scarcely were able to move. One-third of the animals had their hind hoofs unshod by delay delivery of horseshoes, so that many wore out.[15]

French Cavalry Corps Sordet

Elements of the French Cavalry Corps reached the outskirts of Liège at about 1930 hours. They identified enemy road barricades and enemy infantry. Based on the late hour, the decision was made to withdraw to the vicinity of Modave, arriving there just after midnight. While covering one hundred kilometers or more that day, this maneuver was accomplished in intense heat and without pausing to water the horses. It posed high risk to a fragile, already heavily strained, limited asset.[16]

August 9

Einem succeeded in establishing telephonic communication with the city and sent the welcome news to the army commander that the German troops were safe. Five days after invading, Belgian Ninth Army Corps finally had used its telephone detachment to establish communications with the higher HQ. This was an inexplicable and unnecessary delay.[17]

Consolidation continued. Artillery as well as reservists were brought forward. Mobilization and mobilization training, as well as some shelling of the forts in the far north, continued. The Belgians could not confirm or deny rumors of large-scale German crossings of the River Meuse. Although mass crossings did not in fact occur, the Belgian SHQ was assuming twenty thousand German troops had allegedly crossed pontoon bridges established around Lixhe. The Belgians also identified two German cavalry divisions approaching St. Trond, which caused the Belgian cavalry division to fall back behind the Gette and screen the army's left flank.

BEF Embarks

The BEF's embarkation began on August 9 and was accomplished by August 17. On August 20, its concentration at Maubeuge was complete.[18] The location of the BEF was a triangular quandary. Based on cavalry and aviation reconnaissance, the Germans were aware that the Belgian field army was arrayed along the Gette River. It was assumed that the French left wing was somewhere around the Belgian city of Namur. This assumption was not validated by any direct observation. The third force, the BEF, was a complete and total mystery. The OHL believed the British would concentrate around

Lille. This would place them outside of the great German enveloping movement. It would threaten the flank of that envelopment. It would be shorter than joining with the French and would keep the British separate from the French. The other possibilities included a concentration joining the French left flank somewhere around Maubeuge. There was always as well the possibility of a British landing further north on the Belgian coast, threatening the rear of the German army. The danger of this possibility would be increased if the BEF could join with the Belgian forces. Therefore, the Germans had to disperse the Belgian Army before the BEF could join them or before they could withdraw into Antwerp. As First Army had to guard against all three of these possibilities, they often found themselves required to deploy corps in an echelon fashion to cover all the possibilities.

German aviation elements reconnoitered Namur for the first time, showing the intermediate ground between the forts had been fortified and that the forts had armored turrets.[19]

The cavalry divisions experienced improvised campaigning. The logistics of HKK 2 were so bad, it had to declare rest while artillery was repositioning around Liège. One individual cavalry soldier left a poem describing what life was like during this time. These words are hardly immortal verse, but evocative of lost military innocence.

> Before a village, we lay
> On a wide stubble field,
> At crack of dawn
> Horses lined up.
> No time to think about sleeping for now,
> As sun was already to be seen;
> We had to water the horses,
> To enter the village, and go for water.
> There we soon could be found
> At the well,
> Winching up the water,
> We carried to the field
> Back to our mounts
> Quenching their thirst;
> Thereupon we enjoyed
> For breakfast, bread and sausage.
>
> This day stayed in my memory
> As the first Sunday on enemy soil,
> With details engraved in my hearth,
> Found in my mind.
>
> Sun stands brightly at the sky, the blue
> And rays, before the village, a martial scenery;
> In the village, the bell calls men and women to church;
>   outside horsemen, minded to battle.

Yet the commands resound:
"Fertig machen! An die Pferde!" Prepare! To the horses!
Reluctant—I do not deny—
Horsemen rise from the earth.
To life came the wide field,
Where the six Regiments bivouac;
The mounts, still lined up, being prepared to march on.
"Aufsitzen! Anreiten! Die Tête links dreht, March!" Mount! Forward!
  The head to wheel left, March!
Harshly sound the commands from raw throats.[20]

At this point, differing priorities were obvious in the principle HQ around Liège. Second Army had to get the advance moving.

Two brigades under Emmich were inside Liège training reservists and consolidating. Outside of Liège on the eastern side, Einem was organizing and drawing closer to the forts, bringing his artillery to bear. First Army was mobilizing and waiting in line to advance. Two divisions of HKK 2 under the orders of Second Army were leaving Liège, trying to locate the Belgian Army along the River Gette.

French Cavalry Corps Sordet

Trying to centralize his position, General Sordet decided to move to a position where he could meet the enemy whether they came from the west or the north. He decided on a location near Voneche, about fifty miles to the south. His Third Cavalry Division had covered 108 miles in two days for little purpose or reward. The epitaph of *exhausted* began to be applied to the entire corps.[21]

August 10

Now under Einem, Ninth Army Corps (General von Quast) had been assigned the capture of the northern and eastern fronts of Liège: Forts Liers, Pontisse, and Fléron. In addition to his corps' organic artillery, Quast was given operational control over many more artillery units including 42-centimeter guns. General von dem Borne was assigned Forts Chaudefontaine and d'Embourg with 30-centimeter guns provided by Austria-Hungary and a 21-centimeter mortar. The 30-centimeter pieces, however, never participated in the siege, probably because of the blocked rail tunnels and lines.[22]

In the early hours of August 10, Emmich himself brought about his release. Second and Fourth Cavalry Divisions, advancing through St. Trond, drove a part of the Belgian Cavalry Division back on Tirlemont. Belgian cavalry had also been seen at Diest, thirty miles southeast of Antwerp. Ninth Cavalry Division of Marwitz's HKK 2 still had failed to cross the Meuse between Liège and Huy, but north of Liège detachments of Ninth Corps had crossed. The bridge situation was also being resolved. The restoration of the bridge at Visé was not practicable because it was still under fire from Fort Pontisse, and so another temporary bridge was constructed farther north at Lixhe. The bridge at Argenteau had been destroyed, but that at Herstal was now in German possession.[23]

Radio on Patrol

Second Cavalry Division assumed that it was moving to Tirelmont eventually and therefore sent its reconnaissance squadron, Second Squadron Third Uhlan, to patrol this front. Because of its role as a longer-range reconnaissance force, this squadron had taken a mobile radio set with it. Using this device, it was able to report Belgian positions quickly to the division on August 10. This confirmed the main Belgian defenses were along the River Gette. Radio contact with the division was lost that evening and was not re-established for two full days. The squadron finally made contact again on the thirteenth and found that the division was moving north instead.[24] Other actions by Second Cavalry Division achieved additional skirmishing success. In particular, First and Fifth Squadrons Twelfth Hussar Regiment, supported by other cavalry, successfully pushed back Belgian cavalry around the town of Orsmaël-Gussenhoven.

Three-Day Delay

Based on the common misconception of Liège being the objective, there has been a lot of discussion about how long the obstacle of the fortress city delayed the advance of the German forces. The advance was not the objective either. The objective was the Belgian Army. So, if we are asking how much time this obstacle cost the attacking force, it might be a better question of did the fortress city delay or prevent the dispersal of the Belgian Army? There was a three-day delay in the advance of First Army codified by an order from the OHL:

> The march of First Army to its position of deployment abreast of Liège by the roads mentioned in the deployment orders will begin at once. Ninth Corps will still be under the orders of the commander of Second Army. On the arrival of First Army, this corps will clear its front. August 13 was therefore fixed as the date for the march through Aix-la-Chapelle (Aachen) instead of the tenth, and the necessary movements were ordered preparatory to the advance of the corps. Their leading brigades were to reach the following destinations: Second Corps, Herzogenrath; Fourth Corps, Birk; and Third Corps, Weiden. The detrainment of Third Reserve and Fourth Reserve Corps could then take place at stations in advance of the present concentration area, and they would follow the other corps as soon as ready and with at least a day's march interval.[25]

The Belgian field army had just three options left. It could wait for the Germans in a defensive position and hold out there until the French or British reinforcements arrived. It could withdraw due to the approach of German forces, either in the direction of the left wing of the French Fifth Army or toward the BEF. Thirdly, it could finally move to the fortified camp of Antwerp. If the German cavalry approached directly toward Brussels, it would encounter the complete Belgian field army and lack the striking power to break through. If it advanced south of this resistance center—maybe between Jodoigne and Namur—it could threaten the right Belgian flank. In case of an advance north, it would threaten the left Belgian flank. This is what the Belgians feared as most likely, according to the diary entries of the Belgian chief of staff, and in fact the HKK 2 commander decided to outflank the Belgian force to the north. With only two cavalry divisions, Marwitz did not have a force large enough to consider forcing his way through. If he could envelop the Belgians from the north, perhaps he could prevent them from withdrawing along the road into the city of Antwerp. As a German history stated: "Everything depends on hindering it [the Belgian field army] to move to Antwerp and to restrain it until First Army arrives."[26]

HKK 1

Commanded by General Baron von Richthofen, this two-division HKK was the closest cavalry formation to HKK 2. Its mission was "to reconnoitre through the Ardennes forest in the direction of Dinant on the Meuse and beyond." This was a long way from the far right flank. The HKK did not cross the Belgian border until August 10. Prior to that, most of the HKK's time was spent in Luxembourg. Not only did it enter Belgium a full six days after HKK 2, but they immediately became involved in battling French security forces in the town of Simbret, southwest of Bastogne, making it unfavorable to supplement or support Marwitz's overextended formation.[27]

August 11

By late afternoon of August 11, the 21-centimeter mortars had pounded Fort d'Evegnée into submission. Even before the arrival of the main body of the German siege artillery, six of the formidable 21-centimeter mortars had reduced two more adjacent forts on the northeast side of Liège. This created a three-kilometer gap that no Belgian artillery could cover.

The situation around Liège otherwise appeared unchanged. Second Army considered that there was not sufficient heavy artillery, and no one could say how long it might be before the northern forts were captured. Moreover, before they fell, it would be impossible for Ninth Corps to clear the roads between Aachen and the Meuse so that the advance north of Liège could begin. Nevertheless, the Supreme Command had ordered rapid preparations made for that advance. Time was wasting. From information received, the Belgian Army appeared to be deployed on the Antwerp–Louvain–Namur front. The HKK 2 remained east of St. Trond, with its Ninth Cavalry Division southwest of Liège, and HKK 1 was still marching on Dinant.[28]

Aviation

German reinforcing troops started closing up on the eastern and southern fronts. Ninth, Seventh, and Tenth Army Corps had reached their deployment areas, and Guard Corps disembarked near Malmedy. The aerial reconnaissance assets on the right army wing were considerably reinforced by the FFAs of these four army corps. The destruction of three further Meuse bridges was observed: near Amay, at Engis, and the northernmost Liège Bridge. Good aerial photographs were taken of the Forts Chaudfontaine and Flemalle in the Liège fortification belt and of Fort Andoy (southeast of Namur). The FFA 9 conducted sorties in the circular sector of Aachen–Antwerp–Brussels–Namur–Rochefort, also finding and reporting the first sightings of the Belgian field army positions. The observer on a mission of a Rumpler-Taube aircraft along the line Aachen–Antwerp–Brussels–Namur over a distance of 325 kilometers (201 miles) located the Belgian field army near Tirlemont. An airfield with three airplanes and dense troop movements in Leuven indicated the presence of the Belgian SHQ, positioned there six days earlier on August 5. The road leading to Tirlemont (*Tienen*) was packed with troops and vehicles all the way from Boutersem (approximately ten kilometers southeast of Leuven). These were the first signs of the Belgian field army deployment in the Gette River position.[29]

Bivouac

In an endeavor to shift the invasion's priority from tactics and the taking of Liège and onto the operational dimension of reconnaissance, Third, Fourth, Seventh, Ninth, and Tenth Jäger Battalions were detached back to HKK 2. Each was returned, but in various conditions after the losses of the *Handstreich* and the efforts to complete mobilization. Some had to march farther than did the others. Seventh and Ninth Jäger Battalions were up north and had already started joining HKK 2.

It is important to note that when the cavalry divisions did engage an enemy, they broke contact at dusk in order to bivouac, as was their standard procedure. Contact with the enemy was suspended for the night.[30] Fourth

German Cavalry Division stopped and bivouacked at Borgloon (*Looz* on the German maps). This was a small hilltop town in an area covered with high fruit trees. Much German movement was to be seen. From 1500 hours on, swarms of *Feldgrauen* (field grays) had arrived and could be observed moving between the trees. Because the Belgian telephone system was still functioning, it could well be expected that reports of this movement reached the Belgian HQ. Brühe recalled the final bivouac:

> Looz was our day's objective on August 11. We reached it around the third hour after a long and far ride. We set up bivouac before the alleys, nursing the horses that had severely suffered having let out a lot of sweat during the long ride. We were handed our first pay and because the weather was kind to us, we had nothing to do by evening. I went into town not without a weapon but all alone. I only wanted to buy some sweets. I hoped to get chocolate but found only biscuit.[31]

The German Second Cavalry Division had to be taken out of the line due to starving and exhausted horses. The HKK 2 commander lamented his men as well had very little rest and were suffering from the shortage of food and forage: "Advance by these weakened troops seems impossible and their further employment should not be considered." Second Army directed Ninth Army Corps to bring up forage for the horses and instructed HKK 2 to slow down if necessary. Second Army also told the cavalry to "requisition and live off the land." The diet of the horses was bad. The war diary of HKK 2 lamented how the horses had to go hungry because the industrial country did not provide enough food:

> From the rear area, nothing happened to supply enough oat. Repeatedly it was asked for help but the answer was always the same: "Collect and live out of the country," and finally, when we were told that there would be no oat supply for three days, the directive was amended: "Slow down movement, if necessary." But this was very undesirable for operational reasons and was entirely due to the lack of foresight of higher authorities.[32]

As related earlier, the two cavalry divisions pulled back to a bivouac position east of St. Truiden (St. Trond), about halfway between the northern and central roads, where they rested on August 11.[33] By then, the Germans had identified elements of First, Second, Third, Fifth, and Sixth Belgian Infantry Divisions. In addition, the Belgian Army had its Cavalry Division to the north of the infantry divisions. As mentioned previously, Marwitz did not have enough fighting power to engage the infantry directly and so delayed their withdrawal. He decided to go north, or right, and match his two divisions against the one Belgian cavalry division. The Second Army Commander also ordered Ninth Cavalry Division, which for some time had been on the right bank of the Meuse southwest of Liège, to rejoin HKK 2 and Marwitz—a further logistics problem for divisions already suffering from want of oats and ammunition.[34]

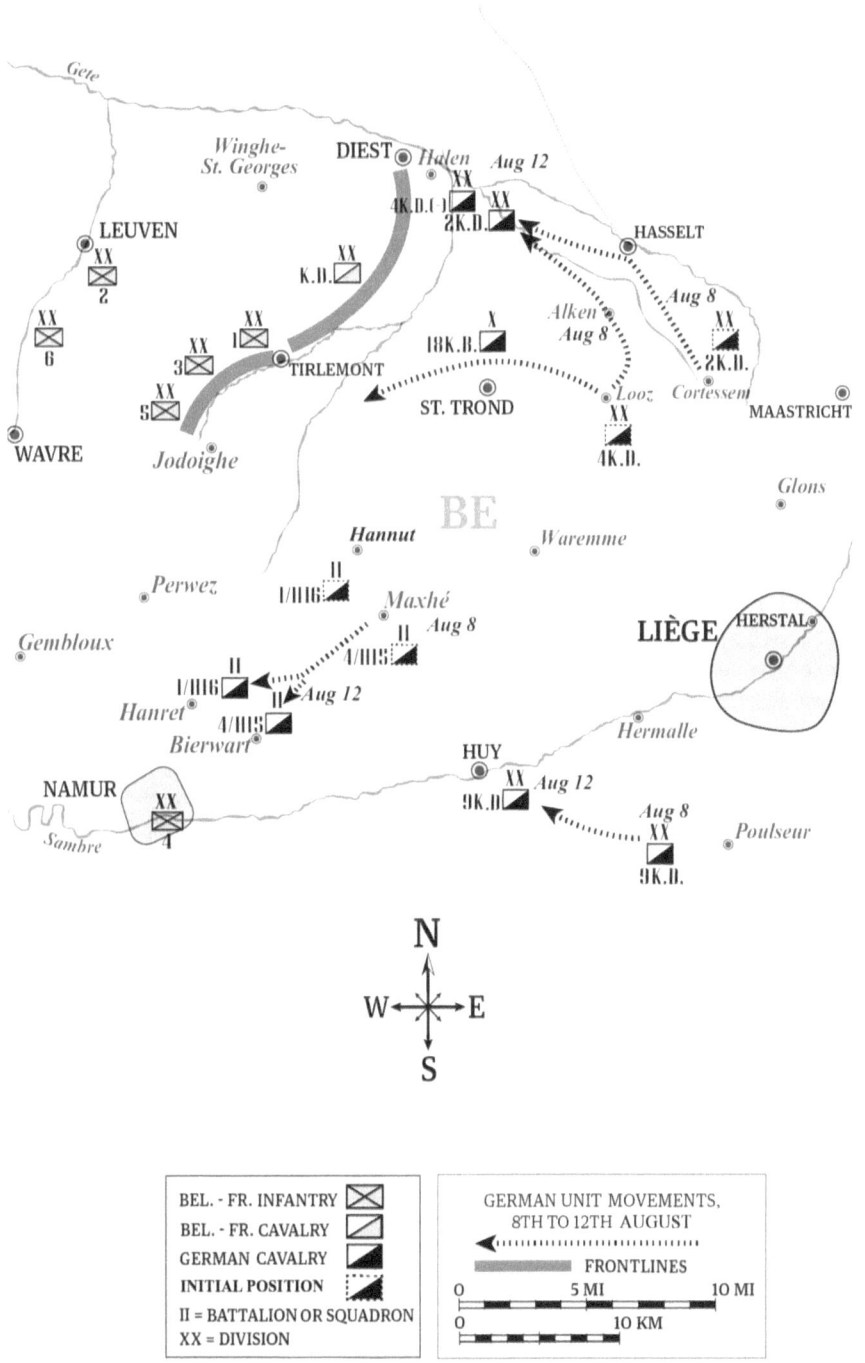

German cavalry movement, August 8–12, 1914

The Germans were consistently trying to move to the right and to the north in an effort to envelop the left flank of the Belgian army. The Belgians were trying to deny the Germans this option and to withdraw into Antwerp. The German intent was somehow to turn the Belgian Army away from Antwerp. If, however, the Germans had in fact imposed themselves between the Belgian Army and the city of Antwerp, what could two cavalry divisions have accomplished? Although the Belgian Army may have been small compared to the main German armies, it certainly was large enough to deal with one understrength HKK. This operational situation literally begged for a second or third HKK, as Schlieffen had envisioned, to provide enough force at least to threaten, and hopefully turn, the left flank of the Belgian army.[35]

Belgians

It can be argued that the German cavalry in 1914 lacked the firepower, the training in dismounted fighting, and the acceptance of a dismounted role to perform after movement successfully even with a larger force. But when the attached Jäger battalions with their machine guns and bicycles are added to the reckoning, German prospects improve. Certainly, the Belgians were worried. On the evening of August 11, the SHQ became increasingly convinced that a great danger existed from a German advance in the direction of Halen-Diest. The retreat of German troops at Orsmaal en Opheylissem on August 10, combined with the vast number of German cavalry identified and intelligence communicated by telephone from the by-now German occupied areas of St. Truiden and Hasselt, clearly proved the danger. Earlier that day, patrols had skirmished near Halbeek farm. The SHQ stipulated in its orders transmitted at 1800 hours "that the direction of Diest would well be the most dangerous one."[36]

7

Prior to the Final Advance

> *It is particularly necessary to watch over the preservation of arms in the interval of a long peace, when they are most likely to degenerate. It is important to foster the military spirit in the armies and to exercise them in great manoeuvres which, though but faintly resembling those of actual war, still are of decided advantage in preparing them for war.* —Jomini[1]

August 12

Aviation

German aerial reconnaissance now focused on the Meuse between Namur and Givet: the area from which relief attempts for Liège could be expected. No activity was observed on roads and railways, however, and no defensive fieldworks were present at the outdated Givet Fortress. However, near Namur, intensified movement and traffic to the east, north, and northwest were spotted. Between Huy and Engis, the Hermalle Meuse Bridge beneath Hermalle-sous-Huy[2] was now reported as destroyed.

Remarkably, the previous day's successful reconnaissance of the SHQ at Leuven was not repeated. This might have been due to the successive costly mishaps that overcame FFA 1. Four aircraft were dispatched but due to the heat and squalls that day, none were able to accomplish its mission. One airplane crashed just after takeoff, killing the two-man crew. The crew of another aircraft was able to rejoin the Abteilung after an emergency landing in enemy territory. These accidents convinced the command of Second Army to direct Einem to use aircraft sparingly, "especially as reconnaissance—within reach of the aircraft—already had brought useful and clear results."[3]

The same day Einem, commander of Second Army's right wing, issued a *Weißung für die Luftaufklärung*, Directive for Aerial Reconnaissance.

According to this directive, until revoked, the army corps would reconnoiter in following sectors:

- Ninth Army Corps: Dutch border–Hasselt–Diest–Tirlemont (Tienen)– Railway: Lüttich–Tirlemont.
- Seventh Army Corps: Fort Fléron–Meuse bridges in Lüttich–Fort Hollogne exclusively the Meuse Line, western border of the Tirlemont– Namur line.
- Heeresabteilung Emmich: Beyond the line Diest–Tirlemont–above Brussels–Antwerp only.
- Tenth Army Corps: Esneux–Fort Boncelles–Meuse line Huy–Namur– Dinant.

With this directive, the aerial reconnaissance sectors for Ninth, Seventh, and Tenth Army Corps were pinpointed at approximately sixty kilometers (37½ miles) in depth, measured from the eastern line of the Liège forts. The FFA 9 was tasked with long-distance reconnaissance of about 150 kilometers (ninety-three miles) beyond the line Diest–Tirlemont–Namur–Dinant up to Antwerp and Brussels. This order regulated aerial reconnaissance within Second Army comprehensively and systematically, for the first time from all points of view. With its issue, all Second and Third Army FFAs were operational for reconnaissance in front of the German right wing.

Halen

In addition to the aviation directive of August 12, a watershed event known as the Battle of the Silver Helmets took place at Halen. The HKK 2 sought to unhinge the Belgian defensive positions along the River Gette. Storming across the river at the village of Halen was intended to be the first stage of forcing the defensive position and outflanking the Belgian Army. No less than eight separate charges were conducted that day, and two entire brigades of German cavalry were decimated as they "tried and tried again." These cavalry charges were the ones often imagined in peacetime, with hundreds of horses thundering into combat as their riders wielded sabers and lances. This was the last time the German cavalry would try to force a position with mounted cavalry against a dismounted opponent. The small, untried Belgian forces inflicted a crushing defeat on the premier land army of its time. As a matter of comparison, the Charge of the Light Brigade involved six hundred men. A German cavalry regiment consisted of over seven hundred troopers. During the battle of Halen, four German cavalry regiments charged and were destroyed. The entire right wing of the invasion had only nine brigades of cavalry. Two of them were badly mauled for no result in one day. This was only eight days after the start of the war.[4]

7. Prior to the Final Advance

The attack was conducted by two brigades of Fourth German Cavalry Division (Seventeenth and Third). Seventeenth Cavalry Brigade, composed of Seventeenth and Eighteenth Dragoner Regiments, came from Mecklenburg. Although the units were organized and trained under a common Prussian system, Mecklenburg had its own Grand Duke and, without question, was the most backward province in all of Imperial Germany. It did not even have a parliament, and its social system was very much like serfdom. In an anecdote attributed to Bismarck, he said, "When I am dying, I want to move to Mecklenburg because everything happens there one hundred years late." Third Cavalry Brigade consisted of Second Kürassier Regiment and Ninth Uhlan Regiment. Second Kürassier Regiment was the regiment dedicated to the Prussian Queen. They wore steel helmets with a distinctive scroll commemorating the regiment's heritage during the time of Frederick the Great. Of the four German cavalry regiments that took part in the Battle of the Silver Helmets, this was the only regiment that actually wore silver helmets. Ninth Uhlan Regiment was nicknamed, *Weissen von der Peene*, the White Ones of the Peene, based on the color of their old uniform.

The troopers were led into the combat by Ninth and Seventh Jäger Battalions. Both Ninth and Seventh Jäger Battalions had been committed to Liège as part of the Army of the Meuse. Ninth Jäger Battalion was known as the Lauenburg Jäger. It was already on its second commander of the war, Major Herbig. The Ninth was reinforced by a consolidated company: all that remained of Seventh Jäger Battalion after its mauling in the battle with the Liège forts. Only two companies had remained and those were merged into one.

Fourth German Cavalry Division was supported by the horse artillery battalion of FAR 3. Second German Cavalry Division had the horse artillery battalion of FAR 35; it too came forward and participated in the battle. Combined, these two units provided twenty-four artillery pieces available to the German forces. An independent machine-gun battalion was also assigned to each division.

The Belgian Cavalry Division included two brigades, a battalion of Cyclists, and a horse artillery battalion of twelve guns divided into three batteries. The two cavalry brigades consisted of First Cavalry Brigade (First and Second Guides Regiment) and Second Cavalry Brigade (Fourth and Fifth Lancers Regiments), each with a section of Hotchkiss machine guns. There was also a company of Engineers Cyclists. In contrast to the German field gray, all of the Belgians wore colorful uniforms harkening back to the Napoleonic wars—and offering inviting targets to modern rifles.

Reinforcing the Belgian Cavalry Division during the afternoon of the battle of Halen was Fourth Mixed Brigade, consisting of the Fourth and Twenty-Fourth Line Infantry Regiments. Both regiments had two battalions each instead of the standard three. Cadre personnel authorizations had not been met, especially in the officer positions. There were a company of Hotchkiss machine guns, a company of Maxim machine guns, and a three-battery artillery battalion with twelve guns. The machine-gun companies formed as late as August 9 and also did not have full complements—a bad omen for a technical branch.

After German Jäger took the village of Halen, Eighteenth Cavalry Brigade entered the narrow streets and began a series of charges against the dismounted Belgian Cavalry Division. The Belgians repulsed each charge. Then, Third Cavalry Brigade crossed the Gette River on pontoon bridges and tried to flank the Belgian defenses from the other direction; again, with no results. In total, the Germans conducted eight charges in vain. Belgian reinforcements arriving in time to see the last charge were handled roughly by the German machine guns.

Forty-four years after the battle, Arthur Brühe of Second Kürassier Regiment returned to the scene. He wrote down his remembrances in an unpublished manuscript of which only ten copies ever existed. Brühe was captured the day after the battle and spent the entire war in a British prisoner of war camp. His memoirs provided a vivid backdrop to questions about the engagement.

> The Haelen [sic] attack was one of the first, perhaps even the first, attacks of a mounted German cavalry regiment against an enemy that was not only equipped with the standard rifles but that also fired the newly issued machine guns. Because of our heavy losses sustained during these attacks, no longer would other cavalry attacks against machine-gun-supported infantry positions be conducted on other parts of the German western front. Since then, the era of cavalry armies and cavalry attacks has ended forever. Never again will there be the sight of the mounted squadrons on the march going into manoeuvres, as I often witnessed in my youth. Never again will we see the romance of a cavalry bivouac with the rows of tied mounts and the cooking over the campfires enlightening the darkness.[5]

At the end of the day, twenty-four German officers, 468 men, and 843 horses were lost—a handful, paling in comparison with future endeavors. However, the loss of nearly one thousand horses took two cavalry brigades off the operational board. Yet, they still existed but in an absolutely crippled state. Seventeenth and Eighteenth Dragoons, Ninth Uhlans, and Second Kürassiers had shrunk to two squadrons each. Also, the horse artillery battalion supporting Eighteenth Cavalry Brigade had very high losses. According to the history of Sixteenth Hussar Regiment, the horse artillery battalion Hanstein had marched out with 170 men on August 9 to fulfil a mission. Ten days later, there were just 68 men left. It had lost fifty percent of its horses and had ridden 333 kilometers. Except for the commander, all officers were either wounded or captured.[6] Henceforth, wherever Fourth Cavalry Division was assigned, it would be incapable of covering a full division's worth of ground. Unit symbols on large scale maps give the impression the division was an organization with multiple capabilities. Mounted reconnaissance, however, was severely impacted and that was this division's primary mission.

An example of German arrogance after the battle is provided by one of the destroyed squadron's commander. Rittmeister von Bodecker had led his squadron four abreast down a road and into a barricade. Of the ninety riders, only fifteen returned. He was made prisoner of the Belgian Army and very loudly blamed Belgium for having declared war on Germany. He also stated that the Germans would be in Brussels by August 15 and in Paris ten days later.[7] Arrogance, yes—but arrogance arguably fueled by the exhaustion that led Bodecker to ride into the trap.

The Germans held the field but then abandoned it, moving east back across the Gette to bivouac and reorganize—again, standard operating procedure. The Belgian Cavalry Division was certainly on its back foot. Belgian Fourth Mixed Brigade, also roughly handled by the German machine guns at Halen, was in a state of disarray. If there had been another HKK to support and develop the attack, the consequences might well have been considerably different. Between August 13 and 19, the Belgian field army held the positions on the River Gette, and the German cavalry was not able to fill in the vacuum west of Halen. Had the cavalry forces Schlieffen envisioned been available, they might have had enough strength to cross the River Gette at Halen and thereafter the flank of the Belgian field army itself—feeling its way, untried, poorly trained, and lacking junior leaders. Might its organization have collapsed and its cohesion dissolved? The possibility cannot be dismissed out of hand. But the Belgian flank was not turned.

Liège

Meanwhile, German artillery started the final silencing of the surviving Liège forts. Because the Aachen–Liège rail line was unserviceable, the 42-centimeter battery unloaded at Herbesthal on the border, and by 2200 hours, had road-marched a respectable fifteen kilometers. The 42-centimeter battery went into an open-firing position on high ground five hundred meters northeast of Mortier and fired eight shells at Fort Pontisse. French Cavalry Corps Sordet conducted security operations by their cavalry against the advancing German cavalry screen. Fog and friction shaped the results about the condition of the reconnaissance forces on both sides.

> It is hot; our horses are very tired. To water them during the route, we disobey orders, for we are forbidden to stop. Enormous losses! Outside of animals that die suddenly on the road, many are those that we find stopped on the edge of a ditch, head carried low, within the flanks, dying eyes looking for a place to fall. It seems that our squadron melts quickly on these marches and we feel that our horses, still up, have not the strength of the past week.

The fact that it was midsummer and the heavily laden horses became tired easily in the heat made frequent watering all the more necessary. The routes became marked by horses in agony, who, partly from lack of water—unable to throw off the poisons which fatigue had accumulated in their system—were seized by rigor mortis before dying.[8]

Replacement mounts were provided for but not in sufficient numbers. They were also considered to be mediocre, out of condition, and with limited or no training as troop horses. As a rule, they lasted for about ten days before dying or being abandoned. This had two significant operational impacts. Both French and German columns were forced to resort to walking horses and leading them by their reins, which slowed movements. As horse losses were far more significant than the loss of the riders, the count of horses became most important.[9]

August 13

Liège

Forts Chaudfontaine, Embourg, and Pontisse fell. Adding to the fire of the 21-centimeter guns, the 42-centimeter monsters continued shelling Fort Pontisse, firing another forty-three rounds. The shocked Belgian defenders then surrendered. This was a tactical victory: Pontisse offered the best possible opportunity for interdiction of the northern road that the Belgians still possessed. Fort d'Embourg and Fort Chaudefontaine surrendered after being bombarded by 21-centimeter mortars. These two forts straddled the main rail line into Liège. The victory was tempered, however, by the fact that the Nasproue Tunnel would not be open for another two days. The main double-line track between Aachen and Liège was still closed far east of the bridge.

> At 1725 hours, Second Army Headquarters reported the capture of Fort Pontisse. Situated in a commanding position on the left bank of the Meuse, it had till now barred the section of the river between Liège and the Dutch frontier which had to be crossed by First Army. The passage of the river by large bodies of troops was now rendered feasible, and valuable time was thus gained for the deployment of First Army and the development of the plan of campaign in the west. General von Emmich, with Generalmajor Ludendorff as Brigade Commander, had broken the chain of forts on the northeastern front of the fortress, in spite of their modern construction. Forts Liers and Lantin, west of Pontisse, were still temporarily a disturbing factor in the calculations of the [First] Army Commander.[10]

First Army began its advance through Aachen on August 13. Second Army had by then vacated the roads north of Liège, allowing First Army to pass. Second, Third, and Fourth Army Corps marched first; Third and Fourth Reserve Corps followed. Their routes of advance closely paralleled each other.

Based on the resulting congestion, each road was required to support the movement of two separate army corps. Nor could First Army spread out to the right until it had crossed the River Meuse. Although the lead elements reached the river on August 14, it took four to five days to march all of the German troops through Aachen's narrow streets. The active army corps completed their concentration and detraining on August 14, including all ammunition columns and trains. The two reserve corps finished their concentration one day later, on the fifteenth. Despite the possibilities for entanglement, in such a large-scale operation, all of this movement went smoothly—a reflection of the systematic peacetime planning so significantly absent at the sharp end.[11]

BEF

The BEF initially arrived in the harbor of Le Havre on August 13,[12] but Kluck had completely different ideas about its position. The bulk of the BEF crossed the English Channel between August 12 and August 19.[13] Based on newspaper reports, still First Army's best source of strategic intelligence, Kluck thought the British were disembarking in small numbers at Ostend and with larger forces at Dunkirk and Calais. In truth, the BEF did not use these ports.[14]

Aviation

The FFA 9 resumed its reconnaissance missions against the Belgian field army. In Tirlemont, the Abteilung observed the movement of cavalry and baggage trains toward Leuven, as well as concentration of vehicles at the market square and a locomotive under steam at the railway station. These were elements of Belgian Third Division, which had previously departed Liège bound for Leuven. This division was also identified in its encampment east of Leuven, preparing for its departure to Diest. After the Halen fight, the Belgian Cavalry Division had fallen back behind the Gette River near Diest in entrenched positions. The forces were to advance to Winghe–St. Georges/St. Joris–Winge and Aarschot in order to protect the Belgian Army's left wing against the threat of being encircled by HKK 2 from the direction of Diest–Halen. The reconnaissance flights confirming these movements considerably improved German insight into the intentions of the Belgian Field Army—and meant there was no threat for the German troops that stood before Liège.

While effective at the close reconnaissance, the airmen did nothing to extend out long-range and find the BEF or the left wing of the French Army. Due to the structural lack of an aviation staff officer, aviation reports, messages, and intelligence snippets frequently did not find their way to the army intelligence staff officer. These messages often went to staff officers who were otherwise burdened and became neglected or even ignored. A conscious decision had to be made at the corps level to forward air reports to the army level. This was then, of course, subjected to communications shortfalls in mounted messengers and wire. It is claimed that First Army was never made aware of about fifty percent of the air reports.[15]

Due to poor visibility and hazy weather conditions, aerial reconnaissance up to the Nivelles-Maubeuge line ordered by Third Army could gain only meagre results. In the sector of the Lesse River near Houyet southeast of Dinant, a cavalry column moving northwest was sighted—elements of the (French) Sordet Cavalry Corps that had crossed to the west bank of the Meuse River. As the aircrews further reported, the expansion of the southwestern fortress belt at Namur showed progress.[16]

Cavalry Problems

Second German Cavalry Division continued to suffer from severe shortages of supplies and rations for men and horses while still on the eastern bank of the River Meuse. The logistical system was even more haphazard on the west side of the river. The division had progressed only between thirty-five and forty kilometers from the German border—hardly a spectacular advance. Although the shortages most affected Second Cavalry Division, they applied to all HKK elements around Liège at the same time.[17] Ninth Cavalry Division, ordered to rejoin HKK 2, also suffered from logistics difficulties.[18] The condition of Fourth Cavalry Division was lamented in the regimental history of the Eighteenth Dragoons:

> Only a few soldiers had still lances. Almost all of them were broken or lost in Halen. Many helmets had disappeared or had no spike anymore or were replaced by the most fantastic headgears. Horses of all kinds of formations were present in the regiment because everybody tried first thing after the attack to find a replacement for his own dead or wounded horse among the countless horses galloping to and fro. Who did not find one anymore seized a bike at the first opportunity and followed the division in this way. Who considered it possible before that the outward appearance of the regiment would change in this way within ten days?[19]

This did not bode well for its prospects as the cavalry advanced deeper into enemy territory. The shortages soon pushed the First Army Motor Transport commander to mobilize twelve more improvised columns equipped with light civilian vehicles. But this fixed one problem by creating another: these civilian vehicles were not built to withstand heavy-duty military use and quickly broke down.

The one brigade of Fourth Cavalry Division that was not involved in the battle of Halen continued to patrol further to the south. Given that this was somewhat distant from the bulk of the division, they also took a light radio set with them. Fifteenth and Sixteenth Hussar Regiments got involved

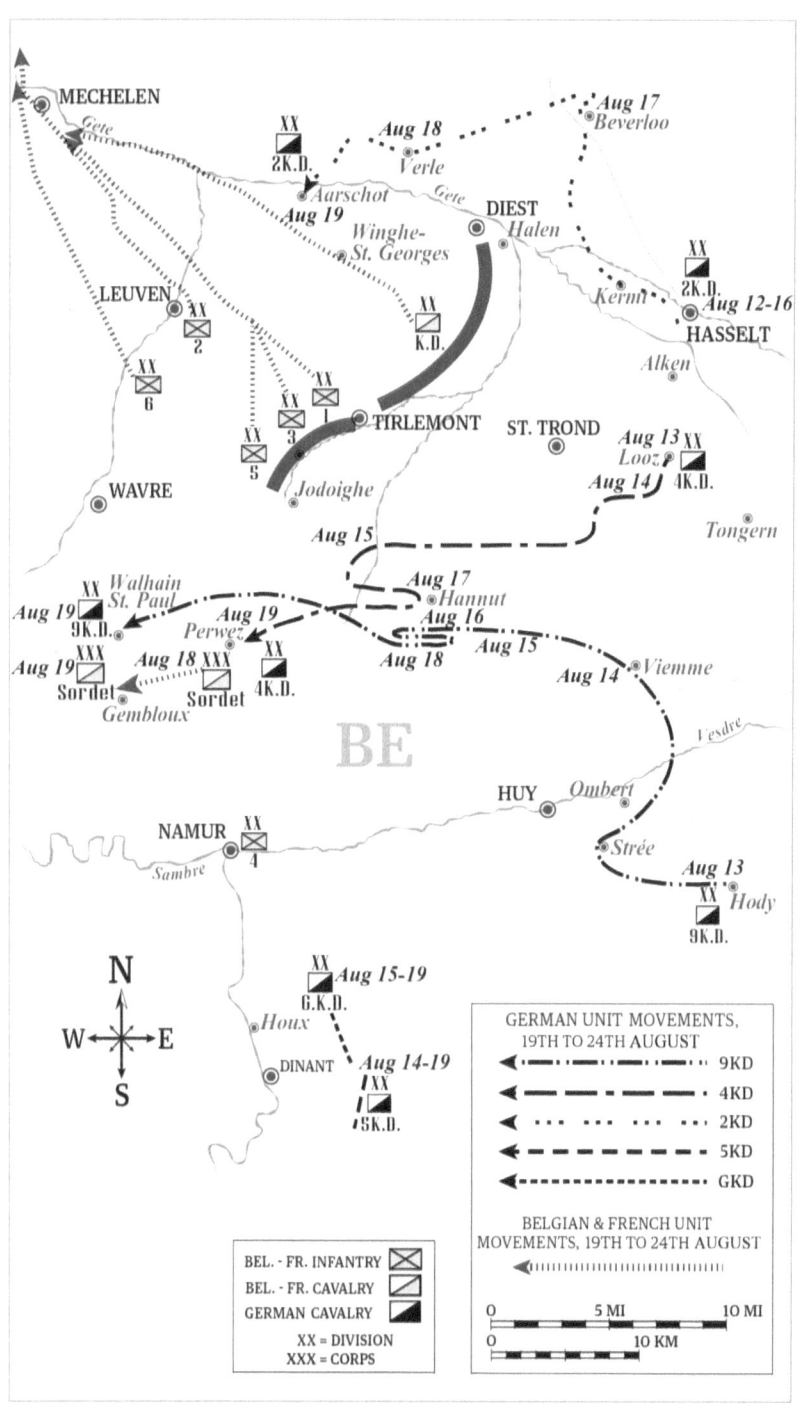

German cavalry movement, August 13–19, 1914.

in a series of engagements which were quickly radioed back to the division HQ. Unfortunately, in addition to many of the troopers, the radio became a casualty. This was one of the two radios available to the division and one of six available to HKK 2.

August 14

Using the 21-centimeter mortars, two additional forts were destroyed—Forts Fleron and Liers fell. The disabling of these fortresses settled into a pattern as infantry closed off the forts and then the artillery pounded them into silence. There were no more nighttime bayonet charges. Casualties diminished. One-half of the fortresses were by now eliminated. The entire northern and eastern sides of Liège were exposed. None of the forts had communication with each other. They were isolated, passively awaiting their turn under the heavy guns. The end of the fighting for Liège was in sight, as on August 14 all forts that blocked First Army marching routes had fallen. Movement into staging positions for the general advance seemed possible, at least to First Army HQ. While Second Army consolidated, First Army continued their march. Second, Fourth, and Third Corps reached the Meuse, and the two reserve corps marching as a second line began to pass the Belgian frontier west of Aachen.[20] Ninth Cavalry Division crossed the Meuse River.

Aerial reconnaissance for the German Army right wing now proved more practical, allowing further observations on the Belgian deployment. In the Gette River sector between Tirlemont and Jodoigne, two divisions were reported. According to Belgian files, these were the First and Fifth in standby positions. Behind these divisions east of Leuven, another division, the Third, was reported assembled. Advanced elements of approximately brigade strength were also sighted near Engelmanshoven southeast of St. Truiden (St. Trond). The Belgian Cavalry Division was observed as it arrived near Papenbroek south of Diest. An additional aviation report stated accurately that the Gette position had been expanded by about thirteen kilometers (eight miles). As reported before, the Namur and Liège Roads were free, and progress was seen on construction northeast and northwest of the Namur forts.[21]

August 15

Artillery

The 21-centimeter mortars and infantry continued to engage Liège's remaining forts. Forts Boncelles and Lantin surrendered. The 42-centimeter mortars joined the 21-centimeter in the destruction of Fort Loncin. This was also Leman's location. Restricted to the fort, it is questionable how much he actually influenced the defense after the *Handstreich*. At 1710 hours, the nineteenth 42-centimeter shell, with a delayed-action fuse, exploded in a magazine containing twelve metric tons of powder, creating a crater thirty meters in diameter and six meters deep. Fort Loncin surrendered, and with this the defense of Liège collapsed. The Army of the Marne was disbanded and FFA 9 assigned to Second Army. Ninth Corps was placed back under the orders of First Army, and the brigades of Third and Fourth Corps, which had been employed against Liège, rejoined their parent formations. First Army was now clear of the gap between Liège and the Dutch frontier, and the OHL gave First Army time to close up, expecting the two armies to be abreast shortly. Finally, the Germans could get going.[22]

How Long Did Liège Delay Germany?

Once Fort Loncin became victim of the enormous power of the 42-centimeter mortars, the route to France lay open. There has been a lot of discussion about how much of a delay the battle of Liège cost the Germans. Many authors had different opinions; not all seem steeped in any kind of logic. If there was a thought that the Belgians would not oppose the Germans, then the general advance would have started days earlier, into a vacuum that the cavalry and the Army of the Meuse could advance unopposed.

But the Belgians decided to defend Liège, making it an academic discussion at best. So how long did the Belgian defense of Liège delay the German Army? This question has an easy answer. Kluck reported, "August 13 was therefore fixed as the date for the march through Aix-la-Chapelle (Aachen) instead of the tenth." So the OHL originally envisioned First Army would begin, not finish, vacating its assembly areas on August 10, taking five days to clear Aachen. That operation was delayed three days—the beginning of active operations as reported by Bergman was August 13.

Could First Army have moved on August 10? Yes. What created the delay was the Belgians and the "technical problems" caused by the defense of Liège. Somewhere between the interdiction of the forts and the destruction of the railroad tunnels, the OHL delayed First Army's movement by three days. The GOH, however, indicated no real delay and asserted that the advance happened just in time. Stig Förster wrote in 1921 that the German deployment timetable had required its armies to reach Mons by the twenty-second day of mobilization (August 23, right on time). The British official history cited a later recollection of Kluck's that gave the defense credit for four to five days. Bülow reported that the OHL had wanted to start movement on August 10 but was forced to delay it until the seventeenth. Both Sewell Tyng and

Strachen claimed a forty-eight-hour delay but focused on the inability of First Army to concentrate all its active forces until August 13. It had always been the plan of the OHL to bring the two armies abreast first and only then begin the general advance. First Army had the longest way to go and would require the most time. So, what becomes paramount is when First Army started to move, not when its last unit left the assembly area—and the OHL delayed the start three days.

8

Advance

There are in Europe many good generals, but they see too many things at once. I see only one thing, namely the enemy's main body. I tried to crush it confident that secondary matters will then settle themselves. —Napoleon[1]

August 16

Liège's remaining two forts finally surrendered—Fort Flemalle after a three-hour bombardment by the 21-centimeter mortars and Fort Hollogne with no bombardment at all. Resistance was ended. The road to central Belgium was open. The mass of the German 21-centimeter siege mortars had opened fire on August 12. By August 16, after five days of bombardment, all eleven remaining forts had been reduced. In total, First Battalion FAR 9 had fired fifteen hundred shells at Liège, and Second Battalion fired 1,007. Short Marine Cannon Battery 3 (42-centimeter) fired seventy shells and participated in the destruction of only two forts.[2]

Imperial HQ remained in Berlin during the period of mobilization and concentration, then departed for the "front"—Koblenz, eight hundred kilometers southwest at the confluence of the Rhine and Mosel. The German General HQ train pulled into Koblenz station the next morning.

Reports about the British continued to be contradictory. They were said to be landing at Ostend, Dunkirk, Calais, and Zebrugge. First Army thought that the BEF was going to march on Brussels to join the Belgians and considered its most important task to be routing the Belgians as soon as possible, before they were able to join their Allied reinforcements. It was further assumed that if the French and British did not arrive soon, the Belgians would retreat toward Antwerp. First Army therefore understood that it had to engage the Belgians in battle as quickly as possible. In Antwerp, they would be an unacceptable threat to the invasion's right flank. A decision was reached correspondingly to move on August 17 onto the line Kermpt–St. Trond, with the intent of fixing the Belgian Army in place by a frontal attack. There was a fear that the German army might run into the British as well as the Belgians but certainly not the French—not yet! Time and space, as always in operations and definitely in 1914, were critical factors.[3]

August 17

German reconnaissance had determined that the five infantry divisions and the cavalry division of the Belgian field army were still at the Gette River position. The expansion of Namur's fortifications with fieldworks and the occupation of the Meuse down to Givet had been identified. Here, however, the OHL appears to have miscounted. Only one division of the Belgian Army, not three as the OHL seemed to believe, was around Namur. Advanced elements of the French Fifth Army and of the Cavalry Corps Sordet were also identified near Namur. The French cavalry corps had approached Liège, then retreated, and was now moving in forced marches, as ordered by General Joffre, to cover the left wing of the French forces. The Germans had their own view about how effective that formation was. "Though it was probably not half starved like our cavalry, it was nonetheless very exhausted and worn out by the extraordinary marches, as reported in a French book about the Cavalry Corps Sordet."[4]

The German First Army continued its advance on the seventeenth, moving abreast of Second Army. Second Army halted in place as First Army pivoted around its right.[5]

Moltke Directive

Moltke issued new orders for the main German thrust into Belgium. At 1630 hours, the following order arrived from Supreme Command:

> First and Second Army and Second Cavalry Corps (HKK 2 Marwitz) will be under the orders of the commander of Second Army during the advance north of the Meuse. This advance will begin on August 18. It is most important that the enemy's forces reported to be in position between Diest–Tirlemont–Wavre should be shouldered away from Antwerp. It is intended to initiate further operations of both [numbered] armies from the line Brussels–Namur, and measures must be taken to secure their flank against Antwerp.[6]

Speed was of the essence. First and Second Army had to pass through a dangerous eighty-kilometer-wide corridor between the fortresses of Namur and Antwerp, all the while securing their left flanks against suspected French forces south of the Sambre.[7] The HKK 2 was supposed to be under the control of the OHL once the advance began. So who was now responsible for finding and tracking the BEF? The Germans were operating with the belief that the Belgian Army would delay in position until the French arrived on their right flank and the British on their left. The exact timing of those arrivals was not known. The overarching thought in German higher HQ was that the Belgians could be dealt with first and then in turn the British, who would have yet to arrive. Dealing with the BEF would in turn provide the opportunity to turn the French left flank.

Kluck argued against being put under the command of Second Army, stating it would have been more suitable if HKK 2 was under command of First Army, and First Army remained independent of Second Army. In Kluck's view, Second Army would then be free to pursue tactical objectives to its front, and First Army could follow the operational objective of falling on the French flank.[8] Although Kluck did not mention this proposed change, he must have intervened at the OHL on August 17, arguing for placing HKK 2 under his command and most probably as well to be released from Second Army control. The result was a compromise. The OHL removed Second Cavalry Division from HKK 2 and attached it directly to First Army.[9]

Disagreement over How to Handle Belgium

A major disagreement increasingly developed between the chiefs of staff of First Army and Second Army. Kuhl from First Army wanted to launch an immediate attack on the Belgian Army. Gen. Otto von Lauenstein, Chief of Staff of the Second Army, agreed with the concept of attack, but wanted to begin with envelopment of the Belgian forces by way of Beeringen-Pael. Kuhl disagreed, saying that the Belgian Army would not wait, but would be able to evade the enveloping movement in plenty of time. He strenuously argued that the only way to keep the Belgians out of Antwerp was to attack them in force at once with First Army, which was ready to launch such an operation. This well-known battle maneuver is designed to deprive the objective army's freedom of movement. Sometimes known in the American vernacular of "holding them by the nose and then kicking them in the ... "[10] The decision was made by Second Army deciding—predictably—to use the envelopment. Classic military tactical and operational planning would tell the perpetrators to fix the enemy front with an attack and then envelop. Bülow and Lauenstein were, seen in retrospect, putting the cart before the horse. Maneuvering against the flank of the Belgians without fixing the front in place assumes they were static, not dynamic. Instead, this decision kept Belgian freedom of maneuver intact. There is always the argument that this decision reflects leadership style. One course of action was very aggressive and the other one very cautious. These were not experienced armies. It is up to readers and analysts to determine if this methodology was reflected in other decisions of timing during the Marne campaign. It reflected a significant, and as of yet unjustified, dismissal of the Belgian Army as an opponent.[11]

Roads held the keys to operational maneuver. A soldier marching on a road could go much faster than marching across an open field. The way that roads were designated by the German military was by listing connecting cities. So, if you read what seems a laundry list of towns, it really is presenting the roads that connect them. Those roads are assigned to a unit, and that unit has priority of movement on the road. The more roads that are available, the easier it is to maneuver. Unit length and road space used is a well-known tool that can be calculated during peacetime. Knowing this is extremely important. A division marching on a road would take up a certain space. The staff officer would look that amount of space up in his handbook (remember the discussion of the red donkey handbook). The handbook was extremely detailed, listing the distances for every conceivable kind of unit. If an army corps was limited to marching on one road, then the amount of road space used would be quite lengthy: first the combat units, which would occupy thirty-one kilometers of road space; then, the logistics units, which would occupy further 21 kilometers of road space. If two roads were available and one division was able to have its own independent road, the divisional alone would take up fifteen kilometers of road space.[12]

The First Army Order for August 18 was issued from its HQ at Glons at 2315 hours on August 17. The inclusion here of the complete order serves two purposes. It shows the high level of detail provided the corps commanders and it sets up the discussion of the orders cycle.

> 1. The enemy is in position on the line Diest–Tirlemont–Wavre with strong forces in rear, probably near Louvain.
> 2. The army will attack tomorrow and envelop the enemy's left wing, driving him away from Antwerp. Second Corps will send one division by Beeringen–Pael–Veerle and the other by Kermpt–Lummen–Diest round the enemy's flank. Fourth Corps will march by Herck la Ville and Rummen toward Haegen and Geet Betz; it will leave three battalions, a section of cavalry, and three batteries of artillery at Stevoort, at the disposal of the army commander, by 0830 hours. Third Corps will move by Nieuwerkerken and Gorssum on Budingen and Neerlinter. Ninth Corps will march from about St. Trond on Oplinter and Tirlemont and will keep a strong reserve on its left flank to act against a possible enemy advance from the area southwest of Tirlemont.
> 3. Second Cavalry Division will be at the disposal of the army commander. It will move past Veerle in order to cut off the retreat of the enemy.
> 4. The corps will cross the line Pael–Lummen–St. Trond at 0800 hours.

5. With the exception of the first-line transport, the train and ammunition and supply columns will not go beyond the line Hasselt–Looz.

6. Air reconnaissance will be carried out by Second Corps to the north of Démer toward Antwerp, by Fourth Corps toward Aerschot and Malines, by Third Corps in the Louvain district, and by Ninth Corps in the area Tirlemont–Wavre.

7. Third Reserve Corps will march by Bilsen on Beverst: Corps Headquarters at Bilsen.

8. Fourth Reserve Corps will march by Argenteau on Tongres: Corps Headquarters at Tongres.

9. Army Headquarters will be at Stevoort at 0830 hours, by which time the corps are to be in telephonic communication with it.

10. Second Army is to reach Vamont with its right wing; Seventh Corps, by midday tomorrow. First Army is to be under the orders of the Second Army commander.

All times will be given according to German standard time.
[Signed] von Kluck.[13]

The movement would start with Second, Third, Fourth, and Ninth Corps marching abreast. Each of these had but one road. Two of these roads, those used by Second and Third Army Corps, were being used by two additional army corps, Third Reserve Corps following Second Army Corps; and Fourth Reserve Corps, the Third Army Corps.[14]

Orders Cycle

In conjunction with this operation, Kuhl tried to explain the problems with the order cycle. Since First Army was under the control of Second Army, he had to get Bülow's permission to issue the concepts for the next day's order. Given decision times and travel times, there was always a problem with issuing the order at a late hour. When the army HQ issued an order at 2300 hours, then it must distribute the order to the army corps, who in turn must prepare an order and issue it to subordinate divisions. They in turn would have to prepare orders and issue them to the regiments, and so on down the chain of command. While peacetime practice had emphasized the early issuance of orders, the timestamps on these documents indicate that this was not the case in practice. As a result, the lower-level organization had zero time or very little time to prepare their own orders and issue them. The net result is that objectives, changes, and timetables will be difficult to implement at the lower levels.[15]

This point may be obvious. It is also continually overlooked in military history writing—at times to the point that some authors in effect assume that when the high-level organization issues instructions, they are promptly transmitted to all the lower levels and promptly implemented. In fact, anyone who has participated in this late-night process of catch-up knows that what it really does is confuse the lower echelons of command and leave the intermediate officers sleepless. That last point is literal. These kinds of orders are disproportionately prepared and transmitted late in the day. Constant tinkering delays inception; concern for making up for lost time leads to prompt dispatch—which usually means after dark. Sleep deprivation and interrupted sleep in turn slow decisions and make them sometimes incoherent. This letter from the chief of staff of Second Army Corps to General von Kuhl is most instructive in not only depicting this problem, but explaining why this corps, assigned a key role in the operation against the Belgian Army, had particular problems complying with the army's scheme of maneuver:

> The tactical orders have hitherto reached us during the night hours. The commander's brief orientation regarding the designs for the following day, and which was exceedingly welcome, has not come in during the last two days. Since the situation did not indicate clearly whether we were to mark or not, the simplest expedient of preparing the troops for the advance in the early morning at a determinate power was not applicable. The wire connection between the army corps and the numbered army is not working. We lacked gasoline for our motor vehicles, and the army has taken no steps to supply this need. This auxiliary means of liaison can accordingly not be utilized. It is therefore impractical for the corps to go for the orders of the army in due time. It is impossible to assure the execution of the orders of the army, either as to time or space.[16]

The problems connected with orders communication and order cycles significantly impact a central issue of this book: developing reconnaissance plans for subordinate units. In this case, the army gives direction to the aviation reconnaissance. Communication and the order cycle would cause problems in just knowing where this aviation reconnaissance is supposed to be. Then there are the problems of execution under high stress and unfamiliar conditions. In particular, coordinating between numbered armies and the HKK posed, as will be seen, critical communication and time issues.

August 18

Failure to Pursue

The first day of the German general advance was a failure. Its consequences would prove vitally important. Yet, compared to all the work done on the German decisions at the Marne, this has been paid almost no attention. Perhaps this is because it predated the German's battle with the BEF. In his order of August 17, Moltke, stressed that the result of keeping the Belgians away from Antwerp was "most important." The subordinate orders and concepts were focused on keeping the Belgian Army out of Antwerp. Its intention was to turn the Belgian's left flank, cutting off their line of retreat. Second Cavalry Division had been sent widely to the right with specific orders to cut off any withdrawal. This was in turn key to an intended *Vernichtungsschlacht*: finishing the Belgians before turning against their allies. Instead, the Germans failed completely in this task. The Belgians got away and established a position on the vulnerable right flank of the German Army. It was incumbent upon First Army to limit the Belgian Army's freedom of maneuver. The way to do this was to fix the Belgian front. Even under the conditions imposed by terrain and firepower, the cavalry could have then cut it off from behind. That did not happen. This is all Kluck said about it:

> The enemy withdrew in places before contact with the attacking troops, though in front of Second Corps at Diest and of Ninth Corps at Tirlemont considerable resistance was first offered. The retirement of the enemy's center was carried out in good time, and the resistance on the flanks showed good leadership and answered the enemy's purpose. The Belgian Army retired to an apparently prepared position on the line Rillaer–Winghe St. Georges—high ground west of Tirlemont.
> By the evening of the eighteenth, the pursuing troops of First Army had reached the line Hersselt–Montaigu–Winghe St. Georges–Glabbeek Suerbempde–Tirlemont. No French troops had been observed with the Belgians. The cautious withdrawal of the Belgian Army led to the conclusion that ... [they] preferred to take advantage of the Brialmont defenses round Antwerp rather than accept an unequal combat in the field. A further rapid advance of First Army toward Brussels would no doubt clear up the situation.[17]

That last sentence combined wish and hindsight. The objective of this operation was the army—the force—and not the city of Brussels, which lay in the wrong direction. As Clausewitz said in *On War*, Book 7, Chapter 6: "Destruction of the enemy's armed forces is the means to the end." Why would it now be appropriate to leave a strong enemy on your flank and rear, strong enough that you were required to commit forces to keep it bottled up? Now there was a sudden new task and a major one. Task: keep the Belgian Army contained in Antwerp. Purpose: to keep the Belgian Army from attacking First Army's flank and rear. The force required eventually amounted to more than two reserve army corps. This should have been a very aggressive pursuit designed to deny the Belgians freedom of movement—and the Germans certainly missed the opportunity. There was no quid pro quo. The Germans had gained nothing from this and now had to deal with the threat. The earlier objectives had been laid out pretty clearly—disperse the Belgian Army. But who was in charge? Which direction were the Belgians going? Had the objectives changed? The aggressiveness Moltke required failed to impress Bülow, given *Auftragstaktik*. "Most important" to the boss did not matter to Bülow.

The Belgians had cooperated with the German Army. They had stayed outside of the Antwerp redoubt and were very catchable. Had the direct approach been used, this entire drama might well have been avoided and decided much earlier. There is a school of thought that says such a pursuit could not succeed in 1914 because cavalry lacked the combat power needed to overcome infantry forces and survive in the face of modern fire.[18] Clausewitz counters by explaining the power of parallel lines for pursuit. Gross reinforces that notion by highlighting the mobility of the pursuing forces. Parallel pursuit is to have a separate column moving on a parallel road overtakes the retreating force and, if the pursuer's mobility is adequate get behind the withdrawing force. A speed advantage is essential and the strength of the force must be sufficient to get the enemy to stand and fight.

Criticism of this tactic in the present context can best be laid at the feet of insufficient force structure. If the direct approach and the five divisions of cavalry projected by Schlieffen had been involved, there would be no question. Second Cavalry Division by itself, however, was certain to be found wanting in combat strength. The question is, how much contact does this more mobile force need? The retreating force would not know the size and composition of the pursuer. To use the analogy of the early chess grandmaster Aron Nimzowitsch, "The threat is stronger than the execution." Outflanking cavalry, using parallel lines that were available in abundance, did not have to fight through infantry forces. The threat should be enough. The Germans did not execute.[19]

Repeating the late-night orders drill, First Army issued its next order at 2200 hrs. Each of the corps had a different objective. This was the norm. The catchphrase hammered into every German staff officer's mind was, "March separately but fight together." The objective was to provide as many roads as possible separately to the different army corps. Each would march along its own dedicated road and then come together at a critical point for combat. Gerhard von Scharnhorst taught military thinkers about this concept using the term *concentric warfare*. Each division would have its own road; therefore, the army corps would travel ideally on two roads. As a general rule, the ideal was spread out carefully while forcing the enemy to do the very same thing and then to attack individual elements in a concentrated manner.[20]

The separate routes led the different army corps through different villages. Reconnaissance was supposed to identify critical points should the army corps have to consolidate for battle. All of this had to be worked out prior to issuing the orders. Sticking with this concept, Second Corps was to march by Aerschot–Wesemael–Wegegabel (south of Werchter)–Thieldonck–Vierstratten; it had to protect its right flank against Antwerp, where the fortress guns covered the northern roads west of Aerschot. Fourth Corps was to march to Winghe St. Georges–Linden–on the north side of Louvain–

Velthem. Third Corps was to march by Bautersem–on the south side of Louvain–Berthem. Ninth Corps was to march by Meldert–Tourinnes–Mille–Neerysche–Loonbeck. The two reserve corps were in a second wave following along behind active corps that was on the same road. Third Reserve Corps was to move through Hasselt. Fourth Reserve Corps was to march to St. Trond. There was no thought of using the cavalry division for pursuit of the Belgian Army. Second Cavalry Division was to advance through Aerschot toward Brussels, reconnoitering toward Antwerp and westward on both sides of Brussels. Army HQ was to be at Winghe St. Georges, and all corps were required to be in telephonic communication with it by 1030 hours. Air reconnaissance was to be carried out by Second Corps toward Antwerp; by Fourth Corps in a westerly direction past the north of Brussels; by Third Corps in a westerly direction south of Brussels; and by Ninth Corps in a southwesterly direction over Wavre.[21]

The HKK 2 skirmished with French Cavalry Corps Sordet at Perwez.[22] Kluck described this encounter as forcing the French Fifth Cavalry Division away from the town of Perwez (Pervez) with heavy losses. Sordet's Corps was indeed driven back, even though they fielded three divisions. Kluck went on to say that serious interference with the advance from the forces in Antwerp could not be feared![23]

Change in the Concept of the Operation

The concept of the operation had changed with the successful Belgian retreat; it was now irreconcilable with previously established intentions. As detailed by the First Army Commander, "The ultimate objective ... was to disperse first the Belgian Army, then the British Expeditionary Force, and finally to fall on the French armies."[24] Moltke saw this requirement on August 17 and ordered its accomplishment as "most important." The Germans let the Belgians escape and then minimized the impact. Without the Belgian Army, the course of the war would have been dramatically altered. An aggressive pursuit at this time might well have caught, fixed, and perhaps scattered the Belgians as they attempted to withdraw into Antwerp. Many historians have debated the German decision to retreat from the Marne. It has been proposed that that was a failure to enforce will because of *Auftragstaktik*. What about this one!

What was the ultimate objective now that the concept of operations no longer included the Belgian Army? Contain the Belgian Army? Fall on the BEF? Turn the flank of the French Army? Where was Moltke to apply and enforce his will? Now the Belgian Army had to be screened, placed in a bottle and corked up. This was a long-term task that would significantly affect the calculations of time, space, and forces. The Belgian Army could not be let

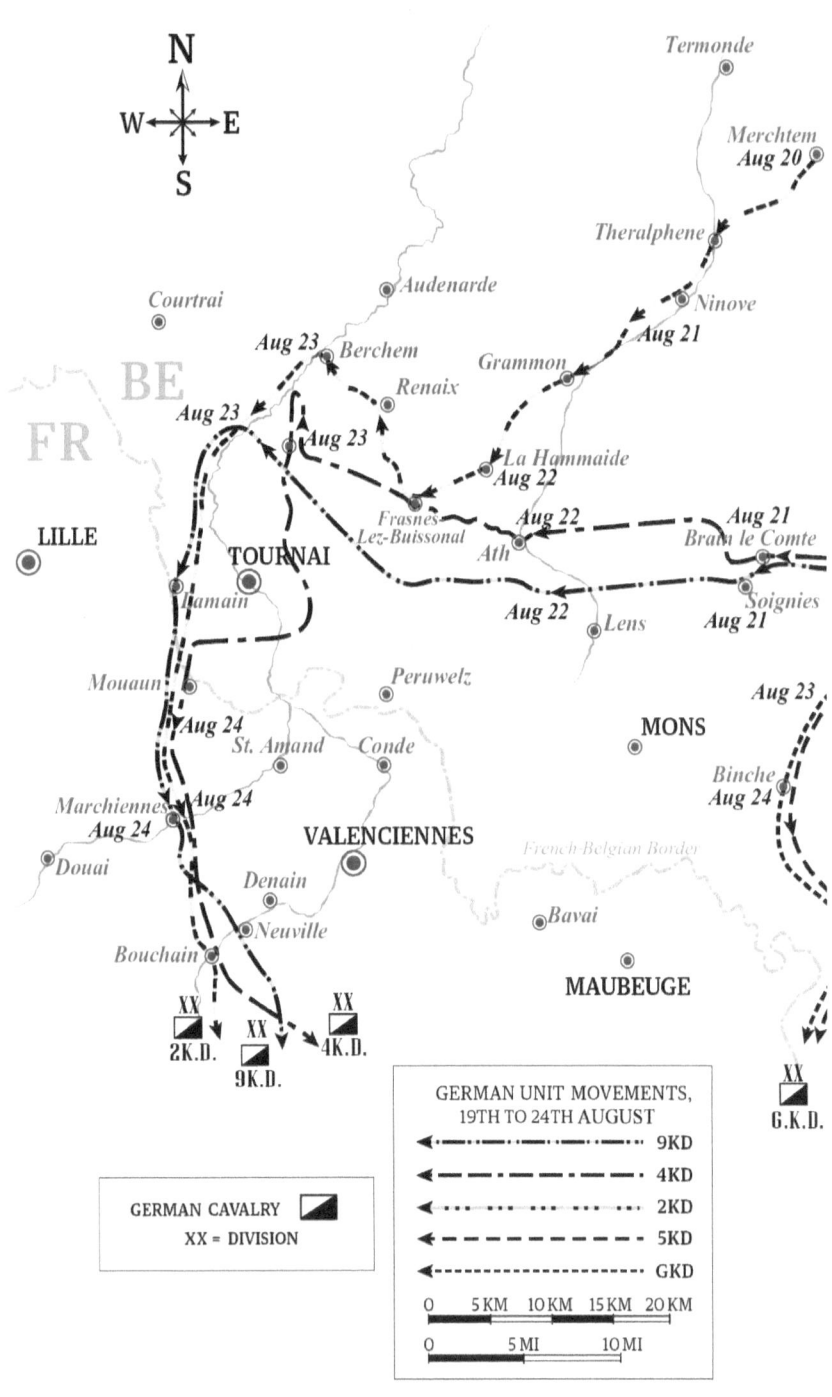

Above and opposite: German cavalry movement, August 19–24, 1914.

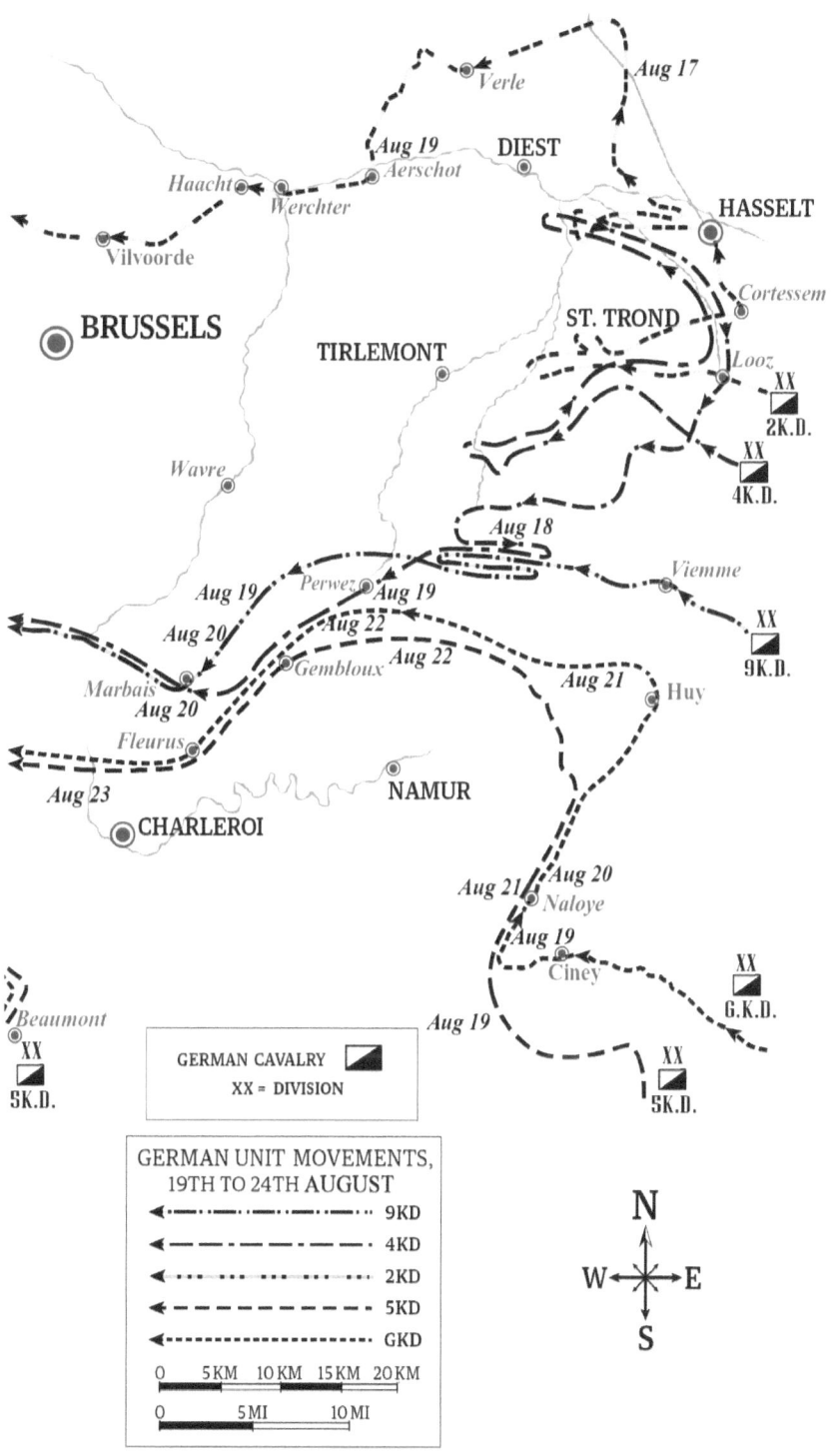

out of the bottle without opening the German logistical rear area to complete destruction. Sorties from behind the fortifications would actually be attempted three times. Screening would take a huge number of troops. Much has been made of the decision by Moltke on August 20 to send two army corps to the east front. Here in Belgium, two more army corps, albeit reservists, as well as some Landwehr were diverted from the primary stated mission. Far too little has been made of this screening operational issue. There seems to have been no serious consideration of reducing the forts of Antwerp. This would be relative to the overall strategic situation, an extremely long-term project. If it was to be considered, which HQ would do it? Would another ad hoc HQ be created? Paradoxically, Kluck also maintained tunnel vision relative to his main goal. Would he have enough force to outflank all of his opponents after leaving behind elements to screen Antwerp? This question never arises in the relevant papers.

August 19

On August 19, Second Army reached the line between Wavre and Namur. First Army was driving west of Louvain. Both were still a significant distance east of Brussels. There was one cavalry division (Second Cavalry Division) in the far north assigned to First Army. Two more divisions (Fourth and Ninth) were assigned to HKK 2, positioned in front of Second Army. Those two cavalry divisions had been skirmishing with the French, losing strength, and fighting power incrementally. Very far to the south were the two divisions of HKK 1, still in the area of Dinant, certainly too far away to reinforce the overworked troopers in central Belgium.[25]

Scrambling to cover long range reconnaissance, First Army started sending out single aircraft on two-hundred-mile trips to the coast of the English Channel. They desperately were trying to find the BEF. First Army's FFA 12 sent an aircraft on a long-distance patrol on the line Namur–Ostend–Bruges. During the flight, the plane ran out of gas and was forced to land in neutral Holland, where the crew was interned for the duration of the war.[26]

The hard-pressed Second Cavalry Division was once again brought to a standstill due to supply difficulties. Ironically, the loss of one thousand horses on August 12 by Fourth Cavalry Division made the requirement for fodder less acute in that organization.[27] The HKK 1 held the high ground to the east of Dinant and used the day to focus on maintenance: horseshoe repair and sharpening lance points. Of the five divisions between the two HKK, three were stopped for the day. No patrolling. This makes operational reconnaissance quite ineffective.[28] Second Cavalry Division's situation became even more problematic for First Army. It was suffering from a shortage of oats and was lagging behind the right flank. It did not arrive at Wolverthem until the twentieth. As has been noted, changes in the command relationship had a direct impact on the logistics of the division. "A change in the command to which the Army cavalry is assigned usually leads to different employment and to its being shoved about from place to place, which is detrimental to its efficiency." The commander of First Army now saw the role of Second Cavalry Division as advancing between Antwerp and Brussels, specifically to observe the approach of the British. With rumors flying about the location of the BEF, reconnaissance of the area between Antwerp and Brussels was vital. The Germans really had no idea where they might be. Aviation and cavalry reconnaissance both had distance limits. Negative reports of contact could not be accepted carte blanche.[29]

The Belgian Army, which been defending the River Gette, continued to fall back toward Antwerp. The Germans' failure to shoulder it away from Antwerp resulted in a force in being that could sortie dangerously against the German flank. In order to contain the Belgian Army, Third Reserve Corps was detached from the main body of First Army, and later augmented by Ninth Reserve Corps from northern Germany. Ninth Reserve Corps was the strategic reserve of the OHL. Its use against this threat was considered more vital by the OHL than the coastal security mission it had previously planned for. The loss of Third Reserve Corps would be a telling reduction in the forces trying to sweep around the French left flank. Based on some intercepted letters, the German staff started to believe that the British could be in Antwerp on the left flank of the Belgian field army. There was no direct confirmation of this but it certainly posed a new threat.[30] One major accomplishment of Second Cavalry Division was its reconnaissance toward Antwerp. First Squadron, Lifeguard Second Hussar Regiment was able to report that the British had not landed at Antwerp and that there were no British troops in the city at this time. But if the British were not there, where were they? It is instructive to note that in October 1914, the Royal Naval Division was sent to Antwerp. Far too late for this operation, however; proof that the British were not a static opponent.[31]

9

Bad Deployment Strikes Back

The greater conditions of warfare have remained unchanged. The battle of extermination may be fought today according to the same plan as elaborated by Hannibal in long forgotten times. The hostile front is not the aim of the principal attack. It is not against that point that the troops should be massed and the reserves disposed; the essential thing is to crush the flanks.—Schlieffen[1]

August 20

On the eastern front, the German army sustained a setback in the battle of Gumbinnen. The overall German strategy was to send troops to the east following initial, decisive victories in the west. Capturing terrain was not a decisive victory. The Belgian, British, and French armies still existed. Yet there were no contingency plans in case of a failure of the strong right. Whether that failure was a lack of quick victory or total failure, there was no "Plan B."

Huge Change for HKK 1

Not surprisingly, the OHL expeditiously determined the force structure problem. They realized they had insufficient cavalry on the right wing and tried to fix it. Especially when trying to screen his two armies on the far-right flank, Bülow complained vehemently about his shortage of horsemen.

The OHL ordered a change for HKK 1 on August 20. Moltke responded that "strong cavalry force west of the Meuse is desirable. Therefore, HKK 1 will clear away from the front of Third and Fourth Army and begin moving around the northern side of Namur. Once it has arrived on the right bank of Meuse, it will pass under orders of Second Army."[2]

This directive from the OHL was remarkable: It indicated that only two days after the general advance started on the right wing, Moltke must have realized his deployment of cavalry divisions was wrong and ordered HKK 1 to move to the right of Second Army—changing armies and calling it a "long detour" around Namur. Operationally, this redirection was huge. Freiher von Troschke, who wrote the history of cavalry on the right wing of the German army, was of the opinion that Moltke wanted to have the same five-division cavalry strike force that Schlieffen had in his original plan. There was a realization that the cavalry would do little good sandwiched between the French and German armies as the front line grew closer. The HKK 1 was badly needed in the open fields of Belgium. Based on the current deployment, it was situated in rough terrain with little chance to use their high mobility.

Having the cavalry on the front lines did no one any good. This truth had been inculcated in the training of all cavalry officers for perhaps centuries. All of the military theoreticians wrote about this. Schlieffen taught repeatedly about this:

> Big cavalry formations are only useful at the front line if the hostile armies are still far away from each other. Later the cavalry belongs on the wings in order to attack the flank and the back of the enemy and to contribute to decisions. In future wars, the cavalry will not only gather intelligence. During the decisive phase of the battle, its position is in the back of the enemy.

As Bernhardi wrote:

> Several cavalry corps have to be united in one strategic direction and this cavalry unit has to be concentrated where it can be assumed from the general operational situation that cavalry can enter the (rear of the) main operational area of the enemy. Furthermore, stronger infantry and artillery have to follow and to overflow as large areas as possible.[3]

Translated to specifics, Moltke was ordering a cavalry force of two divisions to break contact, withdraw several miles, and conduct a major river crossing. After crossing the river, they would come under the operational control of Second Army. That meant HKK 1 was to move at a ninety-degree angle across the communications zone of Second Army without disrupting the flow of troops and supplies, also avoiding entrapment in the developing siege of Namur. Next, HKK 1 was to move entirely around the communications zone of Second Army, establish two cavalry divisions on the right flank of Second Army, and make contact with the enemy. As a result, Poseck said, "much time was lost and the HKK was able to work its way only slowly toward the front of the [Second] Army, with the result that the HKK was again until August 28 making its way to the front of the army advance." It took eight days to complete this maneuver at a time when hours were proving vital![4]

Richthofen moved by forced marches around Namur from the left to the right wing of Second Army. Bülow expected HKK 1 was then supposed to take over the reconnaissance in front of the left wing of the First and the right wing of the Second Army, as well as along the line Condé–Maubeuge and east of it.[5] This assumption turned out to be wrong because First Army did not turn to the right but to the left, toward the approaching British army. The first day was a day of heavy marching, from about 0400 hours until 1900 hours. There was a repeated complaint that the horses had been through heat, rain, and dirt and were rapidly losing their conditioning.[6]

> Cavalry Corps Richthofen [HKK 1] was stuck between the marching columns of Second Army in a most unfortunate way. Now he had no space to move freely and had to squeeze through with his exhausted horses, without having any aim and everywhere regarded with disapproval. But this was not the fault of the cavalry leader.... We will later see how this happened repeatedly in the following days and how it affected the whole negatively.[7]

The roads designated for this maneuver were absolutely clogged. The HKK 1 had to find clearance space not only around the combat troops, but all of the wagon trains in the communication zone bringing supplies to the front of Second Army. What HKK 1 had to do was to approach each of these roads at ninety degrees and try to cross the road when another unit had priority. Think of it as a 1914 game of Frogger. Based on the way logistics were organized, the cavalry divisions had to get supplies by changing army corps as they moved. This accounts for the comment about being unwelcome.

HKK 2

On August 20, Second Army also issued an order directing Second Cavalry Division to remain ahead of the right wing of First Army, coordinating with Second Army Corps about how the limited available roads were to be used. Second Cavalry Division began operations around the village of Wolverthem, pursuing the most important mission of reconnoitering for approaching British forces between Brussels and Antwerp.[8] In a skirmish with the Lifeguard Hussar Brigade, the Belgian cavalry lost one of the squadron standards for the Fifth Lancers to the Second Cavalry Division.[9] The HKK 2 also skirmished with Sordet's French Cavalry Corps. Long-range patrols were sent out to the south. It is instructive to note that when Fourth Cavalry Division withdrew into bivouac, they went all the way behind Second Army's infantry. What that often required was a retrograde march of about thirty kilometers. The distance would have to be traversed again the following day.[10]

Late in the afternoon of August 20, Ninth Cavalry Division reached Marbais. There, Captain von Lobbecke, commanding Fifth Squadron Thirteenth Uhlans, received orders to reconnoiter westward in the area: Marbais–Nivelles–Braine le Comte (north boundary)–old road Marbais–Binche (south boundary). The same evening, the patrol on the left flank of the reconnaissance squadron clashed with hostile French outposts on the banks of the Pieton River west of Gosselies. As these outposts were not British, the reconnaissance zone for August 21 was limited in the south to the Canal du Centre as far as Condé, but prolonged in the north to Lille.[11]

On August 20, Sordet's French Cavalry Corps, on the point of ineffectiveness from being overmarched and undersupplied, withdrew across the Charleroi–Brussels canal in the direction of Fontaine l'Eveque and occupied the canal crossings between Marchienne-au-Pont and a point south of Seneffe.

First and Second Army

First Army continued its advance to the west. "According to press reports received at army headquarters on August 20, the BEF had completed its disembarkation in French ports on August 18 [in reality, August 16]. The direction of the BEF's advance was still unknown but it had to be assumed that it might close up via Lille."[12]

First Army correspondingly eyed the horizon warily for the potential arrival of the British from the west. Headquarters now entertained a different fear that an advance to Ninove would be too far forward and expose the army's flank to attack by the British. Second Corps went to Vilvorde and Koningsloo, guarding its flank against Antwerp and Ganshoren (northwest of Brussels); Fourth Corps to Kortenberg–center of Brussels–Anderlecht (west of the capital); Third Corps to Tervueren–Boitsfort–Droogebosch (south of Brussels); Ninth Corps by Overysche Hoeylaert–La Hulze–Waterloo. Second and Fourth Corps were expected to arrive on a level with Brussels by noon, Third Corps would cross the Brussels–Gembloux railway at 1030 hours, and Ninth Corps would cross it at 0930 hours. Brussels was the intellectual and financial center of Belgium as well as its capital. It had 650,000 inhabitants. Nevertheless, Fourth Army Corps entered the city without struggle, marching in parade review past the commander Sixt von Arnim.[13]

Bülow now instructed First Army to hold both of its reserve army corps in readiness for use against Antwerp. Remember, Kluck had said that the forces in Antwerp could no longer be feared. Their presence was clearly scaring somebody. This raised the issue of splitting up forces for accessory tasks. First Army began to wonder if it had enough troops for a broad sweeping movement. The fear of moving the right flank forward to Ninove became a subject of discussion and disagreement between the liaison of Second Army and First Army HQ. As a result, the commander of First Army, General von Kluck, issued a short order. "To be prepared for its further tasks, First Army will make only a short march forward on the twenty-first, covering toward Antwerp."[14]

Aviation

Undeterred by the loss of long-range reconnaissance on the nineteenth, First Army HQ's FFA 12 sent another sortie over Ghent–Bruges–Ostend, an unusually long flight of three hundred kilometers. Upon returning, the observer reported the entire area "free of the enemy." Further air reconnaissance was carried out by Second Corps over the railways and roads in the area Vilvorde (northeast of Brussels)–Termonde–Alost–Ninove–Brussels and Louvain–Antwerp; by Third Corps in the area Brussels–Ninove–Renaix–Mons–Brussels; and by Ninth Corps in the area Louvain–Mons–Charleroi–Wavre. All of these were desperately looking for any indication of the BEF or the left wing of the French Army.[15]

Namur

Large numbers of German troops arrived. During the day, Guard Reserve Corps of the German Second Army arrived at the north of the fortress zone and Eleventh Corps of Third Army arrived to the southeast. A siege train including one Krupp 420-milimeter howitzer and four Austrian 305-milimeter mortars accompanied the German troops. On August 20, Belgian outposts were driven in. The next day, the German super-heavy guns began to bombard the eastern and southeastern forts. The Belgian defenders had no means to keep the German siege guns out of range or engage them with counter-battery fire. By evening, two forts had been seriously damaged, and after another twenty-four hours, the forts were mostly destroyed.

August 21

Zeppelins in the Wrong Place

Two German Army zeppelins were brought down over the western front: ZVII and ZVIII. This happened very far away from the right wing. However, it seriously affected the total number of dirigibles available. The pair were sister ships of the "K" class, 150 meters (492 feet) long, and capable of speeds up to eighty kilometers (fifty miles) per hour. Both zeppelins were to find and harass French troops retreating in the Vosges Mountains of Alsace.

Commanded by Hauptmann Geisert, ZVII succeeded in dropping a few artillery shells on the French troops before becoming enveloped in a cloud bank. When she emerged, she was unfortunate enough to find herself directly above the enemy at an altitude of less than eight hundred meters (twenty-six hundred feet). The French immediately responded with massive small-arms fire, perforating the zeppelin's envelope in many places. Leaking lift gas, the airship limped away until the crew made a forced landing near St. Quirin, damaging ZVII beyond any hope of repair.

The ZVIII fared even worse. As she set out on her mission, she was first fired upon by German troops, who scored many hits with small arms and at least one artillery shell. Despite the damage and gas leaks, commander Hauptmann Konrad Andrée decided to proceed with the mission. Ironically, when the airship finally located the French, the French Army below did not fire on the zeppelin, believing it to be a French craft until it started dropping shells. The ZVIII was below four hundred meters (thirteen hundred feet) and no longer able to gain height. Consequently, she was heavily damaged by return fire from the 75-millimeter guns of the Sixty-Fifth *ème régiment d'infanterie territorial*. Pursued by French cavalry and out of control, she began to drift and eventually crashed near Bandonvilliers. The crew attempted to burn the airship to avoid its falling into French hands but was unsuccessful. They then engaged the French in a brief firefight on the ground before escaping into the nearby forest. Fourteen of the crew rejoined German forces. The French captured four others, and sections of the wreckage were taken to Paris and displayed as trophies of war. The loss of these two airships, along with the destruction of LZVI on August 6, left the OHL with only four zeppelins on the entire western front. This number would not allow for any "flooding of the zone" looking for the BEF.[16]

HKK 2

The order from Second Army prepared in the late hours of August 20 was enacted by HKK 2 at 0730 hours on August 21. This order directed HKK 2 to march west and take position in front of the right wing of First Army. This constituted a change in direction, and Fourth Cavalry Division, which had sent distant patrols to the south, had to recall them. These did not rejoin the division until August 22, with some arriving later. In addition, there were some severe road interruptions between the units of Second Army and Fourth and Ninth Cavalry Divisions.[17]

First, Second, and Third Army

On August 21, Bülow ordered First Army to conform to the movement of the Second Army while screening Antwerp. Specifically, First Army was to seal off the north and northeastern approaches to Maubeuge from the area to the west of the fortress in such a way that it could take action to support Second Army if required. Neither Second Army nor the OHL expected the British forces to come into action in the near future.[18]

172 The German Failure in Belgium, August 1914

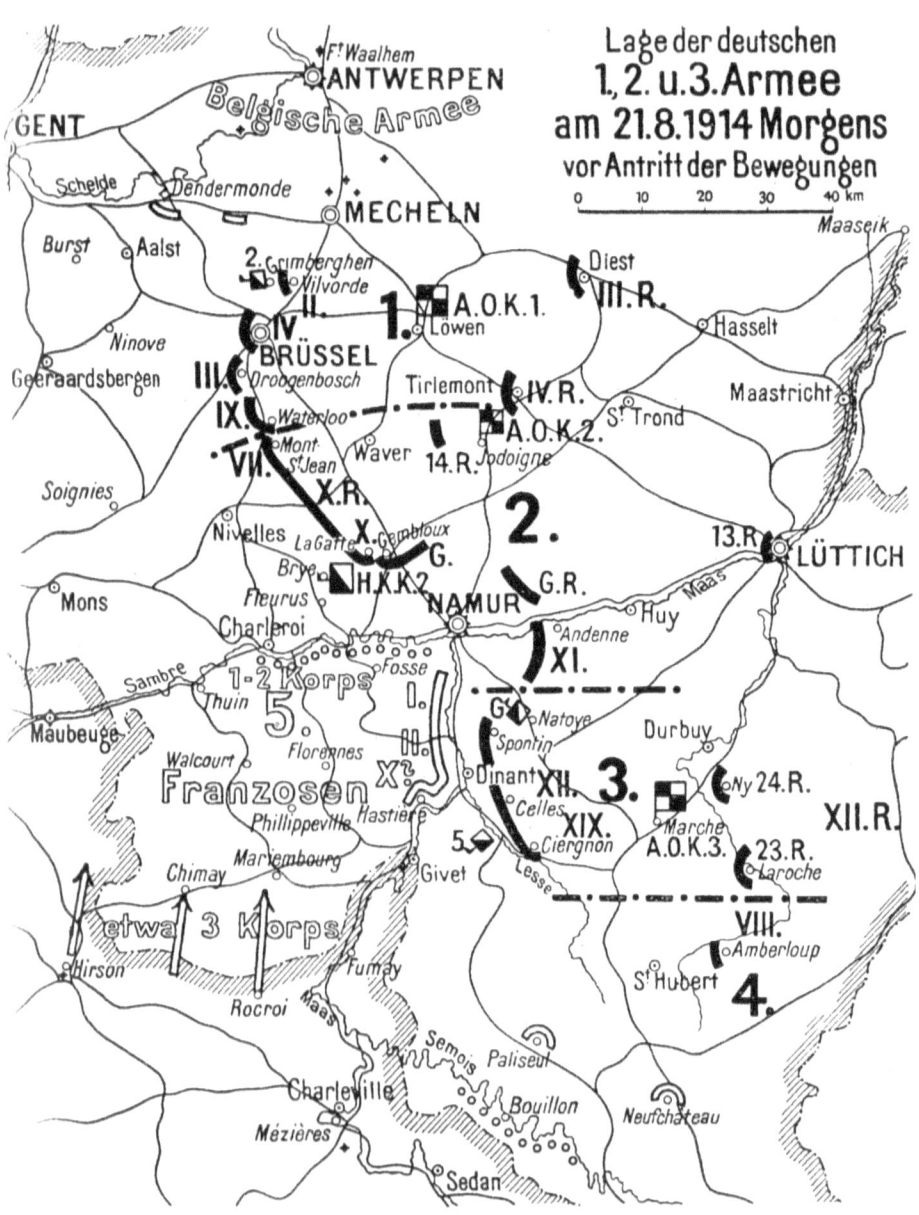

German situation, August 21, 1914.

In an endeavor to cover all three possible BEF deployment scenarios, First Army continued to advance in a strongly refused right echelon. This advance was quite limited, held to about fifteen kilometers per the orders of the commander. Third Reserve Corps, northeast of Brussels, covered the army's right flank against Antwerp. Fourth Reserve Corps reached Louvain. Second Cavalry Division continued to look for the British in the direction of Alost. It was, however, no longer under the command of First Army; assigned once again to HKK 2, which now was ordered to unite the entire HKK at the front of the right wing of First Army in an effort to reconnoiter toward Ath. Searching desperately for the BEF again, First Army stayed deployed in a refused right echelon. This echelon was a safety measure just in case the BEF came straight at the invading army from the English Channel. Using the echelon, First Army could concentrate army corps more easily against a threat to their flank or behind them. The disadvantage or trade-off was that a refused flank such as this made it more difficult to concentrate army corps to threats from the southeast or the southwest. Both of those two possibilities would require much further marching. If the BEF could be discovered, Kluck would know which way to concentrate. Remember, it could be heading for Lille or the French left flank around Maubeuge or directly onto the invasion force's flank literally in the direction of Brussels. A situation report arrived from the OHL cautioning that the British had probably landed at Boulogne and would be employed from the region of Lille. This included the caveat, "There is a tendency here, however, to believe that landings on a large scale have not yet taken place." That caveat was not extremely helpful, the receiving staff probably referred to it with some sort of a modern acronym "CYA."[19]

The lack of an army group HQ combined with the ambivalently nonaggressive approach of the OHL put the entire right wing into an "agreement" mode. Bülow had to plan for the actions of his own army, as well as those of other forces under his command—which was itself ad hoc, temporary, and so less likely to be automatically acknowledged. That had to be done with no additional staff. Kuhl stated that those agreements and understandings were usually arrived at in an incomplete form after a great loss of time. "Each particular army has its own interests and its own conception of the situation. They can be completely harmonized only by a higher authority."[20]

While they generally agreed on French dispositions, there was a significant difference of opinion between First Army and the OHL concerning the British location. They shared a common belief that a strong French army was advancing between the Rivers Meuse and Sambre. Relying on an article published in a newspaper dated August 20, First Army thought the British army had already landed in France but had first to consolidate. As a result,

First Army expected the appearance of the BEF in its sector within the next few days. Kuhl noted that Second Army would be starting its attack on Namur with its left wing and then wheel to the south. He assumed the British had certainly landed but were not expected to arrive from the direction Ghent–Courtrai–Audenard. This view meant there was no longer any danger to his right flank. Kuhl deduced this by thinking that the British would not risk operational isolation by placing themselves that far away from the French left flank. Instead, he expected the BEF to arrive further to the south in liaison with the French left wing. Kuhl saw this as a green light that would allow First Army's right flank, Second Army Corps, to proceed to Ninove and then further onto Ath—slowly eliminating the refused flank of First Army and allowing an easier repositioning to the south. This would allow First Army to maintain contact with Second Army, ready to wheel southward.[21]

Bülow initially had a different concept. He wanted to move south with both First and Second Army and only then, with the greatest possible combination of forces to include Third Army, attack the French between the Rivers Meuse and Sambre—the French Fifth Army. First Army did not want to do such an abrupt swing. They argued it would jeopardize any wide-ranging enveloping movement like Schlieffen's model. First Army wanted their swing to be so broad as would envelop the French left wing whether behind the Rivers Aisne and Somme or behind the Oise or Seine. The OHL left this plan to be agreed on between the armies.[22] Bülow issued this final order on the twenty-first:

> On August 22, Second Army will proceed to the line Binche–Jemeppe for the purpose of advancing over the Sambre on the twenty-third and opening a passage for Third Army over the Meuse. First Army, by covering toward Antwerp and leaving a garrison in Brussels, will participate in this movement so far as to be able in a given case, by investing the north and northwest fronts of Maubeuge, to come into action west of this fortress for the purpose of supporting Second Army.[23]

First Army continued to disagree and sent a liaison officer to argue its position. The Chief of Staff of the Second Army, General von Lauenstein, could not be persuaded. He directed, "Support the attack of Second Army by investing Maubeuge; hence, approach Second Army more closely." The First Army order for the twenty-second accordingly acknowledged, " First Army will wheel to the left to support Second Army." Second Army Corps on the right wing remained far in the rear, going only as far as Ninove. Third Reserve Army Corps advanced more closely toward Antwerp. Fourth Reserve Army Corps was to reach Brussels and press forward, leaving only two battalions as the garrison.[24]

General von Hausen, Commander of the Third German Army, had to release Eleventh Army Corps for the attack on Namur. He would not maximize his strength until he moved forward Twelfth Reserve Army Corps to take its place. That could not take place until the twenty-first at the earliest. However, the agreement between the two armies was not arrived at until the twenty-first. Therefore, the attack by Second and Third Army would not take place until the twenty-third.[25]

The British army cavalry arrived at the area Binche–Canal du Centre screening the advance of the BEF.[26] Meanwhile, French General Joffre ordered Third and Fourth Army to attack into the Ardennes, and Fifth Army to attack and hold the Germans in place.

August 22

Beginning on August 22 and 23, all four First Army corps were able to move on two roads each, or with one division on every route of advance. This meant a reducing of the length of each corps column. Rather than a single route that took over thirty kilometers, now the divisional routes could be taken each at fifteen kilometers. Not only would road space decrease, but the ability to make adjustments laterally increased a great deal with the additional roads. Marching separately and fighting concentrated took on a whole new look. This would also speed up movement as congestion would be reduced.[27] Given the availability of routes, Fifth Squadron Thirteenth Uhlans reached the French frontier south of the line Wiers–Peruwelz–Bernissart at noon August 22. A good twenty kilometers west of Mons, this shows that the cavalry of HKK 2 were well in position to do a wide-enveloping action should an opponent appear in the area of Mons.[28]

Second Cavalry Division was again attached to HKK 2 and had moved north around Brussels. Fourth and Ninth Division moved around Namur, and the three united on August 22 near Ath. The advance west continued with reconnaissance assignments issued to cover the ground between Thourout–Lille–Condé. The HKK 1 was to reconnoiter Condé–Maubeuge–Philippeville. Once again, the theory was to cover the three different approaches that the BEF could take. The HKK 2 would perform reconnaissance to the west as well as cover the expected concentration area of Lille. The HKK 1 was supposed to cover the Maubeuge concentration area. This last expectation was a bit too optimistic. Guard Cavalry Division, after diverting around Namur, arrived at Gembloux with Fifth Cavalry Division far behind. Due to severe road congestion around Namur and behind Second Army, HKK 1 did not believe it had completed the move to the right of Second Army until August 28. As a result, there would be significant gaps in the reconnaissance that HKK1 was expected to conduct in the area around Maubeuge.[29] As of yet, the Germans had no clear intelligence picture of the

The German Failure in Belgium, August 1914

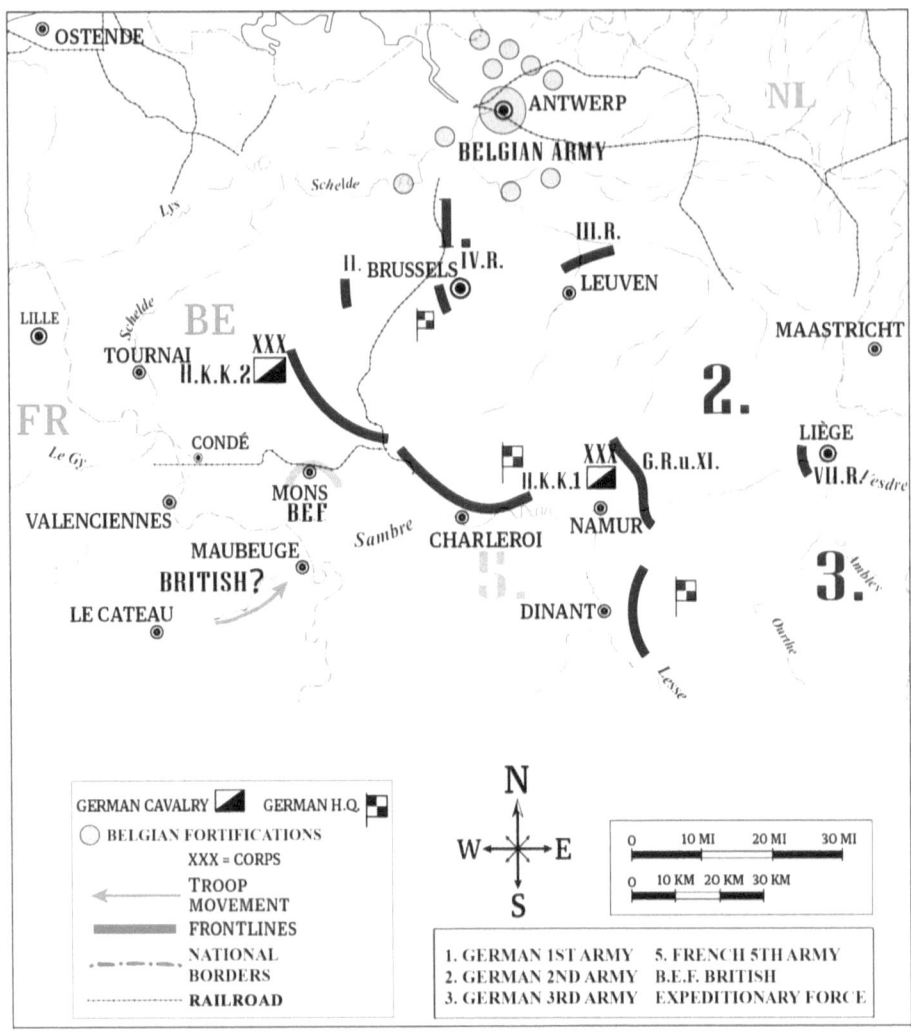

German situation, August 22, 1914.

location of the BEF. For their part, the French became aware of this mass of cavalry but overestimated its strength to be about five divisions. The British were also acutely aware of the potential threat to their open left flank. Haig lamented, "We approach a difficult terrain, a swampy valley. The enemy could stop us with a few forces and with reasonable acceleration surround our left flank by massive troops without the possibility to resist, as far as I know. The approach is aimed on the left flank of the allied armies. The British forces are in a most desperate position."[30]

Contact

The prevailing prewar German hypothesis was that BEF would concentrate around Lille. While that would make them operationally separate from the French Army, this was the overwhelming belief at the OHL still. There was a chance that the BEF might come from the channel ports directly. This possibility caused Kluck to deploy his army with a refused right flank in echelon. There was also a chance that they may come from the south in the vicinity of Maubeuge. Focusing on the Lille expectation, all of the aviation assets of First Army were sent in that direction. The one exception was the flying section of Ninth Army Corps. That unit, FFA 11, was assigned to the area around Mons. All of these aviation elements reported negative contact with the BEF. This included a negative report from FFA 11. The morning report stated, "No military activity in this sector of Mons." Therefore, the staff of First Army still thought the BEF was well south of Mons if located in that direction.

At 1030 hours, Ninth Cavalry Division was informed that a squadron of Eighth Hussar Regiment, as well as a patrol from Fourth Kürassier Regiment, had found British cavalry in the town of Casteau. The village is located between the towns of Mons and Soignies on the road Mons–Brussels. This was immediately reported to First Army.

Then one of the classic moments of fog and friction struck. Around 1500 hours on August 22, one of the aircraft from Ninth Army Corps definitively found the BEF. The aircraft reported large bodies of troops moving to Bavai and from Bavai to Binche. In addition, the aviators found vehicles and wagons on the road from Valenciennes to Mons. This very important aviation report was not, however, forwarded to First Army.[31] Why? As previously explained, the liaison and staff decisions of the intelligence sections officer (Ic) of the German army corps left a great deal to be desired. They were heavily overworked and did not forward an estimated fifty percent of the aviation reports to First Army. The aviation reports were frequently bundled at the end of the day. Telephonic contact was sporadic at best. The lack of a dedicated aviation staff officer at the army level meant that the aviation reports had to be handled by another staff officer who was already overburdened with his traditional tasks. This extremely important report "fell through the cracks."

Reports started coming in by radio. Remember that only the cavalry divisions had radios and they could only report to the numbered army HQ. These broadcasts were available to any receiver and were allegedly broadcast in the clear. It is not certain who the source was on this 1100-hours transmission. "Patrol taken under fire on the canal six kilometers east of Mons. Roeulx—northeast of Mons—clear. Area clear as far as Escot." Now this might

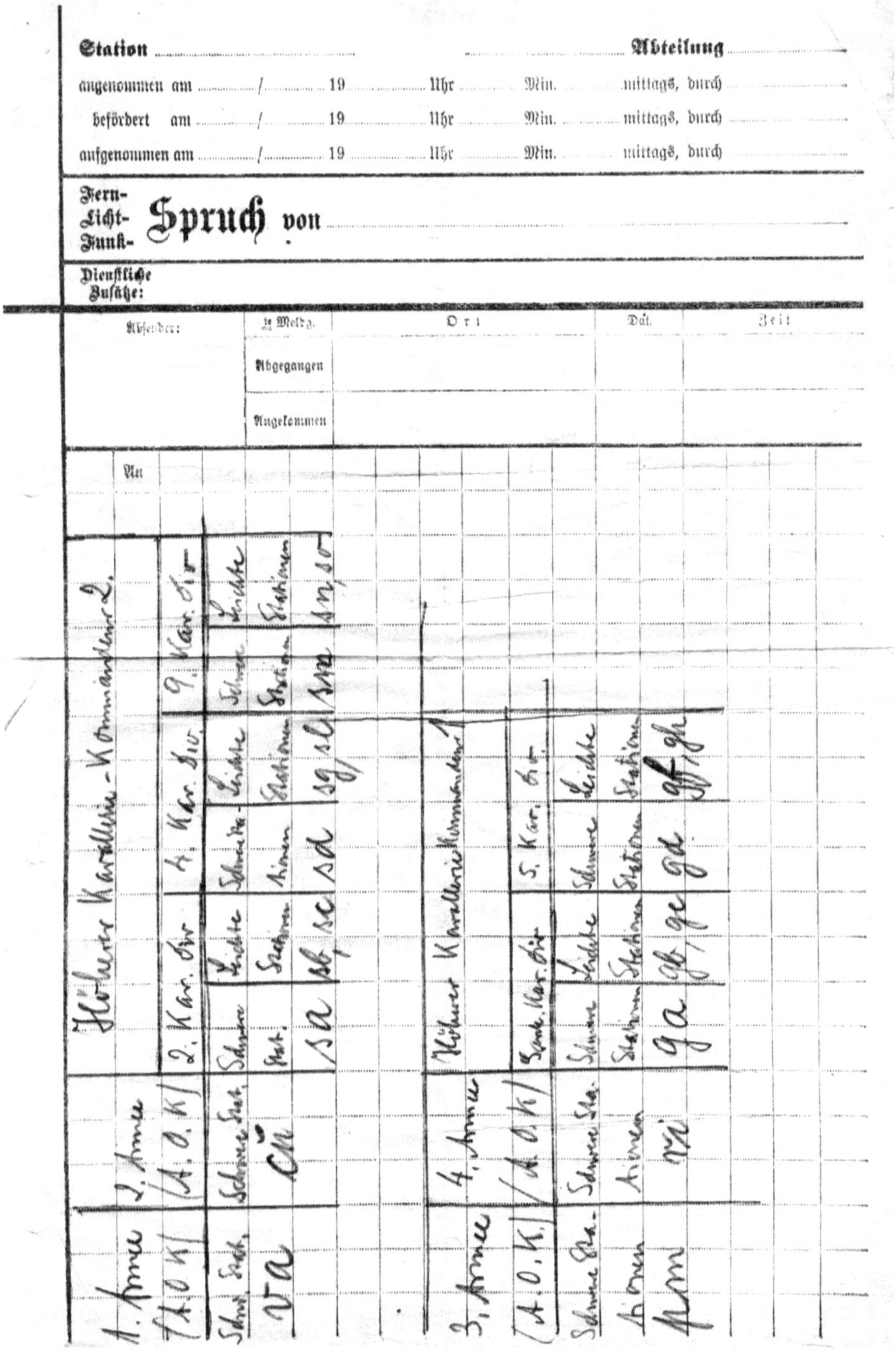

Station .... Abteilung ....

angenommen am ..../.... 19.... Uhr .... Min. .... mittags, durch ....

befördert am ..../.... 19.... Uhr .... Min. .... mittags, durch ....

aufgenommen am ..../.... 19.... Uhr .... Min. .... mittags, durch ....

Fern- Licht- Funk- Spruch von ....

Dienstliche Zusätze:

Absender:	zu Meldg.	Ort	Tag	Zeit
	Abgegangen			
	Angekommen			

An

1. Armee (A.O.K.)	2. Armee (A.O.K.)	Höherer Kavallerie-Kommandeur 2		
		2. Kav. Div	4. Kav. Div	9. Kav. Div
3. Armee (A.O.K.)	4. Armee (A.O.K.)	Höherer Kavallerie-Kommandeur 1		
		Garde Kav. Div	5. Kav. Div	

9. Bad Deployment Strikes Back 179

seem simple enough but it raises quite a few questions. What exactly is meant by Roeulx? There is such a location but it is named La Roeulx. There is another location with just the name Roeulx in the opposite direction, five kilometers southwest of Denain. What is meant by Escot? It is a normal French term used in place of the Scheldt River. It is also an old region of northern France, as well as a village name. All of them are on the west side of the battle zone.

Almost an hour later, at 1150 hours, Fourth Cavalry Division radioed a message: "Patrol of Fourth Cavalry has positively identified an English squadron at Casteau northeast of Mons." Ninth Army Corps sent in a report that arrived at 1500 hours: "According to the declaration of inhabitants, Mons is occupied by English troops." In addition, Fourth Cavalry Division continued to transmit, this time at 1640 hours: "English at Maubeuge." This report was supplemented late in the evening, at 2150 hours: "Passages of the Canal du Centre between Nimy and Ville-sur-Haine are occupied by the British." An aviation report reached First Army at 2145 hours: "No sort of military activity in the sector St. Ghislain–Mons." Other negative reports indicated that the areas Audenarde–Remaix–Grammont, as well as the area Ath–Tournai, were free of enemy troops and that the railroad lines around Lille were quiet. Note the late hour of the aviation reports. This clearly explains the length of time it took to get a report from the airfield up to First Army. Also, a key to the timing is that First Army issued the order for August 23 at 2130 hours on August 22. Recalling the late-night orders drill, we now have to add the issue of time, as reports of contact postdated the issuance of the order.[32]

Third Army Corps shot down a British aircraft. Interrogation of the captured pilot revealed that he was coming from Maubeuge. That gave more credence to the BEF being located in the south. An excerpt from the Army Order of August 22 at 2130 hours states, "A squadron of British cavalry was encountered today at Casteau, northeast of Mons, and a British airplane coming from Maubeuge was shot down near Enghien. In front of Second Army there appear today to be only three cavalry divisions and a weak force of infantry." Clearly, Kluck did not know the strength of the forces in front of him. The subordinate units were told that a British cavalry screen had been encountered. But the Germans at First Army HQ did not know the strength or the exact location of the main body. They did not know how deep the BEF was deployed or how far away. Ninth Army Corps had a better idea about

Opposite: An amazing handwritten note by an unknown GGS officer found within a "red donkey" shows the call signs of every radio of the First through the Fourth German Army and of HKK 1 and HKK 2. There were FEW. The next page showed the call signs from the fortresses.

the BEF and that it was five kilometers away, but not its controlling HQ. A quote from Kuhl's diary confirmed that he thought only cavalry were front of him: "There remains doubt as to what is going on from the English, whether strong forces are there and where."[33]

"The English" were suddenly opposite First Army. The German First Army knew they had found the British but did not know exactly their strength. The assessment of the First Army staff was that the BEF were in the region between Valenciennes and Maubeuge and perhaps even further back. The British intent was interpreted to be coming up on the French left hand and not by way of Lille–Tournai. This analysis supported the view of a wide-enveloping move and that the order issued by Bülow on the twenty-first ordering First Army to invest Maubeuge did not conform or take advantage of the current situation. Oberstleutnant Tappen of the OHL, through a series of relays with corresponding chances of errors, approved the instructions to Second Army and directed First Army to stay in strict liaison with Second Army, directing that the sweeping movement be delayed until the enemy had been beaten. First Army appealed directly to Second Army to no avail. General von Lauenstein did not approve the sweeping proposal but did decide to reduce the force required to invest Maubeuge to a single division.[34]

That night, however, a messenger reached the reconnaissance squadron in the woods northeast of Wadelincourt[35] with the information that the patrols had drawn heavy fire at the outskirts of Condé. The squadron therefore moved on Condé very early on August 23. Its reconnaissance revealed that the vicinity and woods north of Condé were held by French territorial infantry, middle-aged and poorly trained reservists. The enemy was purely on the defensive; there was no reconnoitering cavalry. Simultaneously, it was learned that the Schelde [River] crossings as far as Tournai likewise were occupied by the enemy. The identification of French territorials at Condé was very important information. Territorial troops had never been used previously in the first line of defense. The Germans had identified the eastern flank of the British near Binche and now, with the discovery of French territorials at Condé, the Germans understood that all British forces should be to the east of this point. The extent of the British zone of operations was established because it was also known that a group of French regular army units constituting the left flank of the French Army was concentrated at Charleroi. The British cavalry, after being relieved by infantry, joined the left flank of the British Army, covering the canal crossings as far as Condé.[36]

Dilemma of HKK 2

Marwitz could have approached via Tournai–Denain to the English flank. However, a counterorder arrived from Bülow that ordered the cavalry to move in a northwestern direction instead of to the southwest. The reason was an unproved false report of air reconnaissance that allegedly saw strong English cavalry west of the River Schelde near Courtrai. The HKK obeyed, but Colonel General von Kluck was infuriated. In the early morning hours of August 23, at 0200 hours, a message of the Cavalry Division Garnier arrived: "Up to the River Schelde everything free, English troops at Maubeuge." Kluck therefore messaged to Marwitz: "Intervention from Denain required to cut off the enemy from retreating." Marwitz certainly felt this was the correct option but he had to answer that he had another order from a higher authority. Kluck saw the danger. The cavalry forces that were to be used to envelop the BEF and the French left flank were going the wrong way. First Army could not do it themselves because Second Army Corps was in an echelon right formation too far away from the Mons battlefield.

Kluck cabled back immediately: "Not agreed. English northwest of Maubeuge. First Army is attacking." Shortly afterwards, again: "Right wing Condé! Intervention in direction Valenciennes is necessary." Marwitz's position was extraordinary. Should he follow the orders of the higher authority or the urgent pleadings of Kluck? He struggled and did the first. Then Kluck addressed the Supreme Army Command directly. Pleading that HKK 2 be moved in the direction of Denain, HKK 2 wanted to move to Coutrai. Then finally Moltke gave in—much too late—in a characteristic way: "His Majesty orders that the Higher Cavalry Command [HKK 2] is to be assigned to the command of First Army."[37] "The outcome of the campaign 1914 was not decided at the River Marne, as believed in former times, but on 23rd and 24th of August."[38]

Poseck's statement about the Courtrai incident provides the final punctuation: "Without the waste of time of Courtrai the approach of the Higher Cavalry Command 2 would have resulted in the complete elimination of the enemy."[39]

August 23

First Army

In the morning, First Army HQ moved to Soignes, where a message from HKK 2 arrived. The message reported that since August 22 from Tournai east to Lille, large formations of troops had unloaded from trains. Who? How many? What nationality? The hitherto unresolved question as to whether and where the British would deploy now became even more difficult for First Army. If the army continued its advance in the present manner, and the British appeared from the direction of Lille, the right flank of the army was in danger. The flank was secured against British troops arriving from Lille by the echeloned Second Army Corps and Fourth Reserve Army Corps. But the planned encircling of the left English wing, the operational focus of the Schlieffen-Moltke prewar grand design, could be called into question. Was there only British cavalry around Mons? Not knowing if the British were all in the east or the west, the Third, Fourth, and Ninth Army Corps were held in place temporarily at 0930 hours. After First Army received intelligence from Third Hussar Regiment that thirty thousand British troops had marched up into the area of Mons and HKK 2 reported that Tournai was now free of enemy troops and that a French brigade had fallen back onto Lille, the army resumed its forward movement. Ninth Army Corps was the first to get into action around noon. Third Army Corps followed suit at 1315 hours and covered the nine kilometers it needed to close in on the BEF. Fourth Corps was very late in concentrating for the attack.[40]

About mid-day on the twenty-third, First Army received radio traffic from the OHL directing that it employ Third and Fourth Reserve Corps as a covering force facing Antwerp until Ninth Reserve Corps arrived from Germany. In addition, First Army was ordered to strongly occupy Brussels until further notice. First Army, which was trying to minimize the occupation of Brussels, was required to turn troops around to form a garrison of one brigade. The Belgian Army in Antwerp was certainly causing operational diversions to the objective of the invasion. The brigade stayed there and, on September 5, at the start of the battle of the Ourcq when Fourth Reserve Corps was engaged in heavy fighting, the Brussels brigade had not yet rejoined it.[41]

By the end of August 23, the northern and eastern fronts of Namur were defenseless, with five of the nine forts in ruins. The Namur garrison withdrew at midnight to the southwest and eventually rejoined the Belgian field army at Antwerp; the last fort was surrendered on August 25. The fortress city of Namur had been a continual force drain for both First and Second Army. With the fall of the city, forces that had been diverted to this task were now released to their parent organizations. But then one of the heavily debated decisions occurred about the German forces around Namur. Moltke, on August 24, made the fatal decision to send the two army corps that Bülow freed up after the capture of Namur to the east front. This decision has historically been considered a total misjudging of the situation.[42]

HKK 2 Change of Subordination

Unfortunately, HKK 2 was even now subjected to a series of changes in its chain of command. They constantly flip-flopped between First and Second Army. By August 22, HKK 2 had all three divisions back together but was

9. Bad Deployment Strikes Back

pointed to the northwest by Second Army. On the twenty-third, they were feeding horses along the River Schelde west of Rennaix. Although these were exactly the forces that should have been enveloping the British left flank—the envelopment Kluck was trying to accomplish—all three divisions were in a tight mass far away from the canal. Neither Second Army nor the Supreme Army Command expected the British to come into action in the near future.[43]

Field Marshal Sir John French had about 125,000 men under his command at Mons: four divisions of eighteen thousand, a cavalry division of ten thousand, an extra cavalry brigade, four aircraft squadrons, plus rear area troops. This was a force too formidable to overlook. Its locating and placing had become the cavalry's premier task. But "order–counterorder–disorder" took its toll on the Germans.

An extended quote from Kuhl addressed the command and control of cavalry organizations and demonstrated how daunting the logistical ramifications of a HQ change could be to a cavalry division:

> The Commander of Second Army had temporarily placed the Second Cavalry Division of HKK 2 under the command of First Army, but had later on reunited all three divisions of the HKK 2 under his own command. On August 23, the entire HKK 2 was attached to First Army. On several occasions, these changes of assignment caused difficulties in the employment of the cavalry, resulting in unnecessary marches and overexertion. From this, the lesson may be drawn that the orders for the employment of the independent cavalry must be prepared *with utmost care*. If the cavalry has once been started in the wrong direction, it will often be impossible to remedy the mistake for several days. Thus, when HKK 2, after having been started by the commander of Second Army from Ath on its march on Courtrai, was subsequently attached to First Army, it became necessary to demand of it on August 24 a countermarch toward Denain in order to give it the desired direction.[44]

The diary notes of the Chief of Staff of HKK 2, Major Hoffmann von Waldau, commented when the change of direction was ordered: "Shifting in direction Courtrai. First Army wants us for combat in Valenciennes. Would be the right thing. Second Army insists on approach to River Schelde–Courtrai.... At night, subordination to First Army that commands to engage near Valenciennes via Denain. This joke we could have obtained considerably cheaper."

The First General Staff Officer of Ninth Cavalry Division is still more drastic in his diary: "So the twenty-third of August ended unfortunately with pointless wandering till nightfall."[45]

Meanwhile, a battle was fought at Mons.

Conclusion

The finest theories and most minute plans often crumble. Complex systems fall by the wayside. Parade ground formations disappear. Our splendidly trained leaders vanish. The good men which we had at the beginning are gone. Then raw truth is before us. –Charles O'Daniel[1]

After all this, the Germans almost pulled it off. The great envelopment could have happened on August 23 around the area of Mons. It did not come down to the number of divisions that had been assigned to the right wing. It did not come down to the amount of cavalry on the right wing. It did not come down to an envelopment east or west of Paris; this still happened in Belgium. It did not take forty days. The Germans were able to overcome all of the technical problems associated with Liège. They were also able to overcome the problems associated with letting the Belgian field army get away. They were able to compensate for a complete lack of strategic reconnaissance. They were able to determine methods that would compensate for a lack of communications in their force structure. Had HKK2 swung around into the rear area of the BEF near Mons, World War I might very well have taken a completely different course. Indeed, that result might have been certain.

So are we to conclude that all was well and, without changing anything, the Germans were at the point of complete victory? Given the obvious flaws in the planning and execution of the invasion pointed out in this book, it should be acknowledged that the German near success was the product of a great deal of luck. But luck is in good part the residue of design. And this was the Imperial German Army—an organization fundamentally unlikely to trust blindly to luck. We are therefore constantly plagued by trying to understand why such a flawed plan was allowed. Why was a plan with this many obvious problems and pitfalls allowed to pass for years as the best the GGS could come up with? Hindsight asserts there should be some record that the GGS objected vehemently to this entire concept. Instead, it appears that when

Conclusion   185

the GGS could not solve some questionable aspect of the plan, the accepted solutions were silence and overlooking.

This is not acceptable staff work, let alone something normative in one of the premier staff organizations in the world. Presenting a plan that overlooks or discounts major obstacles to success is by definition risky. Consider the confederacy's Gettysburg campaign, the Third Reich's operation Barbarossa, or SHAEF's "bridge too far" strike for Arnhem and the Rhine in 1944. Imperial Germany's planners should have been able to see—or if necessary forced themselves to see—the relatively obvious ways that the projected invasion of, and sweep through, Belgium could be compromised. If this plan was not the best project or idea, something needed to be developed and presented that had a reasonable chance of success. So, what mindset allowed the GGS to press forward—to internalize, indeed to normalize, this approach to the war plan on which Germany's fate depended? Why would Moltke accept such seemingly obvious flaws? What went on between Moltke and the planners?

Was this some sort of solipsistic syndrome? General Staff officers were trained to come up with similar solutions to a presented problem. A near-inevitable consequence of that is an institutional bias towards "the correct solution." If this is allowed to grow unfettered, it can become a matter of dogmatic acceptance of whatever the General Staff officers tell each other. When the approved solution becomes established, the result might be called, borrowing a familiar movie title song, "The 3:10 to Yuma." Everyone wants to ride the train, but nobody is quite sure why. No one will say anything questioning the journey or the destination. Passengers follow one another blindly. Why are they going to Yuma? When the 3:10 whistles, take that train! Might this be the reason the GGS was allowed to present such a ramshackle solution? A form of group think? A Rubicon mindset crossing a point of no return?[2] Did someone, or enough someones, say that the *Handstreich* might work and so it became an accepted methodology? The overall plan revolved around force destruction of the allied armies: Schlieffen's Cannae. Was the GGS capable of so fundamentally missing the objective and instead focusing on what seemed the less formidable, more familiar mechanics of deploying and moving two armies through a small gap? At some point, did clearing the gap at Liège become the primary objective of the invasion plan, instead of destruction of the enemy force as intended by Schlieffen and directed by Moltke?

Why did the staff fall into the trap of wishful thinking, of assuming away problems? What would have been the response if the four railroad tunnels between the border and the city of Liège had been properly demolished? The German army had no reliable method for seizing these tunnels, no commandos or *spetsnaz*. Securing them was on anybody's essential task list. What about the Belgian field army? What if it initially concentrated to defend the west side of the river Meuse? Why were the defensive forces at the Liège estimated to be so small as to be token, when reliable information existed that they were larger? The Germans knew for five days that the Belgian Third Division had already mobilized and was waiting in Liège! They knew the areas between the forts were fortified. They knew the bridge at Visé had been blown up the night before. The extent of the total damage to the exploded tunnels was unknown. What mindsets led the GGS to internalize, indeed to normalize, this approach to the war plan on which Germany's fate depended? Why would Moltke accept such seemingly obvious flaws?

Whether or not the GGS displayed solipsistic planning behavior, Moltke believed his plan would work. What did Moltke expect? He allowed the GGS to present him with an absolutely horrible plan. We have demonstrated both that the plan was risky and that only Moltke knew in the War Council that the plan was significantly flawed. He did not tell the kaiser. Did he expect that the Belgians would agree to the ultimatum? If that was his belief, it went against everything his soldier's training and general staff experience should have taught him. Nevertheless, he thought it would work:

> However awkward it may be, the advance through Belgium must therefore take place without the violation of Dutch territory. This will hardly be possible unless Liège is in our hands. The fortress must therefore be taken at once. I think it possible to take it by a *coup de main*. Its salient forts are so unfavorably sited that they do not overlook the intervening country and cannot dominate it. I have had a reconnaissance made of all roads running through them into the center of the town, *which has no ramparts* [emphasis added]. An advance with several columns is possible without their being observed from the forts. Once our troops have entered the town, I believe that the forts will not bombard it but will probably capitulate. Everything depends on meticulous preparation and surprise. The enterprise is only possible if the attack is made at once, before the areas between the forts are fortified. It must therefore be undertaken by standing troops immediately [when] war is declared. The capture of a modern fortress by a *coup de main* would be something unprecedented in military history. But it can succeed and must be attempted, for the possession of Liège is the *sine qua non* of our advance. It is a bold venture whose accomplishment promises a great success. In any case, the heaviest artillery must be at hand, so that in case of failure we can take the fortress by storm. I believe the absence of an inner rampart will deliver the fortress into our hands.[3]

For someone generally described and dismissed as a pessimist, Moltke in this case was surprisingly unbothered by worst-case scenarios. Was his intent to launch the *Handstreich* against Belgium and "hope" the Belgians would fold? After all, Germany had to mobilize for a full-scale war, and that would take some time. So perhaps that *Handstreich* was his version of a medieval *coup de main* launched as a forlorn hope—a long-shot gamble that might work. The chief of staff's exact words were, "I think it is possible."

The overall operational plan applied in Belgium in August 1914 was at best a gambler's gambit. As early as August 4, the OHL was considering canceling or delaying the operation. The only definite way to implement the plan was to follow the route originally indicated by Schlieffen. In other and plainer words, Moltke had to cross the Maastricht Appendix. Only in that way did he have reasonable chances to outflank Liège, directly approach the Belgian Army's flank, and assure that the vital logistical lines of communication with Germany would be open. The obvious negative was that would bring the Netherlands into the war. Crossing the Maastricht Appendix would guarantee neither success nor the discovery of the BEF. Militarily, however, it did provide a way to ameliorate all the problems inherent with forcing the gap at Liège. Who should have made this decision? Rather than leave the decision to the political authorities, as Moltke the Elder would probably have done, the junior-version Moltke accepted a high-risk military plan and did not tell his ostensible political superiors of the risks.

The consequences began immediately and then metastasized. German failure to eliminate the Belgian field army early in the campaign and its successful retreat created a consistent, massive force drain culminating in the requirement to watch Antwerp constantly for any possible sortie. What difference might have Fourth Reserve Corps and Ninth Reserve Corps made to the right wing had they not been covering Antwerp?

Moltke put far too few cavalry divisions on the far-right flank—significantly fewer than Schlieffen. The three divisions of HKK 2 could not cover all the tasks assigned. We have shown that additional divisions were available So why did the staff present a plan where eventually there just was not enough cavalry to handle the tasks assigned? After the war, many critics lamented that HKK 3 had been wasted and would have been better utilized in the open spaces of the right wing in Belgium. Moltke realized that his initial deployment was not proceeding as intended. Two to three days after the general advanced started, he tried to move HKK 1 north and combine with HKK 2. This was an overly ambitious correction. It took eight days—"fog and friction" once more determining events in a movement that was incredibly difficult, especially for inexperienced formations and commanders. Then it merely placed HKK 1 on the right flank of Second Army—just outside the cavalry's crucial operational zone.

This could have been avoided had HKK 1 originally been placed at least on the right flank of Third Army. Or, if the plan had followed the intention of Schlieffen, HKK 1 could have started in the same area as HKK 2 and provided more muscle to turn the Belgian field army away from Antwerp. This deployment, however, required crossing the Maastricht Appendix—in 1914, a nonstarter and a classic case of catch-22.

If the German GGS was one of modern history's "perfect organizations," then the bar has been set very low. There are just too many problems with the plan executed by Moltke to give it even a passing grade. The staff failed, the *Handstreich* failed, the reconnaissance failed, the campaign failed. And as near-run things as were the fate of the BEF after Mons and the subsequent battle of the Marne, the campaign's opening events provide significant evidence that the German Army at the decisive point was not configured for success in its first and only great war. In response, the preceding text has developed several points.

First, the German cavalry's mission was *reconnaissance*—not direct battlefield shock action in the fashion of Seydlitz or Murat. That meant finding and feeling out the enemy; maneuvering like a boxer so as to encourage the opponent to set himself up for a decisive infantry-artillery blow. Successful reconnaissance could achieve that in two ways. One involved providing sufficiently comprehensive, sufficiently accurate information to the higher commands to enable them to structure and coordinate their own movements appropriately. The other was playing an economy-of-force role that freed divisions and army corps from subsidiary missions and made them available for the decisive point. In the latter case, for example, the cavalry's rendering unnecessary the diversion of a half-dozen divisions to the siege of Antwerp would have added significant depth, breadth, and impact to the Germans' extreme right wing.

Second, the German cavalry possessed the force structure of an effective, if relatively small, multimission-capable combined-arms team, able to both collect information and fight for it. Horsemen with some ability in dismounted fighting, artillery, machine guns and Jaeger battalions whose training emphasized marksmanship, skirmishing, and endurance demonstrated a flexibility in the August fighting that was often nullified by their limited strength. Had Schlieffen's allocation of cavalry divisions been implemented, opportunities would have been enhanced to surprise and confuse in those first weeks.[4]

Third, the opposition was not exactly characterized by effectiveness. The Belgian cavalry division was a force of civilians in comic-opera uniforms. The French cavalry was not accustomed to dismount and walk; the stench of Sordet's saddle-galled horses could be smelled before the troopers were seen. The British cavalry was the best of the lot, but shortcomings of command and control arguably brought it to the edge of disintegration in the war's first weeks. The Allied armies were vulnerable in other categories as well. Belgium's six divisions brought numbers to the field, but little in the way of effectiveness. The French left flank would have depended heavily on reservists in whom their own army had little confidence The BEF was still finding its feet—literally. Confederate General James Longstreet once described green troops as "as sensitive about the flanks as a virgin." Might German cavalry—employed properly and in strength—have contributed heavily to a catastrophic pattern of order–counterorder–disorder?

Conclusion

The intention of this work has been to present not alternate history but alternate contingencies—contingencies that, while possessing their own risks and shortcomings, offered better German results than those experienced in 1914. In any case, neither the immediate nor the ultimate outcome of the guns of August could have been worse for the Second Reich—or for Europe and the world.

Appendix: Peacetime Organization of the GGS as of May 1, 1914

Chief of General Staff: *Generaloberst von Moltke*
   First Adjutant: Major Tieschowitz von Tieschowa
   Second Adjutant: Hauptmann Köhler
   Central Department (administration and personnel issues) Head: Oberst von Fabeck
   Section IIIb (political issues, military intelligence) Head: Oberst von Bartenwerffer
   Sixth Department (*Kaisermanöver*) Head: not named

General Quartermaster (Generalquartiermeister): not named, later Generalleutnant von Stein
   Adjutant: not named

Senior Quartermaster (Oberquartiermeister) I: Generalleutnant Schmidt von Knobelsdorff
   Adjutant: Hauptmann Wahl
   Second Department (mobilization and deployment department) Head: Oberleutnant Tappen (following Oberst Ludendorff)
   Oberleutant Hentsch (joining July 1), Major Wetzell (joining August 1)
   Railroad Department Head: K. W. Oberleutnant Groener
   Section Ia (review of military transportation regulations)
   Fourth Department, merged with Seventh Department (foreign fortresses) Head: Oberst Buchholtz

Senior Quartermaster (Oberquartiermeister) II: Generalleutnant von Bertrab
   Adjutant: Major von Poncet
   Third Department (France including Marocco; England including Egypt; and Afghanistan) Head: Oberst von Kemnitz
   Ninth Department (Italy, Belgium, the Netherlands, Switzerland, Portugal, both Americas, and German colonies) Head: Oberst Bauer

Senior Quartermaster (Oberquartiermeister) III: Generalmajor (Georg) Graf von Waldersee
　　Adjutant: Hauptmann von Hammerstein-Equord
　　Fifth Department (training and operational studies) Head: Oberst von der Heyde
　　Eighth Department (War Academy and general staff service) Head: Oberleutnant von Winterfeldt

Senior Quartermaster (Oberquartiermeister) IV: Generalmajor von Kuhl
　　Adjutant: Hauptmann von Rundstedt
　　First Department (Russia, Nordic states, East Asia, Persia, and Turkey) Head: Oberst Graf von Posadowsky
　　Tenth Department (Austria-Hungary and the Balkan states) Head: not named

Senior Quartermaster (Oberquartiermeister) V: Generalmajor von Redern (following Generalleutnant von Freytag-Loringhoven)
　　Adjutant: Hauptmann Weyland
　　Military History Department I (contemporary military history starting from mid-nineteenth century) Head: K.W. Oberleutnant Renner
　　Military History Department II (older military history up to Napoleonic wars) Head: Generalmajor von Friedrich
　　Military Archive

Chief of Cartography (Chef Landesaufnahme): Oberst Weidner
　　Adjutant: not named
　　Trigonometrical Department (*Trigonometrische Abteilung*) Head: Oberleutnant Scherenberg
　　Topographical Department (*Topographische Abteilung*) Head: Oberleutnant Launhardt
　　Mapping Department (*Kartographische Abteilung*) Head: Oberleutnant Launhardt
　　Picture and Air Picture Library
　　Colonial Section[1]

Glossary of Terms and Abbreviations

Abteilung: Muti-use German word describing a company- or battalion-sized organization. In a German field artillery regiment, it is a battalion, not a section or detachment.

Albatros: Type of German aircraft.

Aufmarschanweisung: German deployment directives.

Aufmarschplan: German mobilization/deployment plan.

Auftragstaktik: German military philosophy to leave decisions to the subordinate comander.

BEF: British Expeditionary Force.

Denkschrift: German think piece.

Dragoner: German dragoons (a type of cavalry).

Exerzier-Reglement: German tactical drill manual.

FAR: *Feldartillerie Regiment*, German field artillery regiment.

FFA: *Feld-Flieger Abteilung*, German aircraft battalion.

FLA: *Feld-Luftschiffer Abteilung*, German field airship battalion (zeppelins).

francs-tireurs: From the French word for "free shooters," irregular military formations sometimes called guerrilla fighters.

Freiherr: German title of nobility equivalent to Baron.

Garde Civique: Belgian Civil (National) Guard.

Generalinspekteur: German inspector general.

Generalleutnant: German major general.

Generalmajor: German brigadier.

Generaloberst: Field marshal.

GGS: Great General Staff.

Gotha: Type of German aircraft.

Graf: German title of nobility equivalent to count or earl.

Glossary of Terms and Abbreviations

Hauptmann: Captain.

HKK: *Höherer Kavallerie Kommandeur*, in 1914 a cavalry organization. Not a corps; in 1915 named *Heereskavalleriekorps*.

HQ: Headquarter(s).

Jäger: German elite rifle-armed infantry trained to be more independent.

Landwehr: Third level of reserve service.

MG-Abt: *Maschinengewehr-Abteilung*, German machine-gun company.

NCO: Noncommissioned officer.

Oberleutnant: German First lieutenant.

Oberquartiermeister: Senior quartermaster.

Oberst: German colonel.

OHL: *Oberste Heeresleitung*, German Supreme Command.

Radfahrer: German bicyclist infantrymen.

Rittmeister: German cavalry rank of captain.

SHQ: Belgian Supreme Headquarters.

Taube: Type of German aircraft.

Vernichtungsschlacht: German leadership doctrine promoting a battle of annihilation.

Vize-feldwebel: German senior NCO rank equivalent to staff sergeant.

Chapter Notes

Preface

1. Terence Zuber, *The Mons Myth: A Reassessment of the Battle* (Stroud, UK: History Press, 2011), 269.

Introduction

1. Frank Buchholz, Joe Robinson, and Janet Robinson, *The Great War Dawning: Imperial Germany and its Army at the Start of World War One* (Vienna: Verlag-Militaria, 2013).
2. Joe Robinson, Francis Hendricks, and Janet Robinson, *The Last Great Cavalry Charge: The Battle of the Silver Helmets, Halen, 12 August 1914* (Millview, UK: Fonthill Media, 2015).
3. Gerhart P. Gross, "There was a Schlieffen Plan: New Sources on the History of German Military Planning," in *The Schlieffen Plan: International Perspectives on the German Strategy for World War I*, eds. Hans Ehlert, Michael Epkanhans, and Gerhart P. Gross, trans. David T. Zabecki (Lexington: University Press of Kentucky, 2014), 114.

Chapter 1

1. Jay M. Shafritz, *Words on War: Military Quotations from Ancient Times to the Present* (New York: Prentice-Hall, 1990), 363.
2. Carl von Clausewitz, *On War*, trans. Michael Howard and Peter Paret (Princeton: Princeton University Press, 1989), 132, 177.
3. Gerhard P. Gross, *The Myth and Reality of German Warfare: Operational Thinking from Moltke the Elder to Heusinger* (Lexington: University Press of Kentucky, Kindle ed., 2016), 5–10.
4. Dennis Showalter, *Instrument of War: The German Army 1914–18* (London: Bloomsbury, Kindle ed., 2017), loc. 562–63. Moltke ordered the *Ostaufmarsch* to be tabled but not abandoned; no longer updated, but preserved for implementation.
5. Annika Mombauer, "The Moltke Plan: A Modified Schlieffen Plan with Identical Aims?" in *The Schlieffen Plan: International Perspectives on the German Strategy for World War I*, eds. Hans Ehlert, Michael, Epkanhans, and Gerhart P. Gross, trans. David T. Zabecki (Lexington: University Press of Kentucky, 2014), 50–51.
6. Holger H. Herwig, *The First World War: Germany and Austria Hungary, 1914–1918* (London: Arnold, 1997), 46–49.
7. Dennis Showalter, "From Deterrence to Doomsday Machine: The German Way of War, 1890–1914," *Journal of Military History* 64, no. 3(2000): 679.
8. Terence Zuber, *Inventing the Schlieffen Plan* (New York: Oxford University Press, 2002).
9. Gross, "There was a Schlieffen Plan."
10. Hans Ehlert, Michael Epkanhans, and Gerhart P. Gross, eds., Appendix "Deployment Plans, 1893–1914" to *The Schlieffen Plan: International Perspectives on the German Strategy for World War I*, trans. David T. Zabecki (Lexington: University Press of Kentucky, 2014), 424–35.
11. Sewell Tyng, *The Campaign of the Marne, 1914* (New York: Longmans, Green, 1935) e-book, 229–47. The five cavalry divisions in 1905 were increased to six in the deployment plan a year later.
12. Ehlert, Epkanhans, and Gross, "Deployment Plans," 424–35.
13. Herwig, *First World War*, 913–15.
14. Tyng, *Campaign of the Marne*, 282.
15. Annika Mombauer, "The Moltke Plan," 50.
16. Dietrich Gerhard E. T. Tappen, "Letter to the Reichsarchive," (Goslar, GE: 1930). Dietrich Gerhard Emil Theodor Tappen transferred from head of the Second Department to Chief of the Operations Department of the OHL upon mobilization. He was a confidant of Moltke.

17. Terence M. Holmes, "One Throw of the Gambler's Dice: A Comment on Holger Herwig's View of the Schlieffen Plan," *Journal of Military History* 67, no. 3 (2003): 513–6, doi: 10.1353/jmh.2003.0125.
18. Felicity Rash and Falco Pfalzgraph, eds., "Perspectives on the 'Great' War," in *Selected Papers from the World War I International Conference* (Queen Mary University of London, August 1–4, 2014), 55–63.
19. Clausewitz, *On War*, 90–91.
20. Freiherrn Paul von Troschke, *Geschichte des 1.Grossherzoglich Mecklenburgischen Dragoner Regiments Nr. 17* (Berlin: Verlag Bernard & Grase, 1938), Map 2.
21. Ehlert, Epkanhans, and Gross, "Deployment Plans," 427, maps.

Chapter 2

1. Peter G. Tsouras, *Warriors' Words: A Quotation Book: From Sesostris III to Schwarzkopf 1871 BC to AD 1991* (New York: Cassell, 1992), 59.
2. William Balck, *Tactics: Cavalry, Field and Heavy Artillery and Field Warfare*, trans. Walter Kruger, vol. 2. (Fort Leavenworth, KS: U.S. Cavalry Association, 1914), 3.
3. David R. Dorondo, *Riders of the Apocalypse* (Annapolis: Naval Institute Press, 2012), 29.
4. *Ibid.*, 49.
5. Generalinspektion der Kavallerie, *Gesichtspunkte für den Aufklärungsdienst nur für den Dienstgebrauch!* (Berlin: Reichsdruckerei, 1914), 10–13.
6. *Ibid.*, 52–56.
7. *Ibid.*, 16–20. Officer patrols were not considered efficient because they had found it difficult to deliver their reports in time during the 1905 reconnaissance exercise.
8. Maximillian von Poseck, *The German Cavalry 1914 in Belgium and France*, ed. Jerome Howe (Sandhurst, UK: Naval and Military Press, 2007/1921), 230.
9. *Ibid.*, 231.
10. Buchholz, Robinson, and Robinson, *Great War Dawning*, 154–55.
11. Dorondo, *Riders of the Apocalypse*, 40–49.
12. William Balck, *Tactics: Introduction and Formal Tactics of Infantry*, vol. 1. (Fort Leavenworth, KS: U.S. Cavalry Association, 1915), 243.
13. Dennis E. Showalter, "The Prussian Cavalry 1806–1871: The Search for Roles," *Militärgeschichtliche Zeitschrift* 19, no. 1 (1976): doi:10.1524/mgzs.1976.19.1.7.
14. Erich-Günter Blau, *Die operative Verwendung der Kavallerie im Welrkrieg, 1914–1918*, pt. 1, *Friedensvorbereitungen* (Munich: C. H. Becksche Verlagsbuchhandlung, 1934), 24.
15. *Ibid.*, 27, 33.
16. *Ibid.*, 31. Author's emphasis in italics.

17. Johannes Georg von der Marwitz, born July 7, 1856 in Stolp; died October 27, 1929 in Wundlichow. After being educated in the cadet corps, Marwitz joined the Second Garde Ulanen Regiment in Berlin as a Sekondelieutenant in 1875. He attended the War Academy from 1883 until 1886 and successfully graduated. Following a series of appointments alternating between command of troops and the General Staff, he became Commander of the Third Garde Ulanen Regiment in 1900. After five years as a regimental commander, he was selected as chief of General Staff to Eighteenth Army Corps in Frankfurt am Main in 1905. He later took command of First Guard Cavalry Brigade in Berlin and was promoted to Generalmajor in 1908. On March 2, 1911, Marwitz became Commander of Third Division in Stettin, and was promoted to Generalleutnant on March 20, 1911. On November 11, 1912, he became Inspector General (*Generalinspekteur*) of the Cavalry. In 1914, he was mobilized as Commander of HKK 2, responsible for the disastrous combat at Halen on August 12. On December 23, 1914, HKK 2 was disbanded and Marwitz became Commanding General of the newly formed Thirty-Eighth Reserve Corps on the eastern front. He successfully participated in the winter battle in Masuria with the corps.
18. Blau, *Die operative*, 35.
19. Hermann Cron, *Imperial German Army, 1914–1918* (Solihull, UK: Helion, 2002), 94.
20. Großer Generalstab, *Anhaltspunkte für den Generalstabsdienst* (Berlin: Reichsdruckerei, 1914).
21. Poseck, *German Cavalry*.
22. Generalinspektion, *Gesichtspunkte*, 4–5.
23. Zuber, *Mons Myth*, 76.
24. Erich W. L. von Tschischwitz, *General von der Marwitz* (Berlin: Steiniger Verlage, 1940), 17.
25. Some players were changed in accordance with the mobilization plan.
26. Fredrich von Rabenau, *Die deutsche Land und Seemacht und die Berufspflichten des Offiziers* (Berlin: E. S. Mittler & Sohn, 1914), 54.
27. Zuber, *Mons Myth*, 77.
28. Hans von Kuhl, *Der Marnefeldzug, 1914* (Berlin: E. S. Mittler & Sohn, 1921), 86.
29. Hermann von Kuhl and Walter Friedrich Adolf von Bergmann, *Movements and Supply of the German First Army during August and September 1914* (Fort Leavenworth, KS: Command and General Staff School Press, 1929), 10.
30. Martin van Creveld, *Supplying War: Logistics from Wallenstein to Patton* (Cambridge: Cambridge University Press, 1994) 127.
31. Arthur Brühe, "The Experiences of a Pasewalker: 'Königin' Kürassier on his Regiment's Ride Towards its First Defeat" (unpublished memoir, 1984), 14.

32. Hermann von Kuhl and Bergmann, *Movements and Supply*, 8.
33. *Ibid.*, 9–10.
34. Großer Generalstab, *Anhaltspunkte*, 94.
35. Hermann von Kuhl and Bergmann, *Movements and Supply*, 122.
36. *Ibid.*, 120–21.
37. H. J. Vanthuyne, *De dag dat Cavalerie voor 't laatst Storm reed: Halen, 12 augustus 1914* (Halen, BE: Museum Slag der Zilveren Helmen, 1984), 14.
38. *Ibid.*, 8.
39. Großer Generalstab, Kriegsgeschichtliche Abteilung I, *Moltke Militärische Werke*, vol. 4, Kriegslehren, pt. 1, "Die operativen Vorbereitungen zur Schlacht" (Berlin: E. S. Mittler & Sohn, 1911), 287–89.
40. Brühe, "Experiences of a Pasewalker," 18.
41. Creveld, *Supplying War*, 125–27.
42. Gross, *Myth and Reality*, 90.
43. John H. Morrow, Jr., *The Great War in the Air* (Washington, DC: Smithsonian Institute Press, 1993), 6–18.
44. *Ibid.*, 18–19.
45. *Ibid.*, 19–20.
46. James Corum and Richard R. Muller, *The Luftwaffe's Way of War: German Air Force Doctrine, 1911–1945* (Baltimore: Nautical and Aviation Publishing Company of America, 1988), 1 29.
47. *Ibid.*, 38–42.
48. John H. Morrow, Jr., *Building German Airpower, 1909–1914* (Knoxville: University of Tennessee Press, 1976), 72–85.
49. This is a confusing situation in the original text and language. When discussing *Feld-Flieger Abteilung* or FFA, we find *Abteilung* mobilizing *Abteilung*. To keep the hierarchy straight, the authors chose instead to use "battalion" and "company" to show the difference in hierarchy. This is not strictly correct but is easier to understand in the English language.
50. Ernest von Hoeppner, *Germany's War in the Air* (Nashville, TN: Battery Press, 1921), 7.
51. Kriegsgeschichtliche Abteilung der Luftwaffe, *Mobilmachung, Aufmarsch und erster Einsatz der deutschen Luftstreitkräfte im August 1914* (Berlin: E. S. Mittler Verlag, 1939), 105.
52. Hoeppner, *Germany's War*, 7–8.
53. Tyng, *Campaign of the Marne*, 848.
54. U.S. Cavalry Association, *Cavalry Combat* (Harrisburg, PA: Telegraph Press, 1937), 5.
55. Tage Carslward, *Strategic Signal Communications with the German Right Wing and Their Influence Upon the Results of the Battle of the Marne* (Stockholm: U.S. Army War College, 1927), 12.
56. *Ibid.*, 11.
57. *Ibid.*, 6–30.
58. *Ibid.*, 27.
59. Hermann von Kuhl and Walter Friedrich Adolf von Bergmann, *The Marne Campaign, 1914* (Fort Leavenworth, KS: Command and General Staff School Press, 1936), 32–35.
60. Holger H. Herwig, *The Marne, 1914* (New York: Random House e-book, 2009), 1001–7.
61. Carslward, *Strategic Signal*, 11.

Chapter 3

1. Shafritz, *Words on War*, 379.
2. Leon Van der Essen, *The Invasion and the War in Belgium* (London: T. Fisher Unwin, 1917), 39–45.
3. Jeff Lipkes, *Rehearsals: The German Army in Belgium, August 1914*, 2nd ed. (Leuven, BE: Brabant Press, 2014), 822–27.
4. Tyng, *Campaign of the Marne*, 1158.
5. Clayton Donnel, *Breaking the Fortress Line, 1914* (Barnsly, UK: Pen and Sword Military, 2013) 380–85.
6. Poseck, *German Cavalry*, 9–10.
7. Van der Essen, *Invasion and the War*, 45–49.
8. Tyng, *Campaign of the Marne*, 1158.
9. Donnel, *Breaking the Fortress Line*, 696–703.
10. Hew Strachan, *The First World War*, vol. 1, *To Arms* (New York: Oxford University Press, 2006), 216.
11. Lipkes, *Rehearsals*, 685–700.
12. Alexander von Kluck, *The March on Paris: The Memoirs of Alexander von Kluck, 1914–1918* (Chicago: Frontline, 2013/1923), 126.
13. *Ibid.*, 195.
14. Great General Staff, *The Battle of Mons*, trans. Robert Dunlop and Holger Puttkammer (Berlin, 1919), 12–13.
15. Kluck, *March on Paris*, 461.
16. Freiherrn Paul von Troschke, *Die deutsche Heerscavalrie am Entscheidungsflügel, 1914* (Berlin: Verlag Bernard & Grase 1940), 42.
17. Jan Joseph Godfried Baron von Voorst, *The Limburg Maneuver of August 1914* (Limburg, NL: A. W. Bruna and Son, 1919), 16–17.
18. Annika Mombauer, *Helmuth von Moltke and the Origins of the First World War* (Cambridge: Cambridge University Press, 2003), 91–94.
19. Voorst, *Limburg Maneuver*, 12. The five rail lines were: 1) Wesel–Kempen–Goch–Boxtel, Tilbourg, and the single track to Turnhout; 2) Crefeld–Kempen–Viersen–Kaldenkirchen–Venlo-Eindoven, and a single track to Hasselt; 3) Dahlheim–Roermond–Weert–Hamont; 4) Aachen–Maastricht–Hasselt; and 5) the more or less lateral route, Wesel–Venlo–Maastricht–Liège.
20. Maartje M. Abbeennhuis, *The Art of Staying Neutral: The Netherlands in the First*

World War, 1914–1918 (Amsterdam: Amsterdam University Press, 2006), 31–34.
  21. Mombauer, *Helmuth von Moltke*, 94–95.
  22. Jack Snyder, *The Ideology of the Offenses: Military Decision Making and the Disasters of 1914* (Ithaca, NY: Cornell University Press, 1984), 121.
  23. Kluck, *March on Paris*, 195.
  24. Showalter, *Instrument of War*, 554–58.
  25. Tyng, *Campaign of the Marne*, 80.
  26. Gross, "There Was a Schlieffen Plan," 87.
  27. D'état-major Collyns, "La Prise du Premier Drapeau Allemand," accessed March 24, 2016. http://www.arquebusiers.be/Prise-Drapeau-Allemand.htm.
  28. Werner M. Widder, "Auftragstaktik and Innere Führung: Trademarks of German Leadership," *Military Review* 82, no. 5 (2002): 3–9.
  29. Bundesminister der Verteidigung, *HDv 100/100 Truppenführung (TF)* (Bonn: MoD, 1987), 601–11, 711–16. (Similar in the updated 1998 edition).
  30. Michael Geyer, "German Strategy in the Age of Machine Warfare, 1914–1945," in *Makers of Modern Strategy: From Machiavelli to the Nuclear Age*, ed. Peter Paret (Princeton, NJ: Princeton University Press, 1984), 532; Jehuda Lothar Wallach, *Das Dogma der Vernichtungsschlacht* (Frankfurt: Bernard und Graefe Verlag, 1967).
  31. Clausewitz, *On War*, 84.
  32. Hugo von Freytag-Loringhoven, *Generalfeldmarschall Graf Alfred von Schlieffen: Gesammelte Schriften*, vol. 1 (Berlin: E. S. Mittler & Sohn, 1913), 27–30.
  33. Ibid., 30–259.
  34. Shafritz, *Words on War*, 120.
  35. Mark R. Stoneman, "Wilhelm Groener, Officering, and the Schlieffen Plan," (PhD dissertation, Georgetown University, 2006), 187.
  36. Mombauer, *Helmuth von Moltke*, 182–283.
  37. Herwig, *The Marne*, 902–3.
  38. Gross, *Myth and Reality*, 132.
  39. Herwig, *The Marne*, 341–42.
  40. Tyng, *Campaign of the Marne*, 312.
  41. Mombauer, "The Moltke Plan," 34.
  42. The general staff building was destroyed in 1945. Today, the Federal German Chancellery can be found at approximately the same location.
  43. Martin Kitchen, *The German Officer, 1890–1914* (Oxford, UK: Clarendon Press, 1968), 1.
  44. For example, *Vierteljahreshefte für Truppenführung und Heereskund*, a quarterly magazine on military leadership and military sciences, was published between 1904 and 1914.
  45. For example, *Kriegsgeschichtliche Einzelschriften*—studies on military history and *Studien zur Kriegsgeschichte und Taktik*—studies on military history and tactics, publications on the wars of Frederick the Great, the liberation wars, the wars of 1864, 1866, and 1870–1871, and "contemporary" wars.
  46. Stoneman, "Wilhelm Groener." The Railroad Department was one of the departments with the highest workload due to setting up the annual mobilization plan with its complex railroad timetable. However, it was less prestigious than departments dealing with operations, fortresses, and foreign countries. When Groener was assigned to the Railroad Department, he felt he had been shunted away from the center of power.
  47. Hugo Rochs, *Schlieffen: Ein Lebens, und Charakterbild für das deutsche Volk* (Berlin: Vossische Buchhandlung, 1921), 30.
  48. Hansgeorg Model, *Der deutsche Generalstabsoffizier* (Frankfurt: Bernard & Graefe Verlag, 1968), 12. Beginning around 1810, all brigades and fortress governors were assigned a permanent general staff officer who on one hand supported the commanding officer, but on the other hand acted as a kind of extension of the Berlin General Staff into all military formations.
  49. Mombauer, *Helmuth von Moltke*, 34–36.
  50. Kitchen, *German Officer*, 6.
  51. Mombauer, *Helmuth von Moltke*, 94.
  52. James Edmonds, *British Official History*, vol. 1 (London: McMillan, 1922), 42.
  53. Reichsarchiv, *Der Weltkrieg, 1914–1918*, vol. 1, *Die Grenzschlachten im Westen* (Berlin: E. S. Mittler & Sohn, 1925), 667.
  54. Donnell, *Breaking the Fortress Line*, 395–98.
  55. Voorst, *Limburg Maneuver*, 11–12.
  56. Three railway bridges now cross the Meuse in the Liège area, but in 1914 there were only two (the third not having been built until 1939).
  57. Snyder, *Ideology*, 152–53.
  58. Ehlert, Epkanhans, and Gross, "Deployment Plans," 520–21.
  59. Ibid., 510.
  60. Herwig, *The Marne*, 43.
  61. Lipkes, *Rehearsals*, 828–29.
  62. Troschke, *Die deutsche Heerscavalrie*, 34–45.
  63. Buchholz, Robinson, and Robinson, *Great War Dawning*, chap. 11.
  64. Herwig, *The Marne*, 47.
  65. Eric Dorn Brose, *The Kaiser's Army* (New York: Oxford University Press, 2001), 154.
  66. Ibid., 152–53.
  67. Generalstab des Heeres 7 Ab., *Der Handstreich gegen Lüttich vom 3. Bis 7. August 1914* (Berlin: E. S. Mittler 1939), 1–2.
  68. Ibid., 3.
  69. Ibid.
  70. Strachan, *First World War*, 178.

71. Ibid.
72. Herwig, *The Marne*, 35.
73. Hans Delbrück, *History of the Art of War Within the Framework of Political History*, vol. 1 (Greenwood, CT: Greenwood Press, 1975), 319.
74. Gross, *Myth and Reality*, 130.
75. Hermann von Kuhl and Bergmann, *Movements and Supply*, 230.
76. Poseck, *German Cavalry*, 227.

Chapter 4

1. Clausewitz, *On War*, 607.
2. Gross, *Myth and Reality*, 130.
3. David Heal, *Victims Nonetheless: The Invasion of Luxembourg, 1914* (Kindle: 2010), 1139.
4. Ibid., 1436–39.
5. Zuber, *The Real German War Plan, 1904–14* (Stroud, UK: History Press, 2011), 157.
6. Donnel, *Breaking the Fortress Line*, 696–703.
7. Generalstab des Heeres, *Der Handstreich*, 1.
8. See the personal mobilization schedule of Oberst Marquard from July 31, 1914.
9. Reichsarchiv, *Der Weltkrieg, 1914–1918*, vol. 1, *Die Grenzschlachten im Westen* (Berlin: E. S. Mittler & Sohn, 1925), 34. These high-priority war transports required 1,440 standard military trains, of which 340 had to be integrated into the civilian timetable on the first mobilization day.
10. Herwig, *The Marne*, 458–59.
11. Ibid., 392–401.
12. Lipkes, *Rehearsals*, 324–37.
13. Ehlert, Epkanhans, and Gross, "Deployment Plans," 519–20.
14. Lipkes, *Rehearsals*, 376.
15. Ibid., 159–61.
16. Tyng, *Campaign of the Marne*, 1158.
17. Herwig, *The Marne*, 48.
18. Burt Estes Howard, *The German Empire* (London: Macmillan, 1906), Appendix A, 431.
19. Ibid., 36–37.
20. Hans von Kuhl, *Der Marnefeldzug*, 8–14.
21. Ibid., 384–86.
22. Ibid., 387–92.
23. Herwig, *The Marne*, 36.
24. Reichsarchiv, *Der Weltkrieg, Das deutsche*, 26. After the start of the war, it was decided that a significant reduction in the length of the standard military train would achieve a higher level of flexibility.
25. Stoneman, "Wilhelm Groener," 173.
26. Gross, *Myth and Reality*, 131.
27. Generalstab des Heeres, *Der Handstreich*, 4.
28. Heal, *Victims Nonetheless*, 2202–11.
29. Ibid.
30. Herwig, *The Marne*, 21.
31. Zuber, *Real German War Plan*, 157.
32. Generalstab des Heeres, *Der Handstreich*, 5.
33. Hubert Heebouw, *Le réseau ferroviaire liégeois, enjeu de la bataille de Liège en 1914*, accessed April 10, 2016, http://hachhachhh.blogspot.be/2014/08/le-reseau-ferroviaire-liegeois-enjeu-de.html.
34. Verein der Offiziere des Kgl. Prussichen Jäger Bn. no.7, *Der Kgl. Prussichen (Westfäliche) Jäger Bn. no.7 im Weltkeig 1914–1918* (Berlin: Verlag Richard Stalling, 1929).
35. Vanthuyne, *De dag dat Cavalerie*, 13.
36. *De Prins* (Amsterdam: N. J. Boon, August 15, 1914), 100.
37. Heebouw, *Le réseau*.
38. Ibid.
39. Ibid.
40. Ibid.

Chapter 5

1. Tsouras, *Warriors' Words*, 110
2. Troschke, *Die deutsche Heerscavalrie*, 41.
3. Lipkes, *Rehearsals*, 541–51.
4. Herwig, *The Marne*, 109.
5. Kriegsgeschichtliche Abteilung der Luftwaffe, *Mobilmachung*, 12.
6. Van der Essen, *Invasion and the War*, 105–6.
7. Poseck, *German Cavalry*, 10.
8. Many sources used the title Division Garnier used instead of Fourth Cavalry Division. Garnier was Commander of Fourth Cavalry Division. This force had attachments that included a Jäger company of Ninth Jäger Battalion, Bicycle Company of Ninth Jäger Battalion, and some engineers. Garnier was also appointed over some of the elements of Second Cavalry Division.
9. Verein der Offiziere, *des Kgl. Prussichen*, 3.
10. Poseck, *German Cavalry*, 10–11.
11. Curt Badinski, *Erinnerungsblätter des Jäger-Feld-Bataillons Nr. 9. Weltkrieg, 1914–1918. Bd. 1* (Ratzeburg, GE: Lauenburgischer Heima tverlag, H. H. C. Freystatatzky's Buchdruckerei, 1932), 46–50.
12. Edmund Dane, *Hacking through Belgium* (London: Hodder and Stroughton, 1914), 25.
13. Troschke, *Die deutsche Heerscavalrie*, 42–43.
14. Troschke, *Die deutsche Heerscavalrie*, 42–43.
15. *De Prins*, 77.
16. Brühe, "Experiences of a Pasewalker," 14.
17. Verein des Großherzoglich Mecklenburgischen Fusilier-Regiments Nr. 90, *Kriegsgeschichte des Großherzoglich Mecklenburgis-*

chen Fusilier-Regiments Nr. 90 Kaiser Wilhelm, 1914–1918 (Pommern, GE: Verlag Stolp, 1924), 12–15.
18. Generalstab des Heeres, *Der Handstreich*, 5.
19. Freiherr von Rind Valdenstein, *Das Infanterie Regiment Freiherr von Sparr (3. Westfälisches) Nr. 16.* (Oldenburg, GE: Druck und Verlag von Gerhard Stalling, 1927), 17.
20. H. Voigt, *Geschichte des Fusilier-Regiments Generalfeldmarschall Prinz Albrecht von Preußen (Hann.) Nr. 73* (Berlin: Bernard & Graefe, 1938), 8.
21. Offiziere Verein Fusilier-Regiment Prinz Heinrich von Preußen (Brandenburgisches) Nr. 35, *Das Fusilier-Regiment Prinz Heinrich von Preußen (Brandenburgisches) Nr. 35 im Weltkrieg* (Berlin: Verlag Kolk, 1929), 2–7.
22. Claus Just von Lattorff, *Kriegsgeschichtedes Brandenburgische Jäger-Bataillon Nr. 3* (Berlin: Verlag Deutsche Jäger Bund, 1940), 15–24.
23. Terence Zuber, *Ten Days in August* (Stroud, UK: History Press, 2014), 1662–64.
24. Voigt, *Geschichte*.
25. Troschke, *Die deutsche Heerscavalrie*, 43.
26. *Ibid.*, 53.
27. Generalstab des Heeres, *Der Handstreich*, 6.
28. Herwig, *The Marne*, 109–10.
29. *Ibid.*, 112.
30. Brose, *Kaiser's Army*, 188.
31. *De Prins*, 80.
32. Generalstab des Heeres, *Der Handstreich*, 7.
33. Troschke, *Die deutsche Heerscavalrie*, 44.
34. *Ibid.*, 46.
35. Troschke, *Die deutsche Heerscavalrie*, 44.
36. Verein der Offiziere, *Der Kgl. Prussichen*, 25–26.
37. Reichsarchiv, *Die Grenzschlachten*, 111.
38. Generalstab des Heeres, *Der Handstreich*, 9.
39. Adolph Hüttman, *Das Infantrie Regiment von Lützow No. 25 im Weltkrieh 19141918* (Berlin: Verlag Tradition Wilhelm Kols, 1929), 5–7.
40. Generalstab des Heeres, *Der Handstreich*, 10.
41. *Ibid.*
42. Gabrial, *Hannoversche Infanterie-Regiment 74.* (n.d.), 23–30.
43. *Ibid.*, Map 3.
44. *Ibid.*, 34–50.
45. Troschke, *Die deutsche Heerscavalrie*, 43.
46. Herwig, *The Marne*, 108–109.
47. *Ibid.*, 79. See also John Horne and Alan Kramer, *German Atrocities, 1914: A History of Denial* (New Haven, CT: Yale University Press, 2001).
48. Horne and Kramer, *German Atrocities*, 142–43.
49. Kriegsministerium, *Felddienst-Ordnung* (Berlin: E. S. Mittler & Sohn, 1908). The Bavarian Army adopted this issue into the field manual in 1914.
50. Horne and Kramer, *German Atrocities*, 143–49.
51. *Ibid.*, 149–51.
52. Zuber, *Ten Days*, 1834–42.
53. Lattorff, *Kriegsgeschichtedes*, 15–24.
54. Much of this information comes from Horne and Kramer, *German Atrocities*, which is considered the definitive source on German atrocities, despite a few typographical errors concerning the units in the chart on page 435. Researchers should be able to work their way through with little difficulty, but the printed word cannot be accepted carte blanche.
55. Horne and Kramer, *German Atrocities*, 9–23, 435.
56. Lipkes, *Rehearsals*, 141–49.
57. U.S. Cavalry Association, *Cavalry Combat*, 435–38.
58. *Ibid.*, 21–26.
59. Kriegsgeschichtliche, *Mobilmachung*, 13.
60. Donnel, *Breaking the Fortress Line*, 713.
61. Hermann von Kuhl and Bergmann, *Marne Campaign*, 47, 48.
62. Gerhard Wanner, *Die deutsche Stahlrohrlanze* (Reutlingen, GE: Steinach-Verlag, 2005), 5.
63. Heribert von Larisch, *Das Dragoner Regiment number 18* (Oldenburg, GE: Verlag Gerhard Stalling, 1924), 15–19.
64. P. Loodts, "Le sergent van Espen fait 38 prisonniers à Waremme," accessed March 17, 2014, http://www.1914-1918.be/sergent_van_espen_en_chasse.php.
65. *De Prins*, 80. Moving westwards on Voerenstraat, the caption reads, "Lieutenant Sanders, liaison officer, is moving by car from the front to the headquarters—it is clearly visible that the shiny helmets of the Kürassiere that accompany him have been covered with grey fabric. Officer and soldiers are driving through enemy territory with their finger on the trigger." The people in the back are standing on the Dutch border alongside the road; the light colored conical border marker #35 is visible just behind the leftmost civilian. Today, this looks exactly the same—the road, slightly elevated field, and border marker.
66. Buchholz, Robinson, and Robinson, *Great War Dawning*, 362–64.
67. Wanner, *Die deutsche Stahlrohrlanze*, 5.
68. Zuber, *Ten Days*, 2953–84.
69. Troschke, *Die deutsche Heerscavalrie*, 47.
70. Verein der Offiziere, *Der Kgl. Prussichen*, 24–26.
71. Troschke, *Die deutsche Heerscavalrie*, 52.
72. Verein der Offiziere, *Der Kgl. Prussichen*, 16–21.

73. Zuber, *Ten Days*, 3076–95.
74. Valdenstein, *Das Infanterie*, 17–21.
75. Hüttman, *Das Infanterie Regiment*, 5–7.
76. Zuber, *Ten Days*, 3718–845.
77. Ibid., 3845–58.
78. Carslward, *Strategic Signal*, 42–43.
79. Troschke, *Die deutsche Heerscavalrie*, 54.
80. Valdenstein, *Das Infanterie*, 17–21.
81. Tyng, *Campaign of the Marne*, 1245.
82. Reichsarchiv, *Die Grenzschlachten*, 121.
83. Jacques Francois, "Chronique de Waremme," 30 November 2013, accessed May 16, 2014, http://www.chronique-waremme.be/category/militaire/fait-de-guerre/.
84. Kriegsgeschichtliche, *Mobilmachung*, 12–17.

Chapter 6

1. Shafritz, *Words on War*, 387.
2. Showalter, *Instrument of War*, 970–72.
3. Valdenstein, *Das Infanterie*, 17–21.
4. Zuber, *Real German War Plan*, 164.
5. Carslward, *Strategic Signal*, 43.
6. Troschke, *Die deutsche Heerscavalrie*, 58.
7. Carslward, *Strategic Signal*, 44.
8. Tyng, *Campaign of the Marne*, 1267.
9. Marschall von Bieberstein, *Lüttich-Namur* (Oldenburg, GE: Stalling, 1918), 42–44.
10. Lipkes, *Rehearsals*, 872–78.
11. Carslward, *Strategic Signal*, 49.
12. Troschke, *Die deutsche Heerscavalrie*, 61.
13. Kriegsgeschichtliche, *Mobilmachung*, 12–17.
14. Troschke, *Die deutsche Heerscavalrie*, 62–64.
15. U.S. Cavalry Association, *Cavalry Combat*, 431.
16. Ibid., 437.
17. Tyng, *Campaign of the Marne*, 1267.
18. Strachan, *First World War*, 206.
19. Kriegsgeschichtliche, *Mobilmachung*, 12–17.
20. Brühe, "Experiences of a Pasewalker," 15–16.
21. U.S. Cavalry Association, *Cavalry Combat*, 437–38.
22. Zuber, *Ten Days*, 5068–76.
23. Kluck, *March on Paris*, 475–88.
24. U.S. Cavalry Association, *Cavalry Combat*, 18–20.
25. Kluck, *March on Paris*, 475–88.
26. Troschke, *Die deutsche Heerscavalrie*, 60–61.
27. U.S. Cavalry Association, *Cavalry Combat*, 105–6.
28. Kluck, *March on Paris*, 505–11.
29. Kriegsgeschichtliche, *Mobilmachung*, 12–17.
30. Poseck, *German Cavalry*, 17–21, 42.
31. Brühe, "Experiences of a Pasewalker," 20.
32. Troschke, *Die deutsche Heerscavalrie*, 67.
33. Heinz Guderian, *Erinnerungen eines Soldaten* (Heidelberg: Kurt Vowinckel Verlag, 1951), 26.
34. Kluck, *March on Paris*, 553–61.
35. Buchholz, Robinson, and Robinson, *Great War Dawning*, 362–64.
36. Vanthuyne, *De dag dat Cavalerie*, 6.

Chapter 7

1. Tsouras, *Warriors' Words*, 333.
2. Kriegsgeschichtliche, *Mobilmachung*, 12–17, recorded as "Huy."
3. Ibid., 12–17.
4. See Robinson, Hendriks, and Robinson, *Last Great Cavalry Charge*, for an in-depth English-language treatment of the battle.
5. Brühe, "Experiences of a Pasewalker," 6–7.
6. Troschke, *Die deutsche Heerscavalrie*, 81.
7. Robinson, Hendriks, and Robinson, *Last Great Cavalry Charge*, 114.
8. U.S. Cavalry Association, *Cavalry Combat*, 439–40.
9. U.S. Cavalry Association, *Cavalry Combat*, 439–40.
10. Kluck, *March on Paris*, 548–53.
11. Hermann von Kuhl and Bergmann, *Movements and Supply*, 18–25.
12. Peter Hart, *Fire and Movement: The British Expeditionary Force and the Campaign of 1914* (Oxford: Oxford University Press, 2015), 62.
13. Edward Spears, *Liaison 1914: A Narrative of the Great Retreat* (London: Cassel, 2000), 31.
14. Kluck, *March on Paris*, 553–61.
15. Matt Bowden, *The Great War's Finest* (vol. 1), *An Operational History of the German Air Service* (Reno, NV: Aeronaut Books, 2017), 143.
16. Kriegsgeschichtliche, *Mobilmachung*, 12–17.
17. Alexander von Kluck, *Der Marsch auf Paris und die Schlact am Ourcq* (Berlin: Walter de Gruyter, 1926), 23.
18. Kluck, *March on Paris*, 553–61.
19. Larisch, *Dragoner Regiment 18*.
20. Kluck, *March on Paris*, 578–82.
21. Kriegsgeschichtliche, *Mobilmachung*, 12–17.
22. Kluck, *March on Paris*, 582–90.

Chapter 8

1. Shafritz, *Words on War*, 386.
2. Zuber, *Ten Days*, 5927–32.
3. Hermann von Kuhl and Bergmann, *Marne Campaign*, 26–29.

4. Troschke, *Die deutsche Heerscavalrie*, 80.
5. Kluck, *March on Paris*, 590–94.
6. *Ibid.*, 595–99.
7. Herwig, *The Marne*, 2291–96.
8. Kluck, *Der Marsch auf Paris*, 26–27.
9. Poseck, *German Cavalry*, 31.
10. This comes from a technique used to catch cattle known as *snubbing*. American cowboys would get a cow to freeze in place by sticking their fingers up the cow's nose and pulling back.
11. Hermann von Kuhl and Bergmann, *Marne Campaign*, 30–31.
12. Großer Generalstab, *Anhaltspunkte*, 14.
13. Kluck, *March on Paris*, 613–29.
14. Hermann von Kuhl and Bergmann, *Movements and Supply*, 95.
15. Hermann von Kuhl and Bergmann, *Marne Campaign*, 35.
16. *Ibid.*, 34–35.
17. Kluck, *March on Paris*, 642–46.
18. William D. O'Neill, *The Plan That Broke the World: The Schlieffen Plan and World War I (What Were They Thinking?)* (Author, 2014), 134–35.
19. Clausewitz, *On War*, 263–72.
20. Gross, *Myth and Reality*, 35.
21. Kluck, *March on Paris*, 665–82.
22. Poseck, *German Cavalry*, 33.
23. Kluck, *March on Paris*, 689–93.
24. *Ibid.*, 126.
25. Hermann von Kuhl and Bergmann, *Marne Campaign*, 39.
26. Morrow, *Building German Airpower*.
27. Creveld, *Supplying War*, 125.
28. Poseck, *German Cavalry*, 47.
29. Hermann von Kuhl and Bergmann, *Marne Campaign*, 39.
30. Hermann von Kuhl and Bergmann, *Movements and Supply*, ix.
31. Zuber, *Mons Myth*, 103.

Chapter 9

1. Tsouras, *Warriors' Words*, 161–162.
2. Poseck, *German Cavalry*, 47–48; Ian Senior, *Home Before the Leaves Fall* (Oxford, UK: Osprey, 2012), 72.
3. Friedrich von Bernhardi, *Germany and the Next War*, trans. Allen H. Powles (New York: Longman, Green, 1914), 29.
4. Poseck, *German Cavalry*, 48–49.
5. According to the war dairy of Höheres Kavalleriekommando (HKK) 1.
6. U.S. Cavalry Association, *Cavalry Combat*, 108.
7. Troschke, *Die deutsche Heerscavalrie*, 85–86.
8. Kluck, *Der Marsch auf Paris*, 34–35.
9. Zuber, *Mons Myth*, 115.
10. Poseck, *German Cavalry*, 36.
11. von Gonnermann, "Aufklärung vor der Heeresfront," *Militär Wochenblatt* (July 23, 1937).
12. Great General Staff, *Battle of Mons*, 15.
13. *Ibid.*
14. Hermann von Kuhl and Bergmann, *Marne Campaign*, 41–42.
15. Kluck, *March on Paris*, 708–10.
16. Gerhardt Himmelmann, "Another Field," accessed November 3, 2016, http://unaltrocampo.blogspot.com/2014/08/two-german-zeppelins-shot-down.html.
17. Poseck, *German Cavalry*, 37.
18. Great General Staff, *Battle of Mons*, 16.
19. Hermann von Kuhl and Bergmann, *Marne Campaign*, 40–43.
20. *Ibid.*, 40–46.
21. *Ibid.*, 43–44.
22. *Ibid.*, 44–45.
23. *Ibid.*, 49.
24. *Ibid.*, 49–50.
25. *Ibid.*, 45.
26. Gonnermann, "Aufkärung."
27. Hermann von Kuhl and Bergmann, *Movements and Supply*, 96.
28. Gonnermann, "Aufklärung."
29. Poseck, *German Cavalry*, 33–37, 48–49.
30. Troschke, *Die deutsche Heerscavalrie*, 86.
31. Bowden, *Great War's Finest*, 122–125.
32. Hermann von Kuhl and Bergmann, *Marne Campaign*, 50–51.
33. Hans von Kuhl, *Armeeoberkommando 1, Kreigstagbuch v. 2.0.-20.10.1914* (1914/1935), August 3–22.
34. Hermann von Kuhl and Bergmann, *Marne Campaign*, 50–53.
35. This has proven a difficult location to track down. Finding definitive locations seems to be elusive in this case, but the name appears to be synonymous with Hainaut province.
36. Gonnermann, "Aufklärung."
37. Troschke, *Die deutsche Heerscavalrie*, 86–87. Details according to the War Diary of the HKK 2.
38. Troschke, *Die deutsche Heerscavalrie*, 88.
39. *Ibid.*, 92.
40. Hans von Kuhl, *Armeeoberkommando 1*, August 23.
41. *Ibid.*, 81–82.
42. Troschke, *Die deutsche Heerscavalrie*, 93.
43. Great General Staff, *Battle of Mons*, 16.
44. Hermann von Kuhl and Bergmann, *Movements and Supply*, 25–26.
45. Troschke, *Die deutsche Heerscavalrie*, 87.

Conclusion

1. Tsouras, *Warriors' Words*, 127.
2. Dominic D. P. Johnson and Dominic Tierney, "The Rubicon Theory of War: How the

Path to Conflict Reaches the Point of No Return," *International Security*, 36 (2011): 7–40.

3. Gerhad Ritter, The Schleiffen Plan (London: Oswald Wollf, 1958), 165.

4. Nikolas Gardner, "Command and Control in the "Great Retreat" of 1914: The Disintegration of the British Cavalry Division," *Journal of Military History* 63 (1999): 29–54.

Appendix

1. Frank Buchholz, "Gab es einen Schlieffenplan?" *Gessellschaft für Heereskunde* (Bundesarchiv/Militärarchiv PH 3/124, 2009). Compare with J. von Pflugk-Hartung, *Die Heere und Flotten der Gegenwart, Band I Deutschland* (Berlin: Verlag Schall & Grund, 1896), 77–79 for the organization of the General Staff in the 1890s. See also Wiegand Schmidt-Richberg, "Die Regierungszeit Wilhelms II," in *Handbuch zur deutschen Militärgeschichte 1648–1939*, ed. Militärgeschichtliches Forschungsamt (Munich: Bernard & Graefe Verlag, 1979), 70. Due to confidentiality reasons, the Rangliste did not reflect the organization of the GGS in as much detail as it did the organization of the War Ministry.

Bibliography

Abbeennhuis, Maartje M. *The Art of Staying Neutral: The Netherlands in the First World War, 1914–1918.* Amsterdam: Amsterdam University Press, 2006.
Badinski, Curt. *Erinnerungsblätter des Jäger-Feld-Bataillons Nr.9. Weltkrieg 1914–1918. Bd. 1.* Ratzeburg, GE: Lauenburgischer Heimatverlag, H. H. C. Freystatatzky's Buchdruckerei, 1932.
Balck, William. *Tactics: Cavalry, Field, and Heavy Artillery and Field Warfare.* Translated by Walter Kruger, vol. 2. Fort Leavenworth, KS: US Cavalry Association, 1914.
_____. *Tactics: Introduction and Formal Tactics of Infantry,* vol. 1. Fort Leavenworth, KS: US Cavalry Association, 1915.
Bernhardi, Friedrich von. *Germany and the Next War.* Translated by Allen H. Powles. New York: Longman, Green, 1914.
Bieberstein, Marschall von. *Lüttich–Namur.* Oldenburg, GE: Stalling, 1918.
Blau, Erich-Günter. *Die operative Verwendung der Kavallerie im Welrkrieg 1914–1918,* pt. 1, *Friedensvorbereitungen.* Munich: C. H. Becksche Verlagsbuchhandlung, 1934.
Bowden, Matt. *The Great War's Finest* (vol. 1), *An Operational History of the German Air Service.* Reno, NV: Aeronaut Books, 2017.
Brose, Eric Dorn. *The Kaiser's Army.* New York: Oxford University Press, 2001.
Brühe, Arthur. "The Experiences of a Pasewalker 'Königin' Kürassier on His Regiment's Ride Towards its First Defeat" (unpublished memoir), 1984.
Buchholz, Frank. "Gab es einen Schlieffenplan?" *Gessellschaft für Heereskunde.* Bundesarchiv/Militärarchiv PH 3/124, 2009.
Buchholz, Frank, Joe Robinson, and Janet Robinson. *The Great War Dawning: Imperial Germany and Its Army at the Start of World War One.* Vienna: Verlag-Militaria, 2013.
Bundesminister der Verteidigung. *HDv 100/100 Truppenführung (TF).* Bonn: MoD, 1987.
Carslward, Tage. *Strategic Signal Communications with the German Right Wing and Their Influence upon the Results of the Battle of the Marne.* Stockholm: US Army War College, 1927.
Clausewitz, Carl von. *On War.* Translated by Michael Howard and Peter Paret. Princeton: Princeton University Press, 1989.
Collyns, Charles. "La Prise du Premier Drapeau Allemand." Accessed March 24, 2016. http://www.arquebusiers.be/Prise-Drapeau-Allemand.htm.
Corum, James, and Richard R. Muller. *The Luftwaffe's Way of War: German Air Force Doctrine, 1911–1945.* Baltimore: Nautical and Aviation Publishing Company of America, 1998.
Creveld, Martin van. *Supplying War: Logistics from Wallenstein to Patton.* Cambridge: Cambridge University Press, 1994.
Cron, Hermann. *Imperial German Army, 1914–1918.* Solihull, UK: Helion, 2002.
Dane, Edmond. *Hacking through Belgium.* London: Hodder and Stoughton, 1914.
De Prins. Amsterdam: N. J. Boon, August 15, 1914.
Delbrück, Hans. *History of the Art of War Within the Framework of Political History,* vol. 1. Greenwood, CT: Greenwood Press, 1975.

Donnel, Clayton. *Breaking the Fortress Line, 1914*. Barnsly, UK: Pen and Sword Mlitary, 2013.
Dorondo, David R. *Riders of the Apocalypse*. Annapolis: Naval Institute Press, 2012.
Edmonds, James. *British Official History*, vol. 1. London: Macmillan, 1922.
Ehlert, Hans, Michael Epkanhans, and Gerhart P. Gross, eds. Appendix "Deployment Plans, 1893–1914" to *The Schlieffen Plan: International Perspectives on the German Strategy for World War I*. Translated by David T. Zabecki. Lexington: University Press of Kentucky, 2014.
François, Jacques. "Chronique de Waremme," 30 November 2013. Accessed May 16, 2014. http://www.chronique-waremme.be/category/militaire/fait-de-guerre/.
Freytag-Loringhoven, Hugo von. *Generalfeldmarschall Graf Alfred von Schlieffen: Gesammelte Schriften*, vol. 1. Berlin: E. S. Mittler & Sohn, 1913.
Gabrial, Mark. *Hannoversche Infanterie-Regiment 74*, n.d.
Gardner, Nikolas. "Command and Control in the 'Great Retreat' of 1914: The Disintegration of the British Cavalry Division." *Journal of Military History* 63 (1999): 29–54.
Generalinspektion der Kavallerie. *Gesichtspunkte für den Aufklärungsdienst nur für den Dienstgebrauch!* Berlin: Reichsdruckerei, 1914.
Generalstab des Heeres 7 Ab. *Der Handstreich gegen Lüttich vom 3. Bis 7. August 1914*. Berlin: E. S. Mittler, 1939.
Geyer, Michael. "German Strategy in the Age of Machine Warfare, 1914–1945." In *Makers of Modern Strategy: From Machiavelli to the Nuclear Age*, edited by Peter Paret. Princeton: Princeton University Press, 1984.
Gonnermann, von. "Aufklärung vor der Heeresfront." *Militär Wochenblatt*, 23 July 1937.
Great General Staff. *The Battle of Mons*. Translated by Robert Dunlop and Holger Puttkammer. Berlin: 1919.
Gross, Gerhard P. *The Myth and Reality of German Warfare: Operational Thinking from Moltke the Elder to Heusinger*. Lexington: University Press of Kentucky. Kindle edition, 2016.
———. "There Was a Schlieffen Plan: New Sources on the History of German Military Planning." In *The Schlieffen Plan: International Perspectives on the German Strategy for World War I*, edited by Hans Ehlert, Michael Epkanhans, and Gerhart P. Gross, translated by David Zabecki, 85–136. Lexington: University Press of Kentucky, 2014.
Großer Generalstab. *Anhaltspunkte für den Generalstabsdienst*. Berlin: Reichsdruckerei, 1914.
Großer Generalstab, Kriegsgeschichtliche Abteilung I. *Moltke Militärische Werke*, vol. 4, *Kriegslehren*, pt. 1, "Die operativen Vorbereitungen zur Schlacht." Berlin: E. S. Mittler & Sohn, 1911.
Guderian, Heinz. *Erinnerungen eines Soldaten*. Heidelberg: Kurt Vowinckel Verlag, 1951.
Hart, Peter. *Fire and Movement: The British Expeditionary Force and the Campaign of 1914*. Oxford: Oxford University Press, 2015.
Heal, David. *Victims Nonetheless: The Invasion of Luxembourg, 1914*. Kindle edition, 2010.
Heebouw, Hubert. *Le réseau ferroviaire liègeois, enjeu de la bataille de Liège en 1914*. Accessed April 10, 2016. http://hachhachhh.blogspot.be/2014/08/le-reseau-ferroviaire-liegeois-enjeu-de.html.
Herwig, Holger H. *The First World War: Germany and Austria Hungary, 1914–1918*. London: Arnold, 1997.
———. *The Marne, 1914*. New York: Random House, e-book, 2009.
Himmelmann, Gerhardt. "Another Field." Accessed November 3, 2016. http://unaltrocampo.blogspot.com/2014/08/two-german-zeppelins-shot-down.html.
Hoeppner, Ernest von. *Germany's War in the Air*. Nashville, TN: Battery Press, 1921.
Holmes, Terence M. "One Throw of the Gambler's Dice: A Comment on Holger Herwig's View of the Schlieffen Plan." *Journal of Military History* 67, no. 3 (2003), 513–6. doi:10.1353/jmh.2003.0125.
Horne, John, and Alan Kramer. *German Atrocities, 1914: A History of Denial*. New Haven, CT: Yale University Press, 2001.
Howard, Burt Estes. *The German Empire*. London: Macmillan, 1906.
Hüttman, Adolph. *Das Infantrie Regiment von Lützow No. 25 im Weltkrieh 1914–1918*. Berlin: Verlag Tradition Wilhelm Kols, 1929.

Johnson, Dominic D. P., and Dominic Tierney. "The Rubicon Theory of War: How the Path to Conflict Reaches the Point of No Return." *International Security* 36, no. 1, 7–40.
Kitchen, Martin. *The German Officer, 1890–1914*. Oxford, UK: Clarendon Press, 1968.
Kluck, Alexander von. *The March on Paris: The Memoirs of Alexander von Kluck, 1914–1918*. Chicago: Frontline Books, 2013. First published 1923 by Edward Arnold.
———. *Der Marsch auf Paris und die Schlacht am Ourcq*. Berlin: Walter de Gruyter, 1926.
Kriegsgeschichtliche Abteilung der Luftwaffe. *Mobilmachung, Aufmarsch und erster Einsatz der deutschen Luftstreitkräfte im August 1914*. Berlin: E. S. Mittler Verlag, 1939.
Kriegsministerium. *Felddienst-Ordnung*. Berlin: E. S. Mittler & Sohn, 1908.
Kuhl, Hans von. *Armeeoberkommando 1, Kriegstagbuch v. 2.0.-20.10.1914*. Originally published in 1914 and copied in 1935.
———. *Der Marnefeldzug, 1914*. Berlin: E. S. Mittler & Sohn, 1921.
Kuhl, Hermann von, and Walter Friedrich Adolf von Bergmann. *The Marne Campaign, 1914*. Fort Leavenworth, KS: Command and General Staff School Press, 1936.
——— and ———. *Movements and Supply of the German First Army during August and September 1914*. Fort Leavenworth, KS: Command and General Staff School Press, 1929.
Larisch, Heribert von. *Das Dragoner Regiment number 18*. Oldenburg, GE: Verlag Gerhard Stalling, 1924.
Lattorff, Claus Just von. *Kriegsgeschichtedes Brandenburgische Jäger-Bataillon Nr. 3*. Berlin: Verlag Deutsche Jäger Bund, 1940.
Lipkes, Jeff. *Rehearsals: The German Army in Belgium, August 1914*. 2nd ed. Leuven, BE: Brabant Press, 2014.
Loodts, P. "Le sergent van Espen fait 38 prisonniers à Waremme." Accessed March 17, 2014, http://www.1914-1918.be/sergent_van_espen_en_chasse.php.
Model, Hansgeorg. *Der deutsche Generalstabsoffizier*. Frankfurt: Bernard & Graefe Verlag, 1968.
Mombauer, Annika. *Helmuth von Moltke and the Origins of the First World War*. Cambridge: Cambridge University Press. 2003.
———. "The Moltke Plan: A Modified Schlieffen Plan with Identical Aims?" In *The Schlieffen Plan: International Perspectives on the German Strategy for World War I*, edited by Hans Ehlert, Michael Epkanhans, and Gerhart P. Gross, translated by David T. Zabecki, 43–66. Lexington: University Press of Kentucky, 2014.
Morrow, John H., Jr. *Building German Airpower, 1909–1914*. Knoxville: University of Tennessee Press, 1976.
———. *The Great War in the Air*. Washington, D.C.: Smithsonian Institution Press, 1993.
Offiziere Verein Fusilier-Regiment Prinz Heinrich von Preußen (Brandenburgisches) Nr. 35. *Das Fusilier-Regiment Prinz Heinrich von Preußen (Brandenburgisches) Nr. 35 im Weltkrieg*. Berlin: Verlag Kolk, 1929.
O'Neill, William D. *The Plan That Broke the World: The Schlieffen Plan and World War I (What Were They Thinking?)*. Author, 2014.
Pflugk-Hartung, J. von. *Die Heere und Flotten der Gegenwart, Band I Deutschland*. Berlin: Verlag Schall & Grund, 1896.
Poseck, Maximillian von. *The German Cavalry 1914 in Belgium and France*. Edited by Jerome Howe. Sandhurst, UK: Naval and Military Press, 2007. Original work published 1921.
Rabenau, Fredrich von. *Die deutsche Land und Seemacht und die Berufspflichten des Offiziers*. Berlin: E. S. Mittler & Sohn, 1914.
Rash, Felicity, and Falco Pfalzgraph (eds.). "Perspectives on the 'Great' War." In *Selected Papers from the World War I International Conference, Queen Mary University of London*, August 1–4, 2014, 55–63.
Reichsarchiv. *Der Weltkrieg, 1914–1918*, vol. 1, *Die Grenzschlachten im Westen*. Berlin: E. S. Mittler & Sohn, 1925.
———. *Der Weltkrieg, 1914–1918. Das deutsche Feldeisenbahnwesen. Erster Band, Die Eisenbahnen zu Kriegsbeginn*. Berlin: E. S. Mittler & Sohn, 1928.
Ritter, Gerhard. *The Schlieffen Plan: Critique of a Myth*. London: Oswald Wolff, 1958.
Robinson, Joe, Francis Hendriks, and Janet Robinson. *The Last Great Cavalry Charge: The Battle of the Silver Helmets, Halen, 12 August 1914*. Millview, UK: Fonthill Media, 2015.

Rochs, Hugo. *Schlieffen: Ein Lebens, und Charakterbild für das deutsche Volk.* Berlin: Vossische Buchhandlung, 1921.
Schmidt-Richberg, Wiegand. "Die Regierungszeit Wilhelms II." In *Handbuch zur deutschen Militärgeschichte, 1648–1939,* edited by Militärgeschichtliches Forschungsamt. Munich: Bernard & Graefe Verlag, 1979.
Senior, Ian. *Home Before the Leaves Fall.* Oxford, UK: Osprey, 2012.
Shafritz, Jay M. *Words on War: Military Quotations from Ancient Times to the Present.* New York: Prentice-Hall, 1990.
Showalter, Dennis. "From Deterrence to Doomsday Machine: The German Way of War, 1890–1914." *Journal of Military History* 64, no. 3 (2000): 679–710.
──. *Instrument of War: The German Army 1914–18.* London: Bloomsbury, Kindle edition, 2017.
──. "The Prussian Cavalry 1806–1871: The Search for Roles." *Militärgeschichtliche Zeitschrift* 19, no. 1 (1976). doi:10.1524/mgzs.1976.19.1.7.
Snyder, Jack. *The Ideology of the Offenses: Military Decision Making and the Disasters of 1914.* Ithaca, NY: Cornell University Press, 1984.
Spears, Edward. *Liaison 1914: A Narrative of the Great Retreat.* London: Cassel, 2000.
Stoneman, Mark R. "Wilhelm Groener, Officering, and The Schlieffen Plan." PhD diss., Georgetown University, 2006.
Strachan, Hew. *The First World War,* vol. 1, *To Arms.* New York: Oxford University Press, 2001.
Tappen, Dietrich Gerhard E. T. "Letter to the Reichsarchive." Goslar, GE: 20 October, 1930.
Troschke, Freiherrn Paul von. *Die deutsche Heerscavalrie am Entscheidungsflügel, 1914.* Berlin: Verlag Bernard & Grase 1940.
──. *Geschichte des 1. Grossherzoglich Mecklenburgischen Dragoner Regiments Nr 17.* Berlin: Verlag Bernard & Grase, 1938.
Tschischwitz, Erich W. L. von. *General von der Marwitz.* Berlin: Steiniger Verlage, 1940.
Tsouras, Peter G. *Warrior's Words: A Quotation Book: From Sesostris III to Schwarzkopf 1871 BC to AD 1991.* New York: Cassell, 1992.
Tyng, Sewell. *The Campaign of the Marne, 1914.* New York: Longmans, Green, 1935, e-book.
U.S. Cavalry Association. *Cavalry Combat.* Harrisburg, PA: Telegraph Press, 1937.
Valdenstein, Freiherr Rind von. *Das Infanterie Regiment Freiherr von Sparr (3. Westfälisches) Nr. 16.* Oldenburg, GE: Druck & Verlag von Gerhard Stalling, 1927.
Van der Essen, Leon. *The Invasion and the War in Belgium.* London: T. Fisher Unwin, 1917.
Vanthuyne, H. J. *De dag dat Cavalerie voor 't laatst Storm reed: Halen, 12 augustus 1914.* Halen, BE: Museum Slag der Zilveren Helmen, 1984.
Verein der Offiziere des Kgl. Pruss. Jäger Bn. no.7. *Der Kgl. Prussichen (Westfälische) Jäger Bn. no.7 im Weltkeig, 1914–1918.* Berlin: Verlag Richard Stalling, 1929.
Verein des Großherzoglich Meckenlenburgischen Fusilier-Regiments Nr. 90. *Kriegsgeschichte des Großherzoglich Meckenlenburgischen Fusilier-Regiments Nr. 90 Kaiser Wilhelm, 1914–1918.* Pommern, GE: Verlag Stolp, 1924.
Voigt, H. *Geschichte des Fusilier-Regiments Generalfeldmarschall Prinz Albrecht von Prußen (Hann.) Nr. 73.* Berlin: Bernard & Graefe, 1938.
Voorst, Jan Joseph Godfried Baron von. *The Limburg Maneuver of August 1914.* Limburg, NL: A. W. Bruna and Son, 1919.
Wallach, Jehuda Lothar. *Das Dogma der Vernichtungsschlacht.* Frankfurt: Bernard & Graefe Verlag, 1967.
Wanner, Gerhard. *Die deutsche Stahlrohrlanze.* Reutlingen, GE: Steinach-Verlag, 2005.
Widder, Werner M. "Auftragstaktik and Innere Führung: Trademarks of German Leadership." *Military Review* 82, no. 5(2002, Sept–Oct):3–9.
Zuber, Terence. *Inventing the Schlieffen Plan.* New York: Oxford University Press, 2002.
──. *The Mons Myth: A Reassessment of the Battle.* Stroud, UK: History Press, 2010.
──. *The Real German War Plan, 1904–14.* Stroud, UK: History Press, 2011.
──. *Ten Days in August.* Stroud, UK: History Press, 2014.

Index

Numbers in **_bold italics_** indicate pages with illustrations

Aachen, GE 10, 41–42, 44, 47, 49, 57, 59–60, 65, 68, 71, 82, 84–85, 90, 92, 94–96, 100, 111, 126, 128, 135, 137, 145–47, 150–51; *see also* Aix-la-Chapelle, GE
Aarschot (Aerschot), BE 147, 157, 160–61
Abteilung 26–27, 36, 58, 90, 125, 141–42, 147, 192, 194
AEG (aircraft) 36, 40, 95
Aerschot, BE *see* Aarschot (Aerschot), BE
Air Fleet League 33
aircraft 20, 32–35, 52, 170
aircraft battalion *see* FFA
Aix-la-Chapelle, GE 44, 47, 135, 151; *see also* Aachen, GE
Albatros (aircraft) 20, **_32_**, 33, 35–36, 193
Albert I, King of Belgium 78–79
Alost, BE 170, 173
Alsace-Lorraine 2, 7, 72, 77, 106, 112, 170
Amay, BE 137
Amblève River 44
Anderlecht, BE 169
Andrée, Konrad, Hauptmann 171
Antwerp, BE 9, 41, 45, 47–50, 62, 73, 78–79, 84, 91, 99, 113, 123–25, 131, 133–34, 136–37, 140, 142, 153–57, 159–61, 164–65, 168–71, 173–74, 182, 187–88
The Ardennes 2, 7, 42, 44, 136, 175
Argenteau, BE 62, 84, 90, 92, 102, 135, 157
Argus (aircraft) **_32_**, 36
army corps 9, 14–15, 17, 20–21, 23–25, 27–30, 36, 38–39, 51, 58, 64–68, 72, 76, 79–80, 112, 121–22, 128, 137, 147, 156–60, 164, 168, 177, 182, 188
army HQ (headquarters) 19, 20, 27, 31, 37, 47–48, 120, 126–27, 150, 157, 161, 169–70, 177, 179, 181
Arnim, Major 117; *see also* Third Infantry Regiment (German)
artillery battery 26, 103, 144, 153

Artillery Inspection Commission 11
Artois, FR 80
Ath, BE 183
atrocity **_97_**, 106–10, **_111_**, 200n54
Audenarde (Audenard), BE 174, 179
Aufmarschanweisung 52–53, 193
Aufmarschplan 9, 53, 64, 193
Auftragstaktik 38, 53–54, 159, 161, 198, 193
Austria-Hungary 8, **_32_**, 74, 134, 170, 192
Aviatik (aircraft) **_32_**, 33, 35–36
aviation 4, 17, 19–21, **_32_**, 33–37, 121, 131–33, 137, 141–42, 147, 150, 158, 165, 170, 177, 179
Aviation Association 33
Ayeneux, BE 103

Baal, BE 62
Baelen, BE 109
Bandonvilliers, BE 171
Bartenwerffer, von (Oberst) 191
Bastogne, BE 136
Baudry (Captain) 44
Bauer (Oberst) 191
Baugnez, BE 83
Bavai, FR 177
Beaupain (Lieutenant) 44
Beeringen, BE 155–56
BEF *see* British Expeditionary Force (BEF)
Bergman, Walter Friedrich Adolf von (General) 72, 151, 196–97, 199–202
Berneau, BE 83, 100–102, 108
Bernhardi, Friedrich von 8, 167, 202
Bernissart, BE 175
Berthem, BE 161
Bethmann Hollweg, Theobald von (Chancellor) 55, 77, 82
Beverst, BE 157
Beyne-Heusay, BE 119–20
bicycle company 92, 95, 199n8

209

210   Index

bicyclist infantryman (Radfahrer) 101, 194
Bilsen, BE 157
Binche, BE 169, 174–75, 177, 180
biplane *see* aircraft
Birk, BE 135
Bismarck, Otto von 50, 143
Bissing, Moritz von (General), German governor 110
Bitburg, GE 131
bivouac 28, 30, 34, 82, 94–95, 130, 134, 137–38, 144–45, 168
Blegny (Blegney), BE 102, 109, 118
Bober (Oberst) 118
Bodecker, von (Rittmeister) 118, 145
Boehm (Rittmeister) 121, 125
Boehm-Bezing, von (Cavalry Captain) 113, 125
Boitsfort, BE 169
Bolland, BE 102
Borgloon, BE 130, 138, 157; *see also* Looz, BE
Boulogne, FR 173
Boutersem, BE 137
Boxtel, NE 197
Braine le Comte, BE 169
Bredow, Ferdinand von (General) 16, 68, 169
Brialmont, Henri (General) 42, 50, 159
bridge: 42, 44, 46, 48–49, 62, 65, 75, 78, 84, 88, **89**, 90–91, **97**, 99, 104–5, **111**, 118, 120, 135, 137, 195*n*56; pontoon 51, 93, 100, **101**, **117**, 128, 132, 144; *see also* Pont de Argenteau; Pont de Fragné; Pont de Halen; Pont de Hermalle-sous-Huy; Pont de Herstal; Pont de Maghin; Pont de Melreux; Pont de Ombret; Pont de Ougrée; Pont de Roi Albert; Pont de Salm; Pont de Seraing; Pont de Val-Benoit; Pont de Val-Saint-Lambert; Pont de Visé; Pont de Wandre; Pont des Arches; Pont Neuf
Bridge Transport Fourteen 93, 101
Bridge Transport Thirteen 93, 101
Britain 8, 43, 50, 56–57, 59, 79, 112–13, 144, 151, 191
British Expeditionary Force (BEF) 2–3, 5–7, 10, 14, 17, 46–47, 52, 54, 56, 73, 78, 80, 112, 126, 132–33, 136, 144, 147, 153–55, 158, 161, 164–66, 168–75, **176**, 177–83, 187–88, 193
Bruges, BE 164, 170
Brühe, Arthur 94, 138, 144
Brussels, BE 9, 47, 49, 69, 74, 78, 82, 99, 124–26, 136–37, 142, 145, 153–54, 159, 161, 164–65, 168–70, 173–75, 177, 182
Buchholtz (Oberst) 191
Bückeburg, GE 84
Budingen, GE 156
Bülow, Prince Bernhard von (Chancellor of Germany) 105
Bülow, Karl Ulrich von (General) 65, 70, 105–6, 123–24, 127–28, 151, 155, 157, 159, 166, 168–69, 171, 173–74, 180, 182

Calais, FR 147, 153

Canal du Centre 43, 91, 169, 175, 177, 179–80
Cannae, Battle of 15, 54, 71, 185
Carabineer Cyclist Battalion (Belgian) 114, 143
Casteau, BE 177, 179; *see also* Soignies, BE
Cavalry Corps Richthofen *see* HKK 1
Cavalry Corps Sordet (French) 110–11, 132–34, 145, 154, 161, 168–69, 171, 188; *see also* Sordet, Jean-François André (General)
Cavalry Division (Belgian) 91, 96, 114, 132, 134, 138, 143–44, 147, 150, 154, 188
Celles, BE 113
Charleroi, BE 2, 47, 82, 99, 124–25, 169–70, 180
citadel *see* fortress
Clausewitz, Carl von 4, 8, 10–11, 14, 49, 54, 74, 79, 87, 193, 196
Collani, von (Oberleutnant) 118
Cologne, GE *see* Köln (Cologne), GE
colors, regimental *see* flag
command and control 67, 74, 100, 105, 122, 183, 188
Condé, FR 167, 169, 175, 180–81
conscription (Belgian) 43
Cortessem, BE 130
Courtrai, BE 174, 181, 183
Crefeld, BE 197*n*2
Crown Council (Belgian) 78

Dahlheim, GE 61, 197*n*3
dem Borne, von (General) 134
Démer River 49, 157
de Moranville, Antonin de Selliers (General) 78
Denkschrift 8, 15, 193
de Ryckel, Louis (General) 78
Dicke Bertha 128
Diekirch, LU 131
Diest, BE 49, 78, 123, 125, 134, 140, 142, 147, 150, 154, 156, 159
Dinant, BE 131, 136–37, 142, 148, 164
Dindal (Lieutenant) 44
dirigible *see* aircraft
Division Garnier 181, 199*ch*5*n*8; *see also* Fourth Cavalry Division (German)
Divisionskavallerie 21
Donalies (Major) 116
dragoner 21, 193
Droogebosch, BE 169
Dujardin (Colonel) 84
Dunkirk, FR 147, 153
Dyle River 83

Eberhardt, Walter von (Colonel), Inspector of Fliegertruppe 37
Egnis, BE 62
Egon Pax (Oberleutnant) 118
Eiffel, Belgian 131
Eighteenth Cavalry Brigade (German) 144
Eighteenth Dragoner Regiment (German) 30, 113–14, 143–44, 148
Eighth Army Corps (German) 68, 100

Eighth Hussar Regiment 177
Eighty-Ninth Infantry Regiment, Grenadiers (German) 94, 98, 100–101, 115–17, 121
Eighty-Second Infantry Regiment (German) 121
Eindoven, NE 197n19
Einem, Karl von (General der Kavallerie) 128, *129*, 132, 134, 141
Eleventh Army Corps 67, 121, 123, 170, 174
Eleventh Infantry Brigade 47, 67, 83, 95, 103–4, 108–9, 119–21, 123, 127
Emmich, Otto von (General der Infanterie) **65, 66**, 67, 70, 75, 82–83, 88, 90–91, 94–96, 120, 124–25, 127–28, 130–31, 134, 142, 146
Enghien, BE 179
Engineers Cyclists (Belgian) 84, 143
England *see* Britain
English Channel
English language 15, 25, 201*ch*7*n*4
Escot, BE *see* Scheldt River
Esneux, BE 104, 109, 142
Eupen, BE 44, 83–84, 95, 128
Exerzier-Reglement 53, 193

Fabeck, von (Oberst) 191
Faismes, BE 99
FAR 26, 143, 153, 193
Federal German Chancellery 198n42
Feld-Flieger Abteilung see FFA
FFA 36, 137, 193, 197n49
field airship battalion *see* FLA
field artillery battalion 26, 69, 193
field artillery regiment *see* FAR
Fifteenth Brigade (Belgian) 78, 122
Fifteenth Hussar Regiment (German) 91, 140
Fifth Army (French) 136, 154, 174–75, **176**
Fifth Army (German) 53, 68, **178**
Fifth Army Corps (German) 68
Fifth Cavalry Division (German) 161, 175
Fifth Infantry Division (Belgian) 83, 138, 150
Fifth Lancers Regiment (Belgian) 143, 168
Fifty-Third Infantry Regiment (German) 94, 102, 118, 121
First Army (German) 9–10, 20, 27, 47–49, 51, 56, 59–61, 64–65, 67, 71–72, 80, 90, 133–36, 146–48, 150–57, 159–61, 164–65, 168–71, *172*, 173–75, **176**, 177, 179–83, 196n29; Motor Transport 148; *see also* von Kluck, Alexander (General)
First Battalion FAR 9 98, 153
First Battle of Ypres 1
First Cavalry Brigade (Belgian) 143
First Guides Regiment (Belgian) 143
First Infantry Division (Belgian) 83
FLA 90, 193; *see also* Zeppelin (aircraft)
flag 40, 98, 101, 103, 105, 114, 116–17, 121, 123, 168
Flying Column *see* bicycle company
Fokker (aircraft) 36
Forêt, BE 103
Fort de Andoy 137

Fort de Barchon (Barachon) 42, 90, 94–95, 102, 109, 118, 123, 126, 128
Fort de Battice 42, 83, 90, 95, 108–9, 118
Fort de Boncelles 91, 95, 104, 142, 150
Fort de Charlemont 141; *see also* Givet, FR
Fort de Chaudefontaine 42, 103, 120, 134, 146
Fort de Eben-Emael 51
Fort de Embourg 42, 91, 95, 104, 134, 146
Fort de Evegnée 90, 102, 128, 136
Fort de Flémalle 42, 62, 137, 153
Fort de Fléron 42, 90, 95, 103, 120, 122, 127–28, 134, 142, 150
Fort de Hollogne 42, 122, 141–42, 153
Fort de Liers 90, 116–17, 134, 146, 149, 171
Fort de Loncin (Lantin) 122, 146, 151
Fort de Pontisse 42, 65, 91–92, 115–17, 134–35, 145–46
Fortieth Brigade (German) 128; *see also* Tenth (Army) Corps (German)
fortin *see* fortress
fortress: 10, *12*, 39–40, 42–43, 51, 60, 64–65, 69–70, 75, 82, **89**, 90–91, **97**, *111*, 116, 124, 126–28, 132–33, 150, 164, **176, 178**; Antwerp 41, 44, 48–49, 78–79, 154, 60, 164; Liège 10, 42–43, 47, 50, 60, 64, 76, 90, 98, 114, 122–24, 128, 131, 134–37, 142–43, 145, 151, 153, 186; Maastricht 50; Namur 43–44, 78, 148, 150, 154, 170, 182
Forty-Third Field Artillery Regiment (FAR) 94
Forty-Third Infantry Brigade (German) 65, 67, 83, 95, 104, 108, 121, 128
Fourteenth Infantry Brigade (German) 47, 67, 83, 94–95, 103, 108–9, *119*, 121
Fourth Army Corps (German) 47, 67, 90, 121, 135, 146, 151, 156–57, 160–61, 169, 182
Fourth Cavalry Division (German) 67, 94, 98, 125, 129, 131, 134, 144, 148, 164, 168, 171, 179, 199*ch*5*n*8; *see also* Division Garnier
Fourth Infantry Division (Belgian) 78, 83, 103
Fourth Jäger Battalion (German) 103
Fourth Kürassier Regiment (German) 21, 28, 94, 143–44, 177
Fourth Lancers Regiment (Belgian) 143, 168
Fourth Line Infantry Regiment (Belgian) 143
Fourth Mixed Brigade (Belgian) 127, 143, 145
Fourth Reserve Corps (German) 135, 146, 156–57, 161, 173–74, 182
Fouque, von (Captain) 120
Fraipont, BE 128
France 2–3, 7–11, *12*, 14–15, 19, 33, 41, 43–48, 52–57, 62, 72, 76–80, 82–83, 88, 94, 106, 110, 112–14; Army 9, 11, 14, 19, 48, 53, 62, *139*, 147, *149*, 161, 170–71, 173, 177, 180
Franco-Prussian War 31, 68, 106, 121
Francorchamps, GE 83, 96, 109
francs-tireurs 106–7, 110, 193; *see also* irregular; resistance
fratricide 94, 105
French, Sir John (Field Marshal) 183

Index

Freytag-Loringhoven, von (Generalleutnant) 192
Friedrich II of Prussia 82
Frontiers, Battle of the 2

Ganshoren, BE 169
Garde Civique (Belgian) **45**, 46, 69, 107, 193; *see also* National Guard (Belgian)
Geet Betz, BE 156
Geilenkirchen, GE 62
Geisert (Hauptmann) 170; *see also* Zeppelin (aircraft)
Gembloux, BE 83, 169, 175
Gemmenich, BE 83, 91
German Air Service 35
German Supreme Command *see* Oberste Heeresleitung (OHL)
Gette River 44–45, 49, 78, 83, 113, 123, 132, 134–35, 137, 142, 144–45, 147, 150, 154, 165
GGS *see* Great General Staff (GGS)
Ghent, BE 170, 174
Givet, FR 83, 98, 105, 141, 153; *see also* Fort de Charlemont
Glabbeek Suerbempde, BE 159
Glider troops (German) 51
Glons, BE 156
Goch, NE 197*n*19
Godin, von (Freiherr) 118
Gorssum, BE 156
Gosselies, BE 169
Goszler, von (Lieutenant) 125
Gotha (aircraft) 36
Gräfenhan (Leutnant der Reserve) 118
Grammont, BE 179
Great General Staff (GGS) 6, 9, 11, 23, 33, 47, 51, 55, 57–59, 63–64, 68–72, 74–77, 80, 82, 96, **178**, 180, 184–87, 191–93, 203*n*1
Groener, K.W. (Oberleutnant) 191
Groener, Wilhelm (General) 54, 63, 198*n*46
Grün und Bilinger (contractor) 86
Guard Cavalry Division (German) 22, 25, 179
Guard Reserve Corp (German) 36, 170
Gumbinnen, Battle of 166

Haegen, BE 156
Hague convention 106–7, 110
Hainaut, BE 202*n*35
Halbeek farm 140
Halen, BE 49, 84, 140, 144; battle of 17, 19, 113, 142–45, 148, 196*ch*2*n*17
Hammerstein-Equord, von (Hauptmann) 192
Hamont, BE 197*n*19
Handstreich 51, 63–64, **65**, 67–70, 75–76, 82, 88–125, 137, 151, 185–88
Hannut, BE 114, 123
Hanover, GE 68
Hasselt, BE 99, 123, 140, 142, 157, 161, 197*n*19
Hausen, von (General) 174; *see also* Third Army
Haute Préalle, BE *see* Préalle
Hautes Fagnes 42

Heeringen, Josias von 33, 55; *see also* Ministry of War (German)
Henri Chapelle, BE 83
Hentsch (Oberleutant) 191
Herbesthal, BE 145
Herbig, Major 143
Herck la Ville, BE 156
Hergenrath, BE 84, 94
Hermée, BE 101–2, 108, 115–17
Herssalt, BE 159
Herstal, BE 62, 84, 92, 108, 117, 135; *see also* Rhées, BE
Hervé, BE 83–84, 90, 95–96, 109; *see also* Julemont, BE
Heyde, von der (Oberst) 192
HKK 17, 19–21, 23–30, 39–40, 72, 140, 145, 147, 158, 194
HKK 1 15, 48, 72, 131, 136–37, 164, 166–68, 175, **180**, 187
HKK 2 15, 25, 27, 47–48, 59, 67, **71**, 72–73, 83, 88, 91–92, 98–99, 101, 106, 118, 120, 124–25, 128, **130**, 131, 133–34, 136–38, 140, 142, 145, 147, 150, 154–55, 161, 164, 168, 171, 173, 175, **178**, 180–84, 187; *see also* von Waldau, Hoffmann (Major)
HKK 3 15, 72, 187, 196*ch*2*n*17
Höherer Kavallerie-Kommandeur see HKK
Holland 4, 9–11, 41, 44, 49–51, 59, 63–64, 67, 93, 115, 142, 146, 151, 164, 186–87, 191, 200*n*65
Hollogne, BE 42, 122
Hombourg, BE 44, 83, 85
Horion, BE 99
horse 17–18, 20, 26–27, 81, 94, **99**, 102, 110, 113, 115, 131–34, 138, 144–46, 148, 164, 168, 188; fodder 20, 27–28, **29**, 30–31, 138, 164; gear 30
Horse Artillery Battalion Hanstein 144
Houyet, BE 148
Hülsen, von (Major General) 67, 95
hussar 21
Hussar Regiment Seventeen 95
Huy, BE 43, 62, 84, 91, 96, 99, 105, 135, 141–42, 201*ch*7*n*2
hygiene 81

Imperial Constitution 79
irregular 106–7, 193; *see also francs-tireurs*; resistance
Italy **32**, 76, 191

jaeger 17, 40, 95, **99**, 100, 140, 188; *see also* jäger
jäger 27, 92, 194; *see also* jaeger
Jagow, von 83
Japan 38, 78
Jemappes (Jemeppe-Seraing), BE 3, 109
Jodoigne, BE 136, 150
Joffre (General) 154, 175
Julemont, BE 83, 94, 123; *see also* Hervé, BE
Jupille, BE 119, 123

Index

kaiser *see* Wilhelm II, Kaiser
Kaisermanöver 21, 58, 191
Kaldenkirchen, GE 61, 197*n*19
Kemnitz, von (Oberst) 191
Kempen, GE 197*n*19
Kermpt, BE 154, 156
Kiel, GE 79
Klawikowski (Vizewachtmeister) 125
Kleffel (Cavalry Captain), reconnaissance squadron commander 113, 121
Kleinschmidt (Hauptmann) 112
Kleist, Georg Fredrich von (General der Kavallerie) 22–23
Kluck, Alexander von (General) 27, 44, 65, 80, 147, 151, 155, 157, 159, 161, 164, 169, 173, 177, 179, 181, 183; *see also* First Army (German)
Koblenz, GE 80, 120, 153
Köhler (Hauptmann) 191
Köln (Cologne), GE 39, 112, 125
Koningsloo, BE 169
Kortenberg, BE 169
Kräwel, von (Kraewel) (Major General) 125, 131
Krupp (manufacturer) 128, 170
Kuhl, Hans von (Major General) 40, 80, 155–58, 173–74, 180, 183, 192
kürassier 21, 28, 94, 143–44, 177, 200*n*65
Kürassier-Regiment "Königin," Pommersches 2 94
Kutzbach (Major) 118

La Gleize, BE 83
La Hulze, BE 169
La Maison Blanche, BE 83
Landwehr 9, 76, 164, 194
Laroche, BE 110
La Roeulx, BE 179
Lauenstein, Otto von (General) 155, 174, 180; *see also* Second Army (German)
Launhardt (Oberleutnant) 192
Le Cateau, BE 2
Le Havre, FR 147
Lehenner, von 118
Leman, Gérard (General) 43–44, 75, 85, 87, 116, 119, 122–23, 151
Leopold II, King of Belgium 41
Les Waleffes, BE 113
Lesse River 148
Leuven, BE 93, 137, 141, 147, 150; *see also* Louvain, BE
Liège, BE 3, 4, 10, *12*, 28, 41–51, 56, 59–70, 75–79, 82–85, 90–97, 98, 99–105, 109–10, *111*, *112*, 113–18, *119*, 120–38, 141–54, 184–87, 197*n*19, 198*n*56; *see also* Lüttich, BE
Liéry, BE 103
Lieth-Thompsen, Herrmann (Major) 33
Lifeguard Hussar Brigade (German) 168
Lifeguard Second Hussar Regiment (German) 165
Lille, BE 82, 133, 169, 173, 175, 177, 179–82

Limburg, NE 50, 59, 64, 83
Lincé, BE 106
Linden, BE 160
Lixhe, BE 51, 62, *93*, *98*, 99–100, 108, *115*, 118, 125, 128, *130*, 132, 135
Lobbecke, von (Captain) 168
Loonbeck, BE 161
Looz, BE 130, 138, 157; *see also* Borgloon, BE
Louvain, BE 83, 137, 156–57, 160–61, 164, 170, 173; *see also* Leuven, BE
Louveigne, BE 83, 95–96, 109
Ludendorff (Oberst) 191
Ludendorff, Erich (General) 69, 118, *119*, 123–24, 127, 146
Luftschiff ZVI 90, 112
Lummen, BE 156
Lüttich, BE 28, 123, 142; *see also* Liège, BE
Luxembourg 44, 47–48, 55, 69, 76–77, 82–83, 136
LVG (aircraft) *32*, 35
Lyncker, von (General Inspector) 33

Maastricht Appendix 4, 10, *13*, 49–50, 52, 61, 71, 187
machine gun 19, 21, 32, 34, 36, 68, 114, 131, 140, 144–45, 188; Hotchkiss 143–44; Maxim 144
machine-gun company 17, 27, 101, 125, 143–44, 188, 194; *see also* MG-ABT
Magnée, BE 103, 108, 120
Malines, BE 157; *see also* Mechelen, BE
Malmédy, BE 42, 44, 83–84, 95, 109, 128, 137
Marbais, BE 168–69
Marchienne-au-Pont, BE 169
Marne, Army of 91, 151
Marne, Battle of 1, 3, 62, 91, 101, 156, 158, 161, 181, 188
Mars-la-Tour, battle of 16, 68
Marwitz, Georg von der (Lieutenant General) 23, 25, *65*, 67, *71*, 73, 91, 101, 120, 124, 131, 134, 136, 138, 154, 180–81, 196*ch2n*17
Massow, von (Colonel) 196*ch2n*17
Masuria, GE 196*ch2n*17
Maubeuge, FR 132–33, 148, 168, 171, 173–75, 177, 179–81
Mechelen, BE 91; *see also* Malines, BE
Mecklenburger 108
Meldert, BE 161
Melen, BE 109
Melreux, BE 87
Mercedes Benz *see* Argus (aircraft)
Metz, GE 39, 47, 68
Meuse, Army of 35, 64, 88, 91, 112, 120, 143, 151; *see also* Tenth (Army) Corps
Meuse River 10, 15, 41–44, 48–49, 51, 60, 62, 64, 67, 75, 78, 83, 90–92, *93*, 94, 96, *98*, 99–101, 104–5, 110, 118, 121–22, 125, 127–28, *130*, 132, 134, 136–38, 141–42, 146–48, 150, 154, 166, 173–74, 198*n*56
MG-ABT 27, 194; *see also* machine-gun company

Index

Micheroux, BE 95, 103, 108
Mille, BE 161
Ministry of Interior, German 45, 107
Ministry of War, German 11, 22–24, 33–35, 45, 55, 57–58, 128, 203*n*1
Modave, BE 132
Moelingen, BE **93**, **98**
Moltke, Graf Helmuth Karl Berhard von (the Elder) 8, 16, 38, 53, 57, 187
Moltke, Helmuth Johann Ludvig von (the Younger) 1, 8, 10–11, 23, 25, 33–34, 37–38, 47, 50–51, 55–57, 59–60, 65, 69–72, 76–77, 131, 154, 158–59, 161, 164, 166–67, 181–82, 185–87, 191, 195*n*4, 195*n*16
Moltke, von (Colonel), Eighty-Third Infantry Regiment commander 95
Moltke Plan 10, **12**, 15, 48, 57, 72, 76, 93, 131, 182, 185
Moltke the Elder *see* von Moltke, Graf Helmuth Karl Berhard (the Elder)
Moltke the Younger *see* von Moltke, Helmuth Johann Ludvig (the Younger)
monoplane *see* aircraft
Mons, Battle of 2–3, 7, 63, 151, 170, 175, 177, 179, 181–84, 188
Montaigu, BE 159
Montjoie, GE 124
Mortier, BE 145
Mortroux, BE 94, 102
Mouland, BE 93, 100, 118
Murat 188

Namur, BE 43–45, 47, 60, 69, 78, 82–83, 96, 99, 105, 113, 131–33, 136–37, 141–42, 148, 150, 154, 164, 166–68, 170, 174–75, 182
Napoleon 21, 38, 54, 88, 126, 143, 153, 192
Nasproué Tunnel 44, 85, 57, 95, 146
National Guard (Belgian) **45**, 93; *see also* Garde Civique (Belgian)
Neerlinter, BE 156
Neerysche, BE 161
neutrality: Belgium 11, 41, 43–44, 55, 77, 79, 88; Britain 77; Holland 4, 10–11, 50, **115**, 164; Luxembourg 77, 82
Nieuwerkerken, BE 156
Nimy, BE 179
Ninetieth Fusilier Regiment (German) 94, 98, 100–104, 115–17, 121
Ninove, BE 169–70, 174
Ninth Army Corps (German) 47, 135, 137, 151, 156–57, 159, 161, 169–70, 179, 182
Ninth Cavalry Division (German) 15, 47–48, 65, 83, 96, 105, 110, 130–31, 134, 137–38, 148, 150, 164, 168, 171, 175, 177, 183
Ninth Jäger Battalion (German) 92, 94, 100–102, 105, 108, 116–17, 122, 137, 143, 199*ch*5*n*8
Ninth Reserve Corps (German) 165, 182, 187
Ninth Uhlan Regiment (German) 143–44
Nivelles, BE 148, 169
Oberste Heeresleitung (OHL) *see* OHL
OHL 20, 23–24, 27, 37, 39–40, 47–48, 60, 64, 80, 83, 96, 112, 120, 125–26, 132, 135, 151–52, 154–55, 165–67, 171, 173–74, 177, 180, 182, 186, 194, 195*n*16
Olnye, BE 103
Ombret-Rausa (Ombret), BE 62, 84, 96, 99, 105
165th Infantry Regiment 95, 103
Orsmaal en Opheylissem, BE 140
Orsmaël-Gussenhoven, BE 135
Ostaufmarsch 195*n*4
Ostend, BE 147, 153, 164, 170
Ourcq, battle of 182
Overysche Hoeylaert, BE 169

Pael, BE 155–56
Papenbroek, BE 150
Paris, FR 7, 11, 14, 145, 171, 184
Parseval (aircraft) **32**, 83, 91, 161
Pepinster, BE 128
Peruwelz, BE *see* Perwez, BE
Pervez, BE *see* Perwez, BE
Perwez, BE 83, 91, 161, 175
Picardy, FR 80
Pieton River 169
Plainevaux, BE 104
Poncet, von (Major) 191
Pont de Argenteau 84; *see also* bridge
Pont de Fragné 62; *see also* bridge
Pont de Halen 84; *see also* bridge
Pont de Hermalle-sous-Huy 62, 84, 141, 91; *see also* bridge
Pont de Herstal 108; *see also* bridge
Pont de Maghin 62, **63**, 113; *see also* bridge
Pont de Melreux 87; *see also* bridge
Pont de Neuf 62; *see also* bridge
Pont de Ombret 62, 84, 96, 99, 105; *see also* bridge
Pont de Ougrée 62, 104; *see also* bridge
Pont de Roi Albert 62; *see also* bridge
Pont de Salm 86; *see also* bridge
Pont de Seraing 62, 84, 104, **109**, 174; *see also* bridge
Pont de Val-Benoit 62, 84; *see also* bridge
Pont de Val-Saint-Lambert 62, 84; *see also* bridge
Pont de Visé 83–84, **85**, 90–91, **92**, 94, 96, 18; *see also* bridge
Pont de Wandre 120; *see also* bridge
Pont des Arches 62, 84, **112**, 113, 120; *see also* bridge
Posadowsky, Graf von (Oberst) 192
Poseck, Maximilian von (General) 24, 72, 113, 167, 181
Poulsen radio 39; *see also* radio
Poulseur, BE 83, 96, 104, 108
Préalle, BE 116–17
prisoner 94, 104, 107, 110, 112–114, 116, 118, 124, 144–45, 179
Prussian Moresnet 83

Quast, von (General) 134
Queue-du-Bois, BE 118–19

Index

radio 19–20, 27, 34, 37, 39–40, 96, 127, 130, 135, 148, 150, 177, 179, 182
Railroad Section/Division (German) 52, 76
Redern, von (Generalmajor) 52, 76
Remaix, BE 170, 179, 183
Renaix, BE *see* Remaix, BE
Rennaix, BE *see* Remaix, BE
Renner, K. W. (Oberleutnant) 192
Repington, Charles (Colonel) 68
resistance *see francs-tireurs*; irregular
Retinn, BE 108, 119
Rhées, BE 117; *see also* Herstal, BE
Richthofen, Baron von (General) *see* HKK 1
Rillaer, BE 159
Ritter, Gerhard 15
Rochefort, BE 137
Roermond, NE 197n19
Roeulx *see* La Roeulx, BE
Romania 41
Romsée, BE 103–4, 108
Royal Naval Division (British) 165
Rummen, BE 156
Rumpler-Taube (aircraft) *32*, 33, 35–36, 137, 194
Rundstedt, von (Hauptmann) 192
Ruoff (Leutnant der Reserve) 118
Russia 8, 10, 16, 55–57, 77, 192

St. Hadelin, BE 103, 108
St. Joris, BE *see* Winghe St. Georges, BE
St. Privat, battle of 68, 121
St. Quirin, FR 171
St. Trond (St. Truiden), BE 90, 99, 114, 132, 134, 137–38, 140, 150, 154, 156, 161
St. Truiden, BE *see* St. Trond (St. Truiden), BE
Salm River 86
Sambre River 43, 154, 173–74
Sanders (Lieutenant) *115*, 200n65
Sart-Tilman, BE 91, 105, 119
Scharnhorst, Gerhard von 160
Scheldt River 50, 179–81, 183
Schell (Hauptmann) 118
Scherenberg (Oberleutnant) 192
Schlichting, Sigismund von 8
Schlieffen, Graf Alfred von 1–2, 8–10, 54, 57–59, 71, 166–67; *see also* Schlieffen Plan
Schlieffen Plan 1–2, 4–5, 7, 9–10, *13*, 14–15, 48, 50, 54, 56–57, 61, 71–72, 74, 140, 145, 160, 167, *172*, 174, 182, 185, 187–88; *see also* von Schlieffen, Graf Alfred
Schmidt von Knobelsdorff (Generalleutnant) 191
Second Army (German) 9, 27, 47–49, 51, 59–60, 64–65, 67–69, 71–72, 120, 123–24, 126–28, 130, 134–36, 138, 141–42, 146, 150–51, 154–55, 157–61, 164, 166–71, *172*, 174, *176*; *see also* von Lauenstein, Otto (General)
Second Army Corps (German) 30, 40, 146, 150, 156, 174–75
Second Cavalry Brigade (Belgian) 91, 98, 113, 143
Second Cavalry Division (German) 47, 67,
91, 130–31, 135, 138, 143, 148, 155–56, 159–61, 164–65, 173, 175, 183, 199*ch*5*n*8
Second Dragoner Regiment (German) 113–14, 125
Second Garde Ulanen Regiment (German) 196*ch*2*n*17
Second Guides Regiment (Belgian) 143
Second Infantry Division (Belgian) 83
Second Kürassier Regiment (German) 28, 143–44
Second Reich 1, 7–8, 17, 189
Sedan, FR 68
Seidlitz *see* von Seydlitz (Seidlitz), Frederich Wilhelm
Seneffe, BE 169
Serbia 74, 76
Seventeenth Cavalry Brigade (German) 113–15, 121, 125, 143–44
Seventh Army (German) 53
Seventh Army Corps (German) 67, 68, 121, 126, 127–28, 137, 142, 157
Seventh Jager Battalion (German) *65*, 84, 94, 100–102, 108, 116–17, 121–22, 125, 143
Seventy-Fourth Infantry Regiment (German) 104–5, 109, 121
Seventy-Third Infantry Regiment (German) 104, 109, 121
Seydlitz (Seidlitz), Fredrich Wilhelm von 16, 188
SHAEF 185
Short Marine Cannon Battery 3 153
SHQ 44, 83, 122–23, 132, 137, 140–41
signal 40, 105; troops 39–40, 67, 120
Silesia 68
Silver Helmets, battle of *see* Halen, BE, battle of
Simbret, BE 136
Sixt von Arnim, Hans-Heinrich 169
Sixteenth Hussar Regiment (German) 145, 148
Sixteenth Infantry Division (German) 76–77
Sixteenth Infantry Regiment (German) 94, 102, 109, 118, 123, 126, 128
Sixteenth Ulanen Regiment (German) 94
Sixth Army Corps (German) 68
Sixth Infantry Division (Belgian) 83, 138
Sixty-Fifth *ème régiment d'infanterie territorial* (French) 171
Sixty-Ninth Infantry Regiment (German) 77
Soignies, BE 177
Soiron, BE 83, 95
Sordet, Jean-François André (General) 110, 132, 134, 145, 148, 154, 161, 168–69, 188; *see also* Cavalry Corps Sordet (French)
Soumagne, BE 95, 108
Spa, BE 42, 83
Sprimont, BE 104
standard, regimental *see* flag
Station Audel, BE 83
Stavelot, BE 83; Stavelot Tunnel 44, 85, 95, 130

Stein, von (Generalleutnant) 91
Stevoort, BE 156
Stoumont, BE 83
Strantz, von (Oberst) 118
Stroedicke 118
Stülpnagelm, von (General Staff officer) 96
Supreme Headquarters (Belgian) *see* SHQ

Tappanasserts, Gerhard (General) 10
Tappen, Dietrich Gerhard Emil Theodor (Lieutenant Colonel) 77, 180, 195n16; *see also Oberste Heeresleitung* (OHL)
Tappen (Oberleutnant) 191
Taube *see* Rumpler-Taube (aircraft)
Telefunken *see* radio
telegraph 38–39, 57, 76
telephone 20, 37, 40, 58, 96, 110, 132, 138, 140
Tenth (Army) Corps (German) 47, 64–68, 70, 75–76, 84, 121, 126–28, 137, 142; *see also* Meuse, Army of
Tenth Jäger Battalion (German) 65, 95, 137
Termonde, BE 170
Tervueren, BE 169
Theux, BE 83, 95
Thieldonck, BE 160
Thionville, FR 47
Third Army Corps (German) 30, 47, 67, 121, 135, 142, 148, 150, 156–57, 161, 169–71, *172*, 174–75, *176*, 179, 182, 187; *see also* von Hausen (General)
Third Cavalry Brigade (German) 143–44
Third Cavalry Division (French) 134
Third Garde Ulanen Regiment (German) 196ch2n17
Third Hussar Regiment (German) 182
Third Infantry Division (Belgian) 69, 75, 78, 83, 91, 117, 119, 122–23
Third Infantry Regiment (German) 117
Third Jäger Battalion (German) 95, 103
Third Reserve Corps (German) 135, 157, 161, 165, 173–74
Third Uhlan (German) 135
Thirteenth Uhlan (German) 159, 175
Thirty-Eighth Infantry Brigade (German) 65, 67, 83, 95–96, 104, 108–9, 114, 121
Thirty-Eighth Reserve Corps (German) 196ch2n17
Thirty-Fifth Infantry Regiment (German) 103, 120–21
Thirty-Fourth Infantry Brigade (German) 67–68, 83, 92, 94, 100–101, 108, 115–18, 120–21, 125, 127, 131
Thirty-Ninth Brigade (German) 67
Thirty-Seventh Brigade (German) 67
Thourout, BE 175
Tienen, BE *see* Tirlemont (Tienen), BE
Times (London) 68
Tirlemont (Tienen), BE 91, 123, 134, 137, 142–43, 147, 150, 154, 156–57, 159
Tongeren (Tongres), BE 90, 118, 157

Tongres, BE *see* Tongeren (Tongres), BE
Tourinnes, BE 161
Transport Inspectorate (German) 33
Triple Alliance 76
Trois Ponts Tunnel 44, 85, *86*, 87
Troisvierges, LU 77
Troschke, von (Cavalry Captain), reconnaissance squadron commander 113, 121, 131, 167
tunnel 44, 49, 62–63, 70, 75, 84–85, *86*, 87–88, 95, 124, 130, 134, 146, 151, 164, 185–86
Turnhout, BE 197n19
Twelfth Hussar Regiment (German) 113, 135
Twelfth Reserve Army Corps (German) 175
Twentieth Infantry Regiment (German) 103, 121
Twenty-Fifth Infantry Regiment (German) *65*, 67–68, 100, 102, 118, 121
Twenty-Fourth Line Infantry Regiment (Belgian) 143
Twenty-Seventh Infantry Brigade (German) 67, 83, 94, 99, 101, 109
Twenty-Seventh Infantry Regiment (German) 103, 118–19, 122

uhlan 21, 135, 143–44, 168, 175
Unger (Lieutenant) 114
Vamont, BE 157
van Billoen (Lieutenant) 44
van Espen, Georges 114, 200n64
Veerle, BE 156
Velthem, BE 161
Venlo, NE 197n19
Verdun, FR 11
Vernichtungsschlacht 54, 159, 194
Verviers, BE 41, 44, 65, 83, 85
Vesdre River 41–42, 44, 65, 128
Viebeg (Leutnant) 118
Viersen, NE 197n19
Vierstratten, BE 160
Ville-sur-Haine, BE 179
Vilvorde, BE 169–70
Vionville-Mars la Tour, FR 16
Visé, BE *85*, 90–91, *92*, 93–94, 96, 100, 121–22, 126, 128, 135, 186
Voerenstraat, BE 200n65
Vosges Mountains 170

Wachter, von (Major General) 103
Wadelincourt, FR 180
Waldau, Hoffmann von (Major) 183; *see also* HKK 2
Waldersee, Graf Alfred von 52
Waldersee, Graf Georg von (Generalmajor) 192
Waldschenke, BE 84
Wallonia, BE 41
War Academy 192, 196n17
War Council (German) 186
Wars of German Unification 16
Warsage, BE 94, 108

Waterloo, BE 88, 169
Wavre, BE 47, 83, 91, 154, 156–57, 161, 164, 170
Weert, NE 197*n*19
Wegegabel, BE 160
Weiden, GE 135
Weidner, Oberst 192
Weisshaus, BE 94
Wellmann, von (Hauptmann) 118
Werchter, BE 160
Werner-Ehrenfeucht (Fähnrich) 118
Wesel, GE 197*n*19
Wesemael, BE 160
Wetzell (Major) 191
Weyland (Hauptmann) 192

Wiers, BE 175
Wilhelm of Lippe, Prince (Colonel) *see* Wilhelm II, Kaiser
Wilhelm II, Kaiser 33, 41, 56, 77, 105, 203*n*1
Winghe St. Georges, BE 147, 159–61
Winterfeldt (Oberleutnant) 192
Wolverthem, BE 165, 168
Wussow, von (Major General) 95, 103

Yorck, Baron von (Cavalry Captain) 11, 114

Zebrugge, BE 153
Zeppelin (aircraft) *32*, 33, 35, 52, 170–71, 193; *see also* FLA; Geisert (Hauptmann)

www.ingramcontent.com/pod-product-compliance
Lightning Source LLC
Chambersburg PA
CBHW032054300426
44116CB00007B/732